Gender in the Middle Ages

Volume 23

PREMODERN MASCULINITIES IN TRANSITION

Gender in the Middle Ages

ISSN 1742–870X

Series Editors
Jacqueline Murray
Diane Watt

Editorial Board
Clare Lees
Katherine J. Lewis
Liz Herbert McAvoy

This series investigates the representation and construction of masculinity and femininity in the Middle Ages from a variety of disciplinary and interdisciplinary perspectives. It aims in particular to explore the diversity of medieval genders, and such interrelated contexts and issues as sexuality, social class, race and ethnicity, and orthodoxy and heterodoxy.

Proposals or queries should be sent in the first instance to the editors or to the publisher, at the addresses given below; all submissions will receive prompt and informed consideration.

Professor Jacqueline Murray, Department of History, University of Guelph, Guelph, Ontario, N1G 2W1, Canada, (jacqueline.murray@uoguelph.ca)

Professor Diane Watt, School of Literature and Languages, University of Surrey, Guildford, Surrey GU2 7XH, UK, (d.watt@surrey.ac.uk)

Boydell & Brewer Limited, PO Box 9, Woodbridge, Suffolk IP12 3DF, UK

Previously published volumes in the series are listed at the end of this book.

PREMODERN MASCULINITIES
IN TRANSITION

Edited by
Konrad Eisenbichler and Jacqueline Murray

THE BOYDELL PRESS

© Contributors 2024

All Rights Reserved. Except as permitted under current legislation no part of this work may be photocopied, stored in a retrieval system, published, performed in public, adapted, broadcast, transmitted, recorded or reproduced in any form or by any means, without the prior permission of the copyright owner

First published 2024
The Boydell Press, Woodbridge

ISBN 978-1-83765-170-2

The Boydell Press is an imprint of Boydell & Brewer Ltd
PO Box 9, Woodbridge, Suffolk IP12 3DF, UK
and of Boydell & Brewer Inc.
668 Mt Hope Avenue, Rochester, NY 14620–2731, USA
website: www.boydellandbrewer.co.uk

A CIP catalogue record for this book is available
from the British Library

The publisher has no responsibility for the continued existence or accuracy of URLs for external or third-party internet websites referred to in this book, and does not guarantee that any content on such websites is, or will remain, accurate or appropriate

This publication is printed on acid-free paper

CONTENTS

List of Illustrations — vii

Notes on Contributors — xi

Acknowledgements — xiii

Introduction — 1
Jacqueline Murray

SHIFTING MASCULINITIES

1 Work, Writing, and Elite Masculinity in the Lyrics of Baudri of Bourgueil — 15
Jonathan M. Newman

2 Masculinity as Competence — 31
Thomas V. Cohen

3 The Many Faces of Qahramān: A Medieval Persianate Romance as a Window on Mongol and Muslim Masculinities in the Volga-Ural Region (1400s–1700s) — 53
Danielle Ross

FLUID MASCULINITIES

4 Marked Differences: Beards in Renaissance Europe — 75
Patricia Simons

5 Spurs and Negotiations of Masculinity in Early Modern England — 101
Hilary Doda

6 Mars Asleep: Discarded Swords in Seventeenth-Century Dutch Art — 125
Martha Hollander

TRANSFORMING MASCULINITIES

7 Military Masculinities in *La Chanson de Bertrand du Guesclin* — 155
Sarah Wilk

Contents

8 From the Knightly Bayard to Captain Monluc: Representations of
  Masculinity in Sixteenth-Century French Military Literature   175
  Benjamin Lukas

9 The Effeminate Man and the Rhetoric of Anxious Masculinity:
  Anton Francesco Doni and Scipione Ammirato   193
  Gerry Milligan

Index   215

ILLUSTRATIONS

FIGURES

Marked Differences: Beards in Renaissance Europe
Patricia Simons

4.1. Wenceslaus Hollar, *Head and Shoulders of a Turk, with a Moustache and a Large Turban*, 1645, etching (third state of three), 3 3/16 × 2 7/16 in. (8.1 × 6.2 cm). Metropolitan Museum of Art, New York (17.3.3117). 77

4.2. Albrecht Dürer (after Gentile Bellini), *Three Turks*, 1496–1497, pen and black and brown ink with watercolour, 30.6 × 19.7 cm. British Museum, London (1895,0915.974). © Trustees of the British Museum. 78

4.3. Bulgarian, *Icon of the Bogolyubovo Virgin*, c. 1570–1650, tempera on wood, 63.2 × 50.5 × 2.2 cm. Royal Ontario Museum, Toronto (978.353.12.A). Courtesy of ROM (Royal Ontario Museum), Toronto, Canada. © ROM. 81

4.4. Cornelis Danckertsz. the Younger (attrib.), *The candle is lighted, we cannot put it out*, c. 1640, etching, 26 × 37.3 cm. British Museum, London (1907,0326.31). © Trustees of the British Museum. 84

4.5. Hans Baldung Grien, *Martin Luther as an Augustinian Friar*, woodcut, 15.5 × 11.4 cm. Albertina, Vienna (DG1929/429). 85

4.6. Petrus Christus, *Portrait of a Young Man*, c. 1450–1460, oil on oak, 35.4 × 26 cm. Salting Bequest, 1910, National Gallery, London (NG2593). 87

4.7. Albrecht Dürer, *Self-Portrait*, detail, 1493, oil on linen (transferred from vellum), 56 × 44 cm. Musée du Louvre, Paris (R.F. 2382). 88

4.8. The Mint of Pesaro, *Medal of Giovanni Sforza*, 1503, cast bronze, 5.4 cm diameter. British Museum, London (1922,0709.3). © Trustees of the British Museum. 90

4.9. Jan Cornelisz. Vermeyen (manner of), *Portrait of Emperor Charles V*, c. 1530, oil on wood, 26.4 × 14 cm. Rijksmuseum, Amsterdam (SK–A–164). 93

4.10. Agnolo Bronzino, *Portrait of Andrea Doria*, c. 1545–1546, oil on canvas, 149 × 199.5 cm. Pinacoteca Brera, Milan (1206). 96

Illustrations

Spurs and Negotiations of Masculinity in Early Modern England
Hilary Doda

5.1. Partial spur buckle found at the Melanson site, Nova Scotia, in the collections of Parks Canada, Object #17B7L3.1. Illustration by Richard Morris, 2023. — 102

5.2. English spur types. Illustration by Richard Morris, 2020. — 105

5.3. "Pair of Rowel Spurs" (c. 1350) of French or Italian origin. Metropolitan Museum of Art. Gift of Amory S. Carhart, in memory of his father, Amory S. Carhart, 1926. Accession Number: 26.80.1–2. Image in the public domain. — 108

5.4. Frontispiece from Samuel Ward, *Woe to Drunkards. A Sermon by Samuel Ward preacher of Ipswich* (1622). Photograph courtesy of Sotheby's. — 114

Mars Asleep: Discarded Swords in Seventeenth-Century Dutch Art
Martha Hollander

6.1. Gabriel Metsu, *Music Party*, 1659. Metropolitan Museum, New York. Marquand Collection, Gift of Henry G. Marquand, 1890. — 126

6.2. David Vinckboons, *The Outdoor Party* (1610). Rijksmuseum, Amsterdam. — 129

6.3. Nicolaes Maes, *The Listening Housewife (The Eavesdropper)* (1656). Wallace Collection, London, UK © Wallace Collection, London, UK/Bridgeman Images. — 130

6.4. Dutch (Delft), *The Terrace* (c. 1660). The Art Institute of Chicago®. — 132

6.5. Rapier. Blade by Johannes Moum. German hilt (c. 1630–1640); blade, seventeenth century. Metropolitan Museum of Art, New York. Rogers Fund, 1904. — 133

6.6. Pieter Paul Rubens and Jan Brueghel, *The Return from War: Mars Disarmed by Venus* (1612–1616). The J. Paul Getty Museum, Los Angeles. Acquired in honor of John Walsh. — 136

6.7. Claes Jansz. Visscher, "Ad pompam tantum." Illustration for Roemer Visscher, *Sinnepoppen*. Amsterdam 1614, p. 54. Rijksmuseum, Amsterdam. — 139

6.8. Frans Hals, *Portrait of Willem van Heythuysen* (1625). Alte Pinakothek, Munich. bpk Bildagentur/Bayerische Staatsgemäldesammlungen/Art Resource, NY. — 141

Illustrations

6.9. Barend Fabritius, *Artist in the Studio* (1655–1660). Musée du Louvre, Paris. © RMN-Grand Palais/Art Resource, NY.   143

6.10. Rembrandt van Rijn, *Portrait of Jan Six* (1647). Metropolitan Museum, New York. Gift of Henry Walters, 1917.   145

6.11. Isaac Oliver, *A Young Man Seated Under a Tree* (c. 1590–1595). Royal Collection Trust, London. Bridgeman Images.   146

6.12. Jan De Heem, *Interior of a Room with a Young Man Seated at a Table* (1628). Ashmolean Museum, Oxford. Bequeathed by Daisy Linda Ward, 1939. Image © Ashmolean Museum, University of Oxford.   147

GRAPHS

Spurs and Negotiations of Masculinity in Early Modern England
   Hilary Doda

5.1. Spur type prevalence over time. Data set of 2,167 spurs and fittings from the Portable Antiquities Scheme. Finds.uk.org.   106

5.2. Percentage of tinned or gilded spurs, variation over time. Same data set as Graph 5.1.   111

All images in this volume are either in the public domain or reproduced with the kind permission of their respective copyright holders. Any reproduction, in whatever form, of the images in this volume that are not in the public domain is strictly forbidden. Every effort has been made to trace the copyright holders; apologies are offered for any omission, and the publisher will be pleased to add any necessary acknowledgement in subsequent editions.

CONTRIBUTORS

Thomas V. Cohen (emeritus) taught History and Humanities at York University. He writes on the political and cultural anthropology of early modern Rome, often in a microhistorical vein. He investigates the fine structure of coalitions, the impromptu rituals of everyday life, the shape of popular memory, the rhetoric of values, and vernacular epistemologies. His books include *Love and Death in Renaissance Italy* (2004) and *Roman Tales* (2019).

Hilary Doda teaches global dress history in Dalhousie University's Costume Studies program, and her research focuses on the material culture of dress and textiles in the early modern Atlantic world. She holds an Interdisciplinary PhD from Dalhousie, and her recent work engages with textile use in diaspora communities. Her first book, *Fashioning Acadians* (2023), examined the development of new clothing vernaculars and the shaping of colonial identity in pre-deportation Acadia.

Konrad Eisenbichler, CM, OMRI, FRSC is Professor Emeritus from the University of Toronto. Eisenbichler works on the intersection of literature, politics, and religion in fifteenth- and sixteenth-century Italy. He is the author, editor, or translator of more than thirty books, including the prize-winning monographs *The Boys of the Archangel Raphael: A Youth Confraternity in Florence, 1411–1785* (1998) and *The Sword and the Pen: Women, Politics, and Poetry in Sixteenth-Century Siena* (2012). More recently, he is the editor of *Masculinities and Representation: The Eroticized Male in Early Modern Italy and England* (2024).

Martha Hollander is Professor of Art History at Hofstra University. She is the author of *An Entrance for the Eyes: Space and Meaning in Seventeenth-Century Dutch Art* (2002), as well as essays on seventeenth-century Dutch art and culture, digital pedagogy, digital humanities, early modern fashion, and costume in art, film, and television. She is currently at work on a book about masculinity and fashion in seventeenth-century Holland.

Benjamin Lukas received his PhD from the University of Toronto after completing his master's degree at McMaster University. His research focuses on the study of published early modern military literature, such as treatises, memoirs, and biographies written by veterans. His dissertation examined the relationship between military reforms and martial gender norms among the French nobility in the sixteenth century.

Contributors

Gerry Milligan is Professor of Italian and Director of Honors at the College of Staten Island–CUNY. His research focuses on the rhetorical construction of effeminacy and masculinity in Italian Renaissance literature. His books include a volume of essays, co-edited with Jane Tylus, *The Poetics of Masculinity in Early Modern Italy and Spain* (2010) and the monograph *Moral Combat: Women, Gender, and War in Italian Renaissance Literature* (2018).

Jacqueline Murray is University Professor Emeritus of History at the University of Guelph. Her research focuses on sexuality and gender in premodern Europe, with a specific focus on men, masculinity, marriage and the family. She is editor of *Patriarchy, Honour, and Violence: Masculinities in Premodern Europe* (2022), *The Male Body and Social Masculinity in Premodern Europe* (2022) and co-editor of *Sex, Gender, and Sexuality in the Italian Renaissance* (2019).

Jonathan M. Newman is Clif and Gail Smart Professor of English at Missouri State University. He has published on the interplay of gender, social discourse, and literary and rhetorical form in medieval Latin, Middle English, and Old Occitan works. He is currently working on a monograph about masculinity and education in medieval Latin letters and poetry.

Danielle Ross is an Associate Professor of Islamic and Russian history at Utah State University. Her research focuses on the social history, religious practice, and literature of the Muslim communities of Russia's Volga Basin and the Kazakh Steppe. She is the author of the monograph *Tatar Empire: Kazan's Muslims and the Making of Imperial Russia* (2020).

Patricia Simons is a Professorial Fellow at the University of Melbourne and Professor Emerita, University of Michigan, Ann Arbor. Her books include *The Sex of Men in Premodern Europe: A Cultural History* (2011) and the co-edited *Patronage, Art, and Society in Renaissance Italy* (1987). Her work on gender and sexuality in visual culture ranges from fourteenth-century Italy to contemporary Australian art.

Sarah Wilk, a student of the martial and emotional values of medieval military men, was educated at the University of Lethbridge, the University of Toronto, and York University. Her PhD thesis was entitled "The Measure of a Medieval Man: The Emotional Community of Military Men in the Fourteenth Century."

ACKNOWLEDGEMENTS

In bringing together this collection of articles, we have incurred many debts with the many colleagues and institutions that have generously and enthusiastically supported both this particular endeavour and the larger project from which it sprang.

The Toronto Renaissance and Reformation Colloquium hosted the international conference on *Masculinities in the Premodern World: Continuities, Change, and Contradictions* we held on 12–14 November 2020 with their usual generosity and wisdom. The pandemic obliged us to transform the planned in-person event into a virtual congress (long before these became conventional) that spanned three continents and crossed twenty-two time zones, but this did not dampen the spirit of the international group of scholars who presented their research and engaged with one another in lively and productive discussions. Their contributions built upon but also challenged recent decades of research on premodern men and masculinities and, in so doing, moved the field forward in new and exciting ways. Their work pointed especially to the flexibility of masculinity and the expectations placed on men over the premodern period. This collection of chapters, focusing as they do on this flexibility, is one of the outcomes of that splendid (and, as it happened, itself also rather flexible) conference.

The conference was made possible through the generous support of many institutions, first among them the Social Sciences and Humanities Research Council of Canada, whose Connections Grant supported not only the conference but also the editing of this volume. We received essential support from Victoria University through its President's Office and its Centre for Renaissance and Reformation Studies. The ever-capable Eva Chivite managed the entire virtual side of the conference. We are also grateful to the Office of the President at the University of Saint Michael's College and to the Praeses of the Pontifical Institute for Mediaeval Studies. Many units within the University of Toronto supported the conference, in particular the Emilio Goggio Chair in Italian Studies, the Centre for Medieval Studies, the Bonham Centre for Sexual Diversity Studies, the Centre for Comparative Literature, the departments of English, French, History, Religion, Spanish and Portuguese, and the Institute for Islamic Studies. We also received considerable support from partners at the University of Guelph through the Dean of the College of Arts, the Department of History, and the Work-Study program. At Saint Jerome's University the Academic Dean and the DRAGEN Lab also came

Acknowledgements

to our assistance. And we are grateful to the Royal Ontario Museum for sponsoring the participation of Professor Patricia Simons and including her plenary presentation in the ROM Connects series of talks.

As editors of this collection, we were fortunate to benefit from the various contributions of Emma Hoffer-Weinper, Susan K. Riggs, and Dr Rachel Stapleton. Dr Dana Wessell Lightfoot also graciously provided us with excellent advice at the eleventh hour.

The double-blind peer reviewers who read through the collection made excellent suggestions that strengthened the chapters and the volume as a whole. Theirs is a thankless job, partly because they are shrouded in anonymity, but it's also a critical contribution to the scholarly enterprise. We appreciate their sharing their wisdom and their time.

We are especially grateful to Caroline Palmer, Editorial Director at Boydell and Brewer, and to the entire team for their support and expertise in bringing this collection into print.

Finally, we would like to acknowledge and thank the colleagues who have contributed their research to this volume, as well as all the conference participants whose research continues to inspire and expand this important area of historical research.

Konrad Eisenbichler	Jacqueline Murray
University of Toronto	*University of Guelph*

INTRODUCTION

Jacqueline Murray

In recent decades, scholars have been re-examining the experiences of men across every historical period and culture, motivated in part by the current so-called "crisis of masculinity."[1] This has involved moving away from previous universalizing perspectives that considered men as both preeminent and normative human beings. Women were gendered, men were human. Happily, this perspective has now evaporated and current historical research approaches men as gendered and masculinity as an historical phenomenon informed by context and subject to change over time. Like femineity, masculinity is intersectional and malleable. Yet, there is little recognition, much less agreement, about the various manifestations of masculinities and what kind of social changes impacted men's internal sense of self and their external performance of masculinity. To what extent does conventional periodization map onto changes in masculinities? Or, put another way, to what extent does masculinity, as gender and as identity, appear resilient and resistant to historical pressures?

Embracing the premodern period as broadly defined, this collection of essays explores questions about masculinities, incorporating the psychological and social perspectives, leading to re-evaluations of the meanings and permutations of masculinity that eventually signalled the transition into a new historical era. Thus, masculinities have a history that can be set against other histories, particularly notable in the transition from the culture and society of the late fourteenth century, through to the end of the sixteenth century. This was a period of radical change, of rupture and upheaval in almost every area of European, and indeed, global society. Christendom, that concept that had united Europe for a millennium, was no longer a unifying force. The Protestant Reformation transformed the Age of Faith into an age of the Wars of Religion.

---

[1] See, for example, Mary O'Connor's recent three-part series "Man Up! The Masculinity Crisis," first aired on 18 May 2023 in the CBC Radio program *Ideas*. Part One of this series focused on masculinities in Antiquity, the Middle Ages, and the Early Modern Period. Online www.cbc.ca/radio/ideas/man-up-masculinity-crisis-part-one-1.6844883.

Jacqueline Murray

Printing fundamentally changed communication, facilitating the spread of new ideas in science and religion, and new values of humanism and law, new forms of art and literature. Innovations in military technology fundamentally altered how wars were fought and destabilized the warrior class and the warrior code; the knights of chivalry were relegated to the pages of romance or dreams of a heroic past. Medieval kingdoms disappeared and nation-states emerged to radically alter the map of western Europe, while the expansion of the Ottoman Empire did the same for eastern Europe and beyond. Neither of these geopolitical changes was quite as dramatic as that occasioned by the oceanic voyages that, within a few decades, opened a global world and new political, economic, and human systems.[2] The sixteenth century, in particular, was also a time of profound transformation of the values and performance of masculinities as men and societies were required to adapt to new circumstances.

It is common to consider the end of the sixteenth century as the beginning of a new historical period, the age of modernity. Such historical labels, however, and indeed the very notion of periodization itself, is a fraught issue. It has very little to do with the past per se. Rather, it is an artificial construction, a means to make sense of the seemingly continuous beginning-ness and ending-ness of the flow of history. It is an attempt to contain time and space and make sense of it, an imposition by the observer in order to divide past and present into manageable, sensible pieces. The fraughtness of periodization is evident in the demarcation of modern and postmodern so noticeable in this millennium.[3] But, as Fredric Jameson has observed, without periodization we cannot perceive change.[4] Our very definition of history, as change over time, is based on periodization and the discontinuities that make one period discernable from another, much like those factors that distinguish the sixteenth from the seventeenth century. While conventional periodization makes sense for many areas of historical research, the traditional demarcations are not always applicable or relevant despite the enduring structuralism of historical research. Arguably, the sweeping economic and political changes that reconfigured the meta-historical systems in the long term had more measured short-term effects on the modes of life at local and modest social levels. So it is with histories of gender: it is both remarkably resilient and resistant to change while also being fluid and transformative.

Gender, the social and cultural identities of men and women, is amorphous and fluid and tends not to align nicely with the standard political, religious,

---

[2] Cameron, ed., *The Sixteenth Century*. Cameron draws together a series of articles that treats virtually all these topics but has little to say about social history, enslavement, the histories of men and women, of sexes and genders, or the cultural milieux that informed daily life. The essays of this collection map questions of gender and masculinities over such traditional analyses of the tumultuous sixteenth century.

[3] See, for example, Hutcheon, *Politics of Postmodernism*; Akinwumi, "Review Article – A Singular Time, or a Separated Continuum?"

[4] Jameson, *A Singular Modernity: Essay on the Ontology of the Present*.

Introduction

and economic markers of historical change. Gender expectations differ not only between men and women, but also across classes and cultures. Yet, for all that, gender is remarkably stable, as much subject to historical continuity as to change over time. Consequently, gender pushes against conventional periodization. For example, the traditional division between "Medieval" and "Renaissance" privileges certain intellectual and cultural perspectives linked to antiquity and its embeddedness in the nineteenth-century views of Jacob Burckhardt.[5] "Medieval" and "Early Modern" have proven equally unsatisfactory, pulling the latter away from the Middle Ages and linking it more closely with the "Modern" through emphases on alterations in political or economic regimes, among other factors.[6]

The discontinuity between medieval and early modern, however, is perhaps more imagined than real in many areas of culture and society that are characterized by similarity and continuity, for example, in daily life or in the experiences of non-elites.[7] For this reason, social and gender historians have long preferred the notion of the "Premodern" in order to stress areas of "social and cultural continuity" from the twelfth through sixteenth centuries.[8] Premodern might be considered a more organic but fuzzy mode of periodization that can variously integrate centuries stretching from the Fall of Rome to the Enlightenment, depending on topic, perspective, and an individual historian's inclination. It does, however, permit a focus on similarity and continuity that fits well with the assessment of gender throughout the premodern period.

Premodern masculinity was always multivalent and dynamic, a series of intersecting, conflicting, and malleable identities that, nevertheless, were distinct and recognizable to individual men and women and their societies. This has been evident since the earlier studies of men and masculinities that appeared in collections throughout the 1990s.[9] This volume, and a number of others that were published in the 2010s and 2020s, represent a virtual second wave of studies about men, less focused on the individual men or the

---

[5] Burckhardt, *The Civilization of the Renaissance in Italy*. The challenges and critiques from the first half of the twentieth century were compiled in Dannenfelt, *The Renaissance, Medieval or Modern?*

[6] See, for example, the criteria discussed above, used by Cameron, *Sixteenth Century*. See also the helpful introduction by Summit and Wallace, "Rethinking Periodization" to a special issue of *The Journal of Medieval and Early Modern Studies* with articles focusing on questions of periodization.

[7] See, for example, Bennett, "Confronting Continuity."

[8] Murray and Eisenbichler, *Desire and Discipline*, xii.

[9] Although many editors locate these studies in the Middle Ages, in truth many of the articles move across what is better termed the premodern world and incorporate experiences of non-Christian, non-heteronormative men. See Lees, *Medieval Masculinities*; Murray, *Conflicted Identities and Multiple Masculinities*; Hadley, *Masculinity in Medieval Europe*; Cohen and Wheeler, *Becoming Male in the Middle Ages*.

universal "man," and moving instead beyond gender binaries, sensitive to the multivalence of masculinities and male intersectionality.[10] Aligned with this subtle "second wave" approach to masculinities, the articles collected in this volume examine a variety of means by which masculinity was constructed, deconstructed, and transformed across time and cultures. They reveal how masculinity was inculcated, performed, and accommodated during the premodern period, a period when masculinities were in transition. They challenge the dichotomous notions of hegemonic masculinity, demonstrating how traditional expressions of masculinity were eroded under pressure from the shifting landscape of sixteenth-century society, making way for new men and new masculine values.

The fundamental premise of this collection is that masculinity is adaptable and adjusts continually to new circumstances and changing values. Together, the articles embrace a chronological and geographical breadth moving across the premodern world from twelfth-century France to sixteenth-century Italy, from the cloister to the world, from the Persian Empire to the Mongol Empire, and from Muslim to Christian cultures. They are in dynamic conversation with each other and with the societies and cultures they examine, united by an understanding of the attentiveness of masculinities to social and cultural diversities and the ability to accommodate both continuity and change.

SHIFTING MASCULINITIES

In order to avoid the pitfalls of universalizing or essentializing, much current scholarship concentrates on specificity and carefully constructed case studies. It is equally important, however, to trace the continuities of masculinities across time, space, and cultures.[11] Premodern masculinity is frequently construed as displays of male dominance; "to be a man" entailed demonstrating power over women and subordinates. This, then, reinforced the patriarchal social structure while validating the masculinity and honour of individual men. Thus, premodern masculinity has been conceived as hierarchical, as a quality that adhered to virile elite secular leaders who wielded socially sanctioned power and authority. The articles in this section challenge this stereotype. Newman demonstrates the appreciation of diverse masculinities within monastic literary circles. Cohen argues for a more nuanced assessment of masculine values that could cross social status, culture, and even sex. Ross traces the shifting nature of masculine qualities conveyed by a single poem that spoke across multiple temporal and cultural divides. Ultimately, in all these examples, masculinity was respected

---

[10] See, for example, Karras, *From Boys to Men* (2003); Rasmussen, *Rivalrous Masculinities* (2019); Murray, *The Male Body and Social Masculinity* (2022); and Murray, *Patriarchy, Honour, and Violence* (2022).

[11] See also Lees, "A Word to the Wise," in Rasmussen, *Rivalrous* Masculinities, 7.

Introduction

when appropriate to a person's place in the world. Such status-based masculinity was flexible but remained recognizable across multiple mutable contexts.

Jonathan H. Newman opens this collection with a study that explicitly challenges periodization by stretching the premodern world back into the twelfth century. Far from being an outlier among studies of the fourteenth to sixteenth centuries, Newman's study of Baudri of Bourgueil and his circle of friends consciously confronts the artificial periodization that separates the Middle Ages from the Early Modern, finding commonality between the classicism and textual communities of Baudri and his friends with those of the fifteenth- and sixteenth-century humanists. For all these premodern men, monastic poets and secular humanists alike, textual composition was a demonstration of intellectual prowess, a means to fashion and exhibit their masculinity into the world. In his lyric poetry, Baudri developed his masculine identity as an able administrator and *paterfamilias* of the monks of his abbey/household. Two aspects of writing emerge, the mental work of composition and the material work of book production, both of which required masculine skills and competence but of different sorts. While Baudri appreciates the masculine competence of the craftsman who fashions the pens and the scribe who wields them, transcribing his words onto the physical page, it is nevertheless the wordsmith, the administrator, the abbot who exercises the greatest masculine authority. This hierarchical masculinity, based on skill or competence, traces across multiple statuses – poetic, clerical, administrative, scribal – was recognized across the premodern world. Thus, masculinity must be assessed from both synchronic and diachronic perspectives in order to identify both contextual specificity and evolution.

The appreciation of competence highlighted by Newman is similarly foregrounded by Thomas V. Cohen in his study of testimony delivered before the criminal courts in sixteenth-century Rome. Cohen considers the distinctive quality of this masculinity to have been *fede*, trustworthiness, challenging the extent to which historians of masculinity focus on honour and violence.[12] He argues that masculinity and femineity were not binary opposites but rather shared many of the same values and behaviours generally attributed to one gender or the other. These could include tact, a sense of timing, loyalty, generosity of spirit, and good sense. Cohen further argues that this wider, values-driven approach allows premodern masculinity to be decoupled from dominant males in their prime. He uses this perspective to analyze the evidence of sixteenth-century Roman court records and reveals the overlapping complexities of gender and the fundamental instability of traditional hegemonic masculinity. Examples of competence, which he identifies with *fede*, could be found in young and old, among both the rich and the poor, between master and servant, as well as in the actions of both men and women. Thus, while premodern masculinities were flexible and multivalent, crucially Cohen challenges the gender and class

---

[12] See, for example, Murray, *Patriarchy, Honour, and Violence*.

binaries that continue to dominate scholarship on the social expectations of premodern men and women.

Like Newman, Danielle Ross uses literature as a point of entry and a means to reflect the values of masculinity in the surrounding societies. Ross examines the shifting of masculinity across time and culture, taking the Persianate poem *Qahramān-I Qātil* as her starting point. She follows the poem's discursive evolution across the fourteenth to seventeenth centuries as it travelled from Persia into Russia's Volga-Ural region. While transitioning across time, geography, religion, peoples, and cultures, the poem continued to be relevant as it was appropriated and reinterpreted across the cultural divides that separated the urbanized Eastern Mediterranean and the nomadic Mongolian steppes. Masculinity was significantly reinterpreted, as well, moving from an urban working class in the original Persianate version to warrior-aristocratic values in the Volga-Ural areas that were more affected by Mongol influences. This cycle of appropriation and refinement, as the poem was adopted by different social and cultural cadres, echoes the hierarchical and class-based observations about masculinity identified by Newman and Cohen. Masculinity could differ according to the individual man's social and cultural position, while still reflecting overarching masculine values. Ross also identifies transitions in the poem's presentation of masculinity as the society of the Mongol warrior incorporated Muslim practices of inclusivity; together they merged into a masculinity that promoted grace and a moral compass. The inclusion of, and interaction with, other peoples in successor states culminated in the incorporation of Russian-Christian values and a masculinity based on inner virtue and self-discipline. Ultimately, the poem *Qahramān-i Qātil* reveals normative masculinity moving from urban Persia, through the warriors of the Golden Horde, Mongol Muslims, and Russian Christians, all the while shapeshifting to incorporate masculine norms that aligned with different cultural contexts, at once reflecting multiple hegemonic masculinities while also demonstrating their fundamental flexibility.

FLUID MASCULINITIES

If, as David Gilmore argues, masculinity needs to be externally visible and recognized by other men,[13] then it follows that premodern society recognized various manifestations across the lived experience of diverse men. At some level, then, premodern people accepted that masculinity was fluid much as contemporary scholarship identifies the multivalence of masculinities. Certainly, men employed various strategies in their presentation of self, an embodied self that could be both conventional and shapeshifting.[14] The articles

---

[13] Gilmore, *Manhood in the Making*, 7–8.
[14] See, for example, Murray, *The Male Body and Social Masculinity*.

Introduction

in this section discuss how social artefacts and visual culture expressed the fluid dynamics of masculinity between subject and viewer. Premodern men were able to assert, manage, and modify their masculinity through embodied symbols, such as the absence or presence of beards explored by Simons. Sartorial artefacts also functioned as symbols of masculinity, easily assumed or discarded. Thus, Doda's discussion of spurs and Hollander's discussion of swords both reveal a fluidity of self-presentation as men employed art and artefacts to convey their masculinity.

The mutability of how masculinities were performed and manifested across time and cultures provides the basis for Patricia Simons' examination of the meanings of men's facial hair in images from the fifteenth and sixteenth centuries. In the fifteenth century, in northern Europe and the Mediterranean, men demonstrated a definite preference to be clean shaven but in the sixteenth century beards came to dominate in paintings and images. Simons explores the ways in which the meanings of beards, their presence or absence, could signal age, status, religious, political, or social contexts. One notable example is found in the great Greek scholar Bessarion, who moved to Italy, left Greek Orthodoxy behind and became a Roman Catholic cardinal. Once touted as a papal candidate, he was ultimately passed over, perhaps because he continued to sport his Greek beard at a time when Latin prelates were clean-shaven, thereby underscoring his "otherness." Protestant Reformers also wore beards to differentiate themselves from their Catholic rivals. Among fifteenth-century secular men, a clean-shaven face indicated "masculinity that was contained, controlled, normative, honourable," while long bushy beards were linked to a more uncontained sexuality and even sinfulness. These perceptions changed in the sixteenth century when a cluster of young rulers – Holy Roman Emperor Charles V, Francis I of France, Henry VIII of England, and Suleiman the Magnificent in the Ottoman Empire – succeeded to power and used facial hair as a means to overcome their youth.[15] By sporting permanent beards, they asserted their authority and virility. Simons' discussion is provocative and important for reading the changes from the fifteenth to sixteenth centuries in men's sense of themselves and their self-presentation, and in the image and meaning they chose to communicate through facial hair.

Hilary Doda similarly examines the fluid meaning of symbols of masculinity, this time in the context of English society. Doda focuses on the external appropriation of artefacts intended to reflect both internal and external aspects of masculinity. Spurs were important external symbols of a constructed masculinity, symbols that were transformed over time from the "Middle Ages" to the end of the "Early Modern" period. The spur survives in various forms from physical artefact through images in paintings and etchings to literary

---

[15] See Lewis, *Kingship and Masculinity*, for an exploration of royal masculinity in an earlier period.

representations. While the specificities of the masculinity represented by spurs was mutable, they were nevertheless always associated with manhood. Moreover, spurs denoted a masculinity that was stable and hierarchical; it could exercise control over the self and over others. While superficially spurs appear to have been linked to knighthood and chivalry, in fact, they were accessible to men of lower stations and different occupations, although the objects themselves might vary in materials and decoration. In the later Middle Ages, spurs were linked to the assumption of full manhood – a boy would "earn his spurs" – later they were sometimes functional and sometimes merely decorative. Moreover, across the period they gradually replaced the codpiece as the symbol of masculine prowess, as Sarah Wilk notes in her own essay, citing a reference to "golden spurs" as a sign of knighthood. By the end of the sixteenth century, however, spurs had lost their association with rank and respectability, transitioning to become symbols of the chaotic and uncontrolled behaviour at dance halls, images of entertainment rather than knighthood. As Doda puts it, spurs were transformed from being armour to being "the leftover symbolism of armour."

Martha Hollander continues the examination of the fluidity of meaning in the depiction of objects worn by men, in this case, swords that were originally associated with military masculinity. From the sixteenth century onwards, swords were a ubiquitous European male accessory and a sign of masculinity not only for the nobility but also for middle-class men, military men, and civilian men. Consequently, the presence of a sword, or its absence, was laden with meaning. Hollander examines paintings and portraits from seventeenth-century Dutch artists to decode the symbolism of discarded and unworn swords. In paintings of love scenes, or scenes suggestive of eroticism, swords were shown lying abandoned or placed suggestively on tables, leaning against furniture, or hung on hooks, with or without the cloaks that often accompanied swords in art as in life. Discarded swords were also portrayed with groups picnicking out-of-doors or dining in household scenes. Together, these images portray how men could take off their public masculine identity by simply removing their sword, perhaps assuming in the process other aspects of private masculinity such as lover, husband, or householder. Thus, Hollander reaffirms that masculinity was indeed transitional, something men could put on or take off as easily as a sword, that most potent and phallic symbol of masculinity's power and performativity. The symbolism of beards, swords, and spurs says much about how men portrayed their masculinity and how their society perceived it.

TRANSFORMING MASCULINITIES

There is a consensus among gender historians that premodern masculinity/masculinities were a product of time and place, people and values. But masculine norms and the experience of their contextual mutability were also lodged in premodern men's unconscious, informing their decisions

Introduction

and experiences, although perhaps not always consciously appreciated. Textual sources allow access to the conscious and unconscious tensions that underlay the traditional and the transformative experiences of masculinity. As Sara Wilks demonstrates, challenges to elite masculinity were reflected in disjunctions between, for example, knightly ideals and the realities of war that were being challenged and transformed as early as the fourteenth century. Moreover, as Lukas argues, these changes had, by the sixteenth century, transformed, and perhaps diminished, the military masculinity that had hitherto epitomized traditional masculinity in the person of the elite noble warrior. Gerry Milligan reflects on how, for some men, the outer self that performed masculinity could also be in tension with the inner self and a man's sense of identity.[16] The transformations of normative and performative masculinities resulted in social and individual anxiety.

Analyzing the portrayal of Bertrand du Guesclin in a fourteenth-century chanson written to celebrate his military masculinity, Sarah Wilk reflects on the personal values required for a man to be considered a good knight. While Guesclin was a valorous warrior for the French crown during the Hundred Years' War, he was also a trusted advisor to the king. Indeed, the poem stresses that Guesclin risked opprobrium and accusations of cowardice by providing honest and temperate advice that contradicted that of more hotheaded and less able knights who were motivated by an ideology of honour rather than pragmatic military strategy. The poem portrays one critical aspect of military masculinity: unconditional loyalty that still allows for following one's inner moral compass, much like the *fede* foregrounded by Cohen. This discussion shows Guesclin's knighthood as nuanced and refined: requiring military skill and loyalty but also allowing him to proffer unpopular advice, knowing that this too was an essential aspect of knightly honour. The strains between Guesclin and his more militant peers reveal older chivalric values being challenged by pragmatism sustained by unswerving loyalty and trust between knight and liege.

Benjamin Lukas moves the discussion of the transformations experienced by knighthood further, juxtaposing the conventional warrior-knight of chivalry with a new conceptualization of knights as leaders of men. The catalyst for this transition was the military revolution that occurred in sixteenth-century France. Lukas examines the careers of two knights, Pierre Terrail and Blaise de Monluc, to demonstrate the dramatic difference between the two. In his biography of Pierre Terrail, Jacques Mailles describes him in the context of traditional chivalric knighthood, paying attention to participation in tournaments and engaging in courtly romance. By comparison, Blaise de Monluc, who wrote his own memoir, consciously chose to echo Julius Caesar rather than the knights of chivalry. Monluc moves far beyond chivalric

---

[16] This tension between masculinity as a social construct and the individual's inner sense of self was explored early on by Neal, *The Masculine Self*.

warrior-knights to present himself and his fellow noble knights not as individual warriors but rather as captains who lead armies of soldiers from the third estate. The transition from warrior to leader demonstrated that a new knightly masculinity had emerged, one that privileged leadership over individual prowess in battle.

The shockwaves that destabilized conventional knightly values and confidence set the scene for Gerry Milligan's examination of its effects on sixteenth-century society. Using texts written in Italy, he provides insights into the stresses and strains that accompanied men's attempts to embrace and embody hegemonic masculinity in times of transition and uncertainty. Milligan uses texts by Niccolò Machiavelli, Anton Francesco Doni, and Scipione Ammirato, all writers who critiqued the effeminacy of Italian men at a time of considerable social and political crisis. These writers used elite men's external presentation of self, including luxurious dress and effeminate mannerisms, to explain the failures of Italian militancy and masculinity. As Milligan notes, "The sight, smell, and sound of men were fodder for some of the most vehement criticisms of masculine gender performance," also implying failures of Christian morality. The three writers suggested that the so-called effeminacy of elite Italian men had led to social breakdown and the resultant weakness that led to myriad Italian military defeats. But, argues Milligan, a social program of remasculinization would have had little realistic effect on the fortunes of war. These criticisms disguised the writers' real concern that the effeminate presentation by elite men was destabilizing traditional, normative, hegemonic binary gender roles. More importantly, external criticisms of male effeminacy would not necessarily have reflected a man's sense of himself and his own masculinity.[17] Milligan suggests that external critiques do not necessarily reveal internal personal anxieties, even though society itself might be experiencing historical anxiety. Masculinity as the internal sense of self did not necessarily align with perceptions of a man's external presentation.

CONCLUSION

With the historical transformation and the cultural anxiety that developed in the course of the sixteenth century, the older premodern values of masculinity became increasingly anachronistic or irrelevant. More importantly, the world had changed and so, too, had the expectations laid upon men and the strategies they used to meet these expectations. Consequently, in the sixteenth century, masculinities were in a state of transition. Diverse masculinities were assumed

---

[17] In this, Milligan provocatively and thoughtfully takes issue with the necessity that masculinity be recognized by other men, as posited by Gilmore, *Manhood in the Making*, 7–8.

Introduction

and enacted by diverse groups, thus redistributing masculinity among various ages, classes, religions, and genders in a way unthinkable to earlier generations. Similarly, masculine self-identity shifted from the demonstration of physical prowess found among premodern warriors and enshrined in chivalric ideals. Masculinity could be signalled by a beard or spurs or a sword. While noble warriors were sidelined, elite men could present an external effeminacy that, while condemned by other men, nevertheless did not necessarily mean they themselves experienced a sense of masculine inadequacy or failure.

Much like patriarchy, profound changes to the social organization and institutions in which masculinity was enacted did not result in its disappearance. As with the flexible and adaptable "patriarchal equilibrium,"[18] so too masculinities experienced multiple transitions, as new values, ideals, and presentations of self were disseminated, adapting to meet new conditions but, like patriarchy, maintaining an equilibrium. By the seventeenth century, those transitions had cumulatively led masculinity to transition into something different but recognizable. However these many adaptive premodern masculinities are understood, together they point to the sixteenth century as a period of male gender transition that paralleled many of the political, economic, religious, and cultural transitions that were rocking the world. This volume sits on the cusp of old worlds and new. It reveals how masculinity experienced continuity and change, transitioning into this new world order.

University of Guelph

CITED WORKS

Printed Sources

Akinwumi, Akinbola E. "Review Article – A Singular Time, or a Separated Continuum? Unthinking Modernity/Postmodernity." *Time & Society* 15.2–3 (2006): 365–372. doi.org/10.1177/0961463X06066953.

Bennett, Judith M. "Confronting Continuity." *Journal of Women's History* 9.3 (1997): 73–94.

———. *History Matters. Patriarchy and the Challenges of Feminism*. Philadelphia, PA: University of Pennsylvania Press, 2006.

Burckhardt, Jakob. *The Civilization of the Renaissance in Italy: An Essay*. Oxford: Phaidon Press, 1981 (first German edition, 1860; first English edition, 1878).

Cameron, Euan, ed. *The Sixteenth Century*. Oxford: Oxford University Press, 2006.

Cohen, Jeffrey Jerome and Bonnie Wheeler, eds. *Becoming Male in the Middle Ages*. New York: Garland, 1997.

Dannenfelt, Carl H., ed. *The Renaissance, Medieval or Modern?* Boston, MA: D. C. Heath, 1959.

---

[18] Bennett, *History Matters*, 80.

Gilmore, David D. *Manhood in the Making: Cultural Concepts of Masculinity.* New Haven, CT: Yale University Press, 1990.

Hadley, Dawn, ed. *Masculinity in Medieval Europe.* New York: Longman, 1999.

Hutcheon, Linda. *The Politics of Postmodernism.* London: Routledge, 2002.

Jameson, Fredric. *A Singular Modernity: Essay on the Ontology of the Present.* London: Verso, 2002.

Karras, Ruth Mazo. *From Boys to Men. Formations of Masculinity in Late Medieval Europe.* Philadelphia, PA: University of Pennsylvania Press, 2003.

Lewis, Katherine J. *Kingship and Masculinity in Late Medieval England.* London: Routledge, 2013.

Neal, Derek. *The Masculine Self in Late Medieval England.* Chicago, IL: University of Chicago Press, 2008.

Murray, Jacqueline, ed. *Conflicted Identities and Multiple Masculinities: Men in the Medieval West.* New York: Garland, 1999.

——. *Patriarchy, Honour, and Violence: Masculinities in Premodern Europe.* Essays and Studies, 57. Toronto: Centre for Renaissance and Reformation Studies, 2022.

——. *The Male Body and Social Masculinity in Premodern Europe.* Essays and Studies, 56. Toronto: Centre for Renaissance and Reformation Studies, 2022.

—— and Konrad Eisenbichler, eds. *Desire and Discipline. Sex and Sexuality in the Premodern West.* Toronto: University of Toronto Press, 1996.

Rasmussen, Ann Marie, ed. *Rivalrous Masculinities. New Directions in Medieval Gender Studies.* Notre Dame, IN: University of Notre Dame Press, 2019.

Summit, Jennifer and David Wallace. "Rethinking Periodization." *Journal of Medieval and Early Modern Studies* 37.3 (2007): 447–451. doi.org/10.1215/10829636-2007-007.

Electronic Sources

O'Connell, Mary, producer. "Man Up! The Masculinity Crisis." CBC Radio program *Ideas*, first aired on 18 May 2023. Online www.cbc.ca/radio/ideas/man-up-masculinity-crisis-part-one-1.6844883.

SHIFTING MASCULINITIES

1

WORK, WRITING, AND ELITE MASCULINITY IN THE LYRICS OF BAUDRI OF BOURGUEIL

Jonathan M. Newman

Despite a century of scholarship troubling the boundary between medieval and early modern, one still encounters Jakob Burckhardt's periodization that sets apart a medieval classicism – distant, reverential, and decontextualizing – from renaissance classicism, which, conscious of historical difference and change, engaged classical authors as peers and familiars.[1] This development was epitomized by Petrarch's letters to Cicero upon his "discovery" of Cicero's familiar letters and was dramatized by Florentines giving orations in ancient Roman dress.[2] Nevertheless, medieval scholars since Charles Haskins have found ever earlier instances of the kinds of discourse and self-representations that get called "humanism," "classicism," "individuality," and so forth.[3] The milieu examined in this chapter, north-western France in the late eleventh century, featured a small group of high-status men, the Loire Valley poets, who imitated classical authors, especially Ovid and Horace. They had a good ear for meter, a refined aesthetic sensibility, and a propensity for reimagining their lives and circumstances through poetic analogy to the lifeworld of high-status Roman men represented by ancient Roman lyric. The Loire Valley poets engaged with the classics in a playful, creative way, treating classical texts not as disembodied, ahistorical authorities offering phrases for colour and pomp, but as living utterance and social performance.

Like their early modern counterparts, highly educated literary men of the late eleventh century played in the wardrobe of personae offered by Roman lyric poetry, and there found costumes from which they fashioned authoritative masculine personae. The Roman patrician masks fit the roles these medieval poets played in their lives – not as spiritual authorities (though they were all highly ranked churchmen), but as heads of households and administrators of material property and ranked hierarchies of men at work. The lyric poetry

---

[1] Burckhardt, *The Civilization of the Renaissance in Italy*.
[2] Wilson, "Petrarch's Queer History," 719; Currie, *Fashion and Masculinity*, 36.
[3] Haskins, *The Renaissance of the Twelfth Century*. For a broad overview of this debate over periodization and *mentalité*, see Benton, "Consciousness of Self and Perceptions of Individuality," 263–298.

they wrote on the playful and even erotic themes were not juvenile exercises to be replaced in maturity by more serious writing; according to internal references, these poets were already abbots, archdeacons, and bishops charged with the care of souls and significant temporal power.

Their poetic exchanges, then, were not then a discursive space of retreat from responsibility, but a signifier of their authority, status, social relations, even partisan affiliation in contemporary controversies over church governance. Their poems enact personae at once unstudied, playful, irreverent, and witty, but also conveying authority and responsibility. The Horatian persona takes ease in his authority and enjoys the upper hand in most interactions. It is a species of elite masculinity, the *paterfamilias*, and their poetry represents an early instance of the recuperation of this mode of masculinity based in learning, administrative competence, and mannered sophistication. In this "Romanesque" period of Latin western Europe, this kind of masculinity coalesced as an alternative to martial or chivalric masculinity. It would later come to be blended with these as the courtly knight became the professional soldier and courtier, and as the lay elites of Europe integrated the documentary administration into its courts and made competence in these affairs a core value. This is a masculinity predicated on writing and literary skill, and enacted through writing, and hedged about with the trappings of sophisticated literacy, and its early instancing here might serve to clarify some of its features as they would appear in coming centuries.

I will focus specifically on the writing of Baudri of Bourgueil (1050–1130); a number of his lyric poems can be designated as belonging to a "writing group." These poems link the immaterial act of composing verses to the production and exchange of material and labour among a community of men sharing a common work culture of books, tablets, styluses, metrical feet, ink – all the material links between Baudri's identity as a poet and his identity as an abbot and cleric. The writing group is central to Baudri's poetic persona and, more specifically, to his precocious instancing of textual clerical masculinity, a form of hegemonic masculinity distinct from already legible forms at the time. These poems show "how textual strategies can create normative ideas of masculinity" that define communities of men of similar training, experience, and status.[4] In the case of Baudri, these normative ideas of masculinity centre textuality itself not just as a means of expression and communication but as the totem of an authority that is social, institutional, and material at least as much as spiritual, and that is gendered as masculine.

At a time when textual administration was expanding rapidly across western Europe, Baudri's interest in making and using texts and his exploration of the possibilities of self-representation in texts were inseparable from his administrative work as an abbot. In his early career, he was educated at the cathedral school of Angers. In 1079, Baudri became the abbot of Saint-Pierre-de-Bourgueil in Anjou; during this tenure he wrote the majority of the 256 lyric poems collected in a

---

[4] Quaintance, *Textual Masculinity*, 30.

single surviving manuscript under the title of *Carmina*.[5] In 1107, he became bishop of Dol, and became involved at the highest levels of church business, travelling frequently and taking part in councils until his retirement. He is well-known among historians for writing an account of the First Crusade drawn from the testimony of eyewitnesses and several historical poems about near-past events, such as the Norman conquest of England.[6]

Saint-Pierre-de-Bourgueil was a rich abbey; it was closely associated with the duchy of Aquitaine and later with the monarchs of the Angevin empire, and records suggest that thanks to his administrative skills Baudri even increased the abbey's wealth.[7] Baudri's poems, many of them epistolary works addressed to friends, scribes, and counterparts at other monasteries and church institutions, offer an idealized view of monastic life as practiced by him and his fellow monks. The ideals he expresses, however, differ in important respects from the rigorous asceticism championed by his contemporary, the abbot Robert de Molesme, who in 1075 tried to restore the "strict observance" of the Benedictine rule. In Baudri's writings we can find devotion and commitment to monastic ideals, but we also find, and in greater measure, the elegance, decorum, and learned self-cultivation of eleventh-century schoolmasters.[8] Baudri stands between the reforming Benedictine monasteries and the secular masters at the cathedral schools of late eleventh-century north-western Europe, both distinct but significant developments in clerical life of the period. C. Stephen Jaeger has discussed the attention to bodily grace, decorum, and presence in writings by and about cathedral school masters and has identified this as one of the origins of courtly self-performance.[9] For Jaeger, the act of writing memorialized the master's charismatic physical authority but did not itself produce it. Writing by and about schoolmasters thus invested contemporary social identity into text and was part of a surge of expressing social selves in writing that included not only the Latin lyrics of Baudri and the other Loire Valley poets, but also the formulae of address and petition in the rapidly developing *ars dictaminis* and in the vernacular and Latin literature in decades to come.[10]

The lyrics of Baudri of Bourgueil instance the poetic investment of a social persona into a textualized self. This persona – moral and decorous, but with an

---

[5] BAV, Reg. lat 1351.
[6] See Baudry, *The Historia Ierosolimitana*; Baudry, *Baldric of Bourgueil "History of the Jerusalemites."*
[7] Dupont, *Monographie du cartulaire de Bourgueil*, 30–31 and 183–186; Baudri, *Poèmes*, vol. 1, vii, 6.
[8] On Baudri's link to the culture of the cathedral schools, both their humanistic study and their cultivation of *mores*, see Jaeger, *The Envy of Angels*, 61.
[9] This thesis runs through *The Envy of Angels*, as well as *The Origins of Courtly Love* and the essays collected in *Scholars and Courtiers*.
[10] The first surviving handbook of the *ars dictaminis* dates from the same decade as Baudri's lyrics, the 1080s. Constable, *Letters and Letter-Collections*, 34–38.

affable and gentle wit – offers a specimen of an emergent "textual masculinity" in Romanesque France, one that would come to much greater prominence as the twelfth century progressed, especially in epistolography. The term textual masculinity is used by Constance Quaintance to describe an identity in an elite society of discourse, the "literary fraternity" of Pietro Aretino and his peers in sixteenth-century Venice.[11] Aretino's circle, like Baudri's, was marked by erudite exchanges that bound the group together "through the repetition of specific themes [...], poetic forms, and subject matter," and erotic or obscene subject matter that offered access "like a secret code" to some and excluded others.[12] Baudri and his monastic colleagues did not indulge in the frank obscenities of Aretino's circle, but they had their own privileged themes and subjects that likewise advertised their affiliation with sophisticated circles. More than anything else, these were the themes and subjects they explored in their sustained imitation and adaptation of ancient Roman poets, especially Ovid and Horace. Baudri and his literary circle were not just "a society of discourse" but a "community of practice" bound through the cultivation and exchange of learned Latin poetry.[13] This learning served the purpose of sociable display, the cultivation of the charismatic self that Jaeger documented so extensively; not simply an ornament or accomplishment, it was a part of leadership and practical administrative work.

MASCULINE AUTHORITY IN ROMANESQUE FRANCE

In medieval western Europe, authority was overwhelmingly masculine and the possible expressions of elite masculinities were multiple and contested. Scholarship on medieval masculinity has burgeoned since the 1990s. Jennifer Thibodeaux, for example, delineates common presuppositions and discoveries of this body of work; first, "masculinity is always tied to a struggle of some kind (manliness is proven by a defense and reinforcement of that particular masculinity)."[14] The prize for this struggle is the enjoyment of hegemonic masculinity, that is, the behaviours and habits that, through consensus rather than coercion, subjugate women to men, femininity to masculinity, and some kinds of men to other kinds of men.[15] Second, there were many kinds of hegemonic masculinity. Vern Bullough identifies traditional lay warrior masculinity with "impregnating women, protecting dependents, and serving as a provider to one's family."[16] In contrast to this Joann McNamara and others have discussed

---

[11] Quaintance, *Textual Masculinity*, 27.
[12] Quaintance, *Textual Masculinity*, 28.
[13] Wenger, *Communities of Practice*; Kopaczyk and Jucker, *Communities of Practice*, 4. More recently, see Vanderputten, Snijders, and Long, eds, *Horizontal Learning in the High Middle Ages*.
[14] Thibodeaux, *The Manly Priest*, 10.
[15] Connell, *Masculinities*, 76–79.
[16] Bullough, "Male in the Middle Ages," 34.

Work, Writing, and Elite Masculinity in the Lyrics of Baudri of Bourgueil

how clerics (especially monks), demonstrated masculinity through mastery over their own bodily desires, desires understood in patristic and scholastic writings as feminine temptations to be dominated by masculine reason and will.[17] Thus, clerical masculinity includes embodied sexuality enacted through struggle and self-mastery. Appropriate expressions of clerical masculinity were debated through writings that adapted authoritative biblical, patristic, and classical texts to underwrite the authority of specific masculine performances.[18] These included writings by a range of reform-minded writers including Peter Damian, Hildegard of Bingen, and others who identified corruption and worldliness in the church with effeminacy.[19] Reformed monks who lived in ascetic discipline were praised as spiritual warriors and soldiers of Christ.[20] Likewise, the warrior masculinity of actual warriors was celebrated not only in the ceremony and material practices of lay nobility, but in the Latin and vernacular textual culture of chroniclers like Geoffrey of Monmouth or Otto of Friesing, sermonizers like Bernard of Clairvaux, and romancers like Chrétien de Troyes.

The two traditionally legible forms of authoritative masculinity, monk and warrior, thus already had textual form, but a third kind of hegemonic masculinity proliferated in the eleventh and twelfth centuries generated within Latin textuality rather than arriving there as an act of translation or adaptation. This variety of clerical masculinity based itself on the act of writing and on mastery over writing rather than on the spiritual athletics of ascetic practice. Textual masculinity is a matter of advertising and sustaining individual and group status through writing and prowess at writing, and, through that practice, establishing and sustaining social connections among men. The textual masculinity built around the imitation of Roman authors learned by clerics in the cathedral schools became the kernel of humanistic culture as well as of the administrative class in subsequent eras of western European history.

One group of writers in this tradition was the coterie of high-ranking clerics to which Baudri belonged. In addition to Baudri, the so-called Loire Valley poets include the schoolmaster and archdeacon Marbode of Rennes (1035–1123) and archbishop Hildebert of Lavardin (1055–1133), but may be expanded to include their influential predecessor Godfrey of Reims (died c. 1094), to whom Baudri pays tribute. All were talented poets, precise prosodists, and greatly influenced by and interested in Ovid and Horace. Their careers offer a template for the kind of humanistic masculinity that would flourish in the early modern period in similar circles of elite educated men.

---

[17] McNamara, "The *Herrenfrage*," 6–9; Miller, "Masculinity, Reform, and Clerical Culture," 25–28; Thibodeaux, *The Manly Priest*, 16–23. On the link between corporeality, desire, and female embodiedness, see Dinshaw, *Chaucer's Sexual Poetics*, esp. 113–131.

[18] Parsons and Townsend, "Gender," 423–424.

[19] On Damian, see Olsen, *Of Sodomites*, 1–12. On Hildegard, see Newman, *Sister of Wisdom*, 238.

[20] See for example Wells, "The Warrior Habitus," 57–85.

Jonathan M. Newman

TEXTUAL MASCULINITY AND ROMANITAS

Clerical celibacy and the contests over sexual values and practices both locally and generally in the Latin church has often been studied, with shifting emphasis, through religious history and theories of gender and sexuality. Literary scholars including Gerald Bond, Ralph Hexter, and Susannah Brower have explored the uses to which Baudri and other clerical authors put Ovidian eroticism in fashioning a textual persona with a sexualized masculine identity.[21] Beyond sexuality, gender also entails social roles including those of protection and provision enumerated by Bullough; these often go along with a competition between men for status and within group coalitions to maintain it. In spite of the premium that Christian discourse puts on humility, the competition for status was a prominent feature of ecclesiastical life; abbeys or episcopal courts furnished elite churchmen with a household where they might exercise the role of *paterfamilias*, the autocratic master of the house. Ancient Latin literature had concepts and postures to offer to the competition and cooperation of such patriarchs.

In some poems, Baudri and the other Loire Valley poets imitate Horace's easeful poetic persona of mastery, comfort, and social graces much more than Ovid's louche playboy. Horatian masculinity revolves around the management and performance of a different set of appetites and dispositions than those specific to sexual relations.[22] The easy authority of the Horatian householder informs Baudri's persona, specifically in the ways his poetry enacts his management of his own household. His lyrics depict him at the top and centre of his abbey, and they perform his pre-eminence in that community through the association of his social and institutional position with his literary virtuosity. A number of the lyrics show him in his public official capacity, such as the many elegiac poems he wrote for mortuary rolls. Other works that show him performing his institutional role include letters of consolation urging young men to take up or remain in the monastic life.[23]

In contrast to these "official" poems, Baudri's lyrics sometimes display an "unofficial" masculine identity that encompasses sexuality and bodily presence. Gerald Bond argues that Baudri uses classicism and the idea of fictional eroticism as literary play, but the playfulness of Baudri's lyrics has other dimensions; his play with the topic of work reveals a conception of work as the foundation of relationships between men, personal and organizational. Michel de Certeau described play as "a stage on which the formality of practices is represented, but the condition of its possibility is that it be detached from actual social

---

[21] Bond, *The Loving Subject*, 64–68; Hexter, "Ovid in the Middle Ages," 422–424; Brower, "Gender, Power, and Persona," passim.

[22] On Baudri's allusions to Horace and invocation of a Horatian ethos, see Otter, "*Sufficientia*," 245–248; and Blänsdorf, "Ancient Genres," 209–218.

[23] Baudri, *Poèmes*, Carmen 91. Translations of Baudri's verse into English are my own, though I have consulted Tilliette's French translations.

practices."[24] Lyric poetry offers Baudri precisely this stage of detachment and formality. For him, writing was social practice: letters advertised affiliations and disputes; charters established property and community rules; sermons circulated intellectual ideas and community ideals. Baudri explores two different aspects of writing in tandem: the material work of making texts and the mental work of composition. Latin distinguishes these acts as *dictare* and *scribere*, the mental work of the master and the material work of the servant. Thus, writing as a social practice coordinates the specific social relations of Baudri's everyday life.

There are enough poems by Baudri about writing, writing practices, and writing materials to constitute a "writing group." An incomplete inventory of this includes Carmen 1 ("Contra obtrectatores"), a dedicatory envoi that addresses the book directly (as with Ovid's *Tristia ex Pontis*). The material work of writing that coordinates physical labour toward the production of such books is addressed by lyrics including the following to be discussed below: Carmen 9 ("Ad Girardum scriptorem"), 12 ("Ludendo de tabulis suis"), 84 ("Ad scriptorem suum"), and 92 ("De graphio fracto grauis dolor"). These poems materially enact Baudri's status as an abbot through his power to coordinate vertically the labour of skilled subordinates.[25]

As with Baudri's textual eroticism, his performative textuality inhabits the boundary between work and play.[26] Lyric poetry is a form of cultivated leisure; it is a textual space for playing with identity and persona. Nevertheless, the textual masculinity it enacts has real and consequential social effects – it is not walled off in a domain of fiction. The self-composed body of the Romanesque scholar-poet is as material and consequential as the holy body of the monk and the dangerous body of the lay noble warrior, but the matter and consequence of this body is not holiness or violence; it is administration. That is to say, it is the ordering and organization of work. The lyrics examined below link writing materials and the labour that produces them, Baudri's own labour as poet and abbot, and the community served by these labours and the texts they produce. In so doing, they represent and reproduce administrative work.

The community of practice represented by Baudri shares above all an affective attachment to textuality and text, not simply as a disembodied sequence of words, but as material objects, scratches on the wax of a tablet, ink and gold leaf on sheets of parchment bound in wood and leather.[27] The materials of writing metonymically signify the monastic and learned communities that they establish, regulate, and regenerate. Writing materials – stylus and tablet, inks and gold foils, bookbinding threads – are also totemic signifiers of administrative power. Baudri's

---

[24] Certeau, *The Practice of Everyday Life*, 135.
[25] Baudri also writes epistolary lyrics about the exchange of poetry and poetic values that affiliate clerics horizontally in peer relationships; these will be treated in future publications.
[26] Brower, "Gender, Power, and Persona," 190.
[27] Kong, *Lettering the Self*, 21–23.

writing communicates this claim through the cultivation of a tasteful appreciation that comprehends all aspects of textual production from the design of a tablet to the metre of elegiac couplets. In his representation of textual materialities, Baudri characterizes the internal hierarchies of his community around the task of making texts and their instruments, but fashions an imaginative alliance between his work as poet-abbot and the work of binders, scribes, even the miners and the smith responsible for the iron stylus with which he drafted letters, charters, poems, sermons, lyric poem, and versified histories. As he represents himself in his *Carmina*, Baudri sits at the centre of this community of practice, a localized prime mover. At the same time, he is one node in a network of practitioners made up of peers at other abbeys and cathedrals, notably his fellow poets Marbode of Rennes and Hildebert of Lavardin. In Baudri's poetry, we also glimpse the activity of women in this network.[28] Their community of affinity is established through the exchange and mutual critique and enjoyment of poetry. Baudri's masculinity is constituted simultaneously through domination over his subordinates and affiliation with a cultivated elite. This study does not afford space to fully examine the social and institutional context of Baudri's writing group, but it will look at Baudri's poems about writing materials – pens and such – as they articulate his dominant position within a community of men at work.

MEDIEVAL OFFICE SUPPLIES

Baudri's lyrics demonstrate an affective attachment to the tools of writing. A basic sense of delight and fascination with the instruments and materials of making written texts pervades the writing group, which represents these attachments as the basis of shared affinities with other men. Poems about a wax tablet, an iron stylus, and the folio of a book refer to at least five artisans whose labour Baudri commands and whose work supports his own; their labour is the material support of his writing, and the material itself of his writing, which he shapes even as they shape notebooks and pens.

Readers of Geoffrey Chaucer may recall the lyric poem "To His Own Adam Scriveyn," in which the poet playfully but sternly admonishes his scribe to transcribe his work correctly. It is not the accuracy of his scribe that Baudri on the other hand remonstrates, but his lack of industriousness:

> May one foot be just like the other for you, my Gerard,
>   Whatever I desire from you: write out my poems.
> I should have added poems upon poems,
>   if the tablets could receive the addition.
> I filled my tablets, while you lazed,
>   and once written, you are slow to copy out those in wax.

---

[28] A famous sequence of letters between Baudri and a nun Constance may be found in translation; see Ferrante, trans., "A Poem from Baudri | Epistolae"; online.

Work, Writing, and Elite Masculinity in the Lyrics of Baudri of Bourgueil

> But as you have opportunity for the wax, transfer my work,
> and prove yourself to shake off your ordinary laziness.[29]

This short poem about writing as the work of producing texts establishes a hierarchy of positions and skills. Despite his complaint about Gerard's scribal slowness, Baudri praises him to a third party in Carmen 1: "The scribe limps like Jacob, since he is disabled in one foot, but with his proper talent, he is most able!"[30] Another reading of "tibi sit pes unus ut alter" implies that Gerard cannot distinguish metrical feet, a fact that itself distinguishes the skill of the poet from that of the scribe. The jest simultaneously suggests the genial intimacy of a master with a servant and the boss's liberty to bully a worker; it opens a poem that expresses impatience about Gerard's slow pace of copying lyrics from Baudri's tablet and thus freeing up space for more writing. This at once displays Baudri's authority with his bald (if humorously couched) directives, his poetic knowledge, and his writerly productivity.[31]

In Carmen 84, Baudri addresses another scribe with this combination of authority, urgency, and humour:

> By entreaty and payment I have retained you to transcribe for me.
> Therefore I promise you for getting on the task right away
> Double the price if you write well,
> and don't inflict the tedium of long period of delay.
> But if you take great pains to write it well,
> Colouring some capital letters with red lead,
> Others with green or bluish-gray or black,
> So that the beginning of a verse always varies nicely,
> I will immortalize your very name through the ages –
> If my poem manages to survive at all![32]

---

[29] "Sic, Girarde meus, tibi sit pes unus ut alter / Quodque tibi cupio: carmina scribe mea. / Carmina carminibus nostris superapposuissem, / Si superapposita susciperent tabule. / Impleui nostras, dum tu pigritare, tabellas, / Dum scriptum, in cera lentus es excipere. / Vt uero ceram uaces, opus excipe nostrum / Vt probus a solita te excute pigritia." Baudri, *Poèmes*, 8.1–8

[30] "Claudicat ut Jacob, quoniam pede claudicat uno/ Scriptor, sed recto praeualet ingenio"; Baudri, *Poèmes*, 1.116–117. Tilliette points out that the reference to feet here in connection to the limping biblical Jacob must refer to a disability of Gerard's; see Baudri, *Poèmes*, 166 n. 2.

[31] Brown and Levinson discuss how *bald* directives, orders and requests made without "face-saving" strategies, are an act of dominance that indicate the speaker's higher status relative to the recipient. Brown and Levinson, *Politeness: Some Universals of Language Usage*, 91–101.

[32] Vtque mihi scribas prece te precioque redemi. / Ergo manus operi tibi protinus apposituro / Polliceor pretium, bene si scribas, duplicandum, / Nec mora longa mihi neque tempus taedia gignet. / Sit tamen id studeas, et cures ut bene scribas, / Altera de minio capitalis littera fiat, / Altera de uiridi glaucoue nigroue colore, / Vt

That "carmina perpetuare" (14) plays on the humanistic trope of verse as immaterial monument, but this monument is grounded, suggests Baudri, in the material text whose existence depends on the artisanal *ingenium*, which Alexander Andrée translates as "aptitude" or in-born talent, of scribes like Gerard and Hugh.[33] To Hugh, the addressee of Carmen 84, Baudri offers not just poetic immortality, but a "special reward" (*munus speciale*): an expenses-paid trip to Rome with Baudri, who desires Hugh's companionship on the road to lighten the toil (*labor*) of traveling with conversations (*mutua uerba*).[34] Baudri expresses more affection and regard for Hugh, but Baudri's superiority remains beyond doubt, underscored by Baudri's transactional patronage evident in the final line: "Meanwhile, please do serve so you may earn it all."[35] Baudri's "seruire uelis" is a vernacularism structured like modern French's "veuillez" plus infinitive – a polite but unambiguous command.[36] Baudri figures himself as the source of poetic fame and material benefit, his lyric thus a complex sign of his material authority as poet-abbot, and the labour of his scribes the vehicles and instruments of that authority; as they reproduce the verse that expresses Baudri's social mastery and education in gold leaf and different coloured inks, the *ingenium* of his workers is intertwined with his own in the totality of the book object. This network of ingenious labour extends to the instruments of Baudri's own composing, the tablet that needs scraping and an iron stylus that needs repairing or replacing.

Poem 12, "Ludendo de tabulis suis," also articulates this network of labour by figuring the materials of writing as the site of exchange and reciprocity. It is a note of thanks suited to an elegant present from another abbot, a writing tablet.[37] Baudri describes this present as being like a bird for a crying child (40) and declares that he will be buried with it:

> Someone has a bigger or smaller notebook than this,
>   But nobody has one of equal beauty.
> It is small of body, but great with the gift of beauty,
>   Which the craftsman's keen attention gave it.
> That hand was indeed so very ingenious
>   That gave this specimen such compact pages.[38]

---

uersus semper uarietur origo decenter. / Ipse tuum / nomen in saecula perpetuabo, / Si ualeant aliquem mea carmina perpetuare"; Baudri, *Poèmes*, 84.5–14.

[33] Andrée, "The Virtues of a Medieval Teacher," 163–171, 165.
[34] Baudri, *Poèmes*, 84.17, 20.
[35] "Interea seruire uelis ut id omne lucreris"; Baudri, *Poèmes*, 84.22
[36] According to Hilbert, Old French structures are present throughout Baudri's verse; see Baudri, *Baldricus Burgulianus Carmina*, 304.
[37] Marilynn Desmond provides a concise account of such objects in Desmond, "Translatio in Wax," 51–76.
[38] "Quisquis maiores habet his tabulasque minores / Aequalis forme non tamen ullus habet. / Corpore sunt parue, sed magne munere forme, / Cura sagax illis quam

The repetition of the word *ingeniosa* (5) (here describing the hand of the tablet's crafter) in Baudri's lyrics suggests a key aesthetic value of his community. Baudri responds to the artisan's ingenuity with his own, an epic simile comparing the construction of the notebook from eight small pieces of wood to the successive waves of the creation of mankind described in Ovid's *Metamorphoses*:

> They say the earth once begat giants,
>   Whose massive bodies provoked the gods;
> At length, when the race of giants had been destroyed by lightning,
>   An ape or dwarf was elevated as a second mankind.
> Then the earth brought forth smaller men,
>   Lest dauntless giants fright the stars with war.
> In such a way, but with the Deity pleased, the attentive
>   Labour of the artisan transformed the pliable wood into
>   something modest.[39]

An Alexandrian aesthetic of modesty and proportion links Baudri's craft with the tablet's maker, expressed in praise for the labour that transforms the world's unruly material into something carefully measured, useful, and appropriate.[40] The mock-epic linking of the creation of the world to the making of a charming notebook also recalls the Alexandrian aesthetic cultivated by Roman poets like Horace and Ovid – the idea of the poet as a maker of pretty little things. Baudri's work pays homage to this Alexandrian poetic by transgressing the boundaries of this aesthetic modesty through playful allusion: "Oh new norm, new form, new race of tablets!"[41] Using the phrase "nova progenies" (12.11) from Vergil's fourth eclogue to describe the tablet humorously links the grand with the minute and, given that Vergil's poem was understood in the Middle Ages to prophesy Christ's birth, Baudri flirts with sacrilege, especially if we recall the Pauline connotations of "noua lex."[42] Baudri pivots, however, from these mythological and biblical excursions about giants, dwarves, and apes to take up a technical discussion of the tablet's construction, which Tilliette describes as unparalleled in its precision in the Middle Ages.[43]

---

dedit artificis. / Illa manus siquidem nimium fuit ingeniosa, / Tam breuibus foliis que dedit hanc speciem." Baudri, *Poèmes*, 12.1–6.

[39] "Vt dicunt, olim generauit terra gigantes / Que commouerunt corpora magna deos˙ / Fulminibus tandem destructa prole gigantum / Simia uel nanus editur alter homo. / Tunc homines etiam produxit terra minores, / Ne bellis audax terrea astra gigas. / Sic sed placata deitate dolatile lignu / Artificis studium transtulit in modicum." Baudri, *Poèmes*, 12.14–20.

[40] Curtius, *Essays in European Literature*, 359.

[41] "O noua lex, noua res, noua progenies tabularum"; Baudri, *Poèmes*, 12.11.

[42] Vergil, Eclogue 4.7.

[43] Baudri, *Poèmes*, 168 n. 1.

Tilliette characterizes writing tools as "instruments of intellectual work."[44] Baudri's poetic treatment of these tools links the labour of the artisan who makes them with his own work, which includes practical administration as well as versifying. Carmen 12 describes the labour of the tablet-maker, probably a monk based on Baudri's designation of him as "our Lambert," the possessive pronoun expressing the kind of subordination and intimacy seen in the lyrics to scribes. The poem celebrates Lambert's work making things from "pliable wood" ("lignum dolatile"). Baudri himself makes things like giants and dwarfs out of the pliable wood of language in peacocking display of poetic skill, simultaneously playing with numbers in terms both of the dimensions of the book and the quantities of poetic metre. He brings into contact the immaterial and material dimensions of writing in a discussion of the notebook's capacity:

> The pages hold scarcely eight verses in length
> and barely a hexameter in width.
> But still, there are eight equal boards in you,
> Which give twice two and ten little pages.
> (The outside boards lack wax on the exterior sides
> So that eight boards makes fourteen pages.)
> Thus they contain twice twelve and a hundred lines.[45]

This exuberant product description scans perfectly, aligning the quantities of poetry with the quantities of the physical artifact, matching *ingenium* with *ingenium*, and an alignment of arithmetical and verbal dexterity that brings to mind the range of intellectual work the abbot does with numbers on his tablet, namely, keeping accounts – in this light it is worth recalling that Baudri's abbey was rich and became richer under his rule.[46]

As an example of precision and ingenuity, the tablet is a metonymical link between artisan and abbot; as a gift, it is a material link between Baudri and his colleague, the abbot of Sées. The work the abbots share as colleagues is managerial knowledge work, not solely the monastic *opus dei* but the administration of property, material, and men that maintains the *opus dei*. His ostentatious erudition associates his work, position, and education with a relatively horizontal community of colleagues maintained through the exchange of writing and writing materials. It also places him (like his peer, the abbot of Sées) once more at the centre of the community of men around him who make writing materials.

This attention to the hierarchical organization of labour that places Baudri atop and at the centre of networks of working men is more explicit in Carmen

---

[44] Baudri, *Poèmes*, 168 n. 1.
[45] "In latum uersus uix octo pagina uestra, / In longum uero uix capit exametrum. / Attamen in uobis pariter sunt octo tabelle, / Que dant bis geminas paginulasque decem. / Cera nanque carent altrinsecus exteriores˙ / Sic factiunt octo, quatuor atque decem. / Sic bis sex capiunt, capiunt et carmina centum." Baudri, *Poèmes*, 12.20–29.
[46] On the flawlessness of Baudri's scansion, see Tilliette, "Culture Classique," 80.

Work, Writing, and Elite Masculinity in the Lyrics of Baudri of Bourgueil

92, "De graphio fracto gravis dolor." This poem eulogizes a broken stylus, the tool used with the tablet to write poems as described in "Ad Gerardum." Carmen 92 describes how the stylus has splintered, then recounts its material history: its iron was first dug from the ground, then cast and forged by a smith. It then expresses the speaker's contemplation of how he shall continue without this pen and finds consolation in the legacy of the poems it helped beget before its end. The poem concludes by appealing to the goddess *Fortuna* to protect the styluses of other poets and requests those same poets share in his mourning at his loss.

Threaded throughout the poem is a learned but playful discussion of materiality and causation that serves to articulate a relationship between Baudri's labour and that of other men. Of the splintered stylus, he writes:

> From iron, a blacksmith fashioned the pen;
> the efficient cause perished, but the material cause remains.
> What remains is iron; the pen is that which lost its being,
> being that the craftsmen's talent hammered out.[47]

The *ingenium* of the craftsman belongs to a chain of labour and exchange in the production of this poem that is linked to Baudri's own *ingenium*. They both accomplish refined work, *labor exquisitus*, reflecting once more Alexandrian aesthetics of polish and refinement. The poet describes mining and fashioning of the pen in terms reminiscent of the forging of a weapon or piece of armour in an epic (in this case, the *Psychomachia*):[48]

> Countless arts, work of unprecedented distinction
> fashioned my pen, which I now mourn.
> The bosom of the earth revealed the iron through digging,
> While the panting man sought it from hiding.
> At last, smelted three days in the flame-spitting furnace,
> He draws the solid iron out of the liquid.[49]

The violence, heat, force, and activity revolving around the panting miner is charged with masculine energy. This raw force and activity is refined by the next stage of labour, the smith's studied care (*sagax cura*) and small hammer (*marculus*). This portrays the work of smithing such a tool as cerebral and precise (like Baudri's poetry) but no less grounded in masculine bodily exertion as the smith conquers iron with iron and fire:

---

[47] De ferro grafium ferrarius effigiauit; / Effigiale perit, materiale manet. / Quod manet est ferrum, stilus, id quod perdidit esse, / Esse quod artificis extudit ingenium." Baudri, *Poèmes*, 92.7–10.

[48] Prudentius Clemens, "*Psychomachia*," 596–603.

[49] "Artes innumerae, labor exquisitus abusque / Confecere meum, quem modo plango, stilum. / Telluris rimando sinus patefecit abissum, / Dum latitans ferrum querit anhelus homo. / Tandem, flammiuoma triduo fornace recoctum / Educit ferrum de liquodio solidum." Baudri, *Poèmes*, 92.15–20.

> But through all the milling, the iron is not yet a stylus;
> It remains for the wise care of a man to make it so.
> The small hammer, as well as the tenacious bellows, anvil, and fire
> are prepared so they might all together subdue the iron.
> Likewise indefatigable, the smith persists at the undertaking
> And conquers iron with iron and fire at once.
> The tired man pants, the anvil rings, the artisan,
> raising high blackened arms, doubles his blows.
> Through various exertions, the pen is at last fashioned;
> so great a toil indeed to make such a pen![50]

This description of the stylus's creation associates Baudri's versifying with the strenuously masculine labour of miners and smiths, an association that in turn recalls the Ciceronian link of writing and rhetoric to the labour of building civilization, a link described in *De inventione*, the *Tusculan Disputations*, and popular eleventh-century school texts.[51] This link is sustained through the pun on *stilum* as both pen and style, and the contiguity between the poet's crafting his *stilum* as style out of the smith's *stilum* as pen; writing – textuality itself – is the final cause and guiding purpose of a civilization organized around the masculine labour that subdues matter. This point is embellished in the quotation in line 30 of Vergil's *Aeneid* 1.33: "tantae molis erat Romanam condere gentem," a line that summarizes the entire plot of the *Aeneid*!

As in the poem about the tablet, mock-epic play with scale characterizes the abbot and his cloistered world as masculinist and heroic, but in a way founded on textual expertise rather than martial prowess or spiritual excellence. It grandiloquently celebrates the work that produced the stylus and the work it enables in the phrase "labor exquisitus" (92.15). Carmen 92 concludes with a collegial wish to fellow poets that "fortune protect their pens." As in the epistolary poem thanking another abbot for the tablet, this mode of address bases fellowship on the tools of textuality through which fellow elite churchmen exercise administrative authority. The space of work – the little pages of the tablet – is also the space of play, and in play these poems reveal a vision of clerical life as a work culture that links literary prowess with heroic masculine labour and forms the foundation of a hegemonic masculinity based on technical accomplishment and learning, one that has persisted, and arguably triumphed over rivals, in the form of the expert and the technician.

Missouri State University

---

[50] "At necdum stilus est per tot molimina ferum: / Instat ut id faciat cura sagax hominis. / Marculus atque tenax, follesque parantur et incus / Et focus, ut ferrum cuncta doment pariter. / Indefessus item ceptis ferrarius instat / Et ferrum ferro unicit et igne simul. / Lassus anhelat homo, gemit incus, duplicat ictus / Alte sustollens brachia nigra faber. / Per uarios nisus tandem stilus effigiatur: / Quippe stilum tantae condere molis erat!" Baudri, *Poèmes*, 92.21–30.

[51] See Newman, "Ciceronian Ethos."

ABBREVIATIONS

BAV   Biblioteca Apostolica Vaticana, Vatican City.

CITED WORKS

Manuscript Sources

Vatican City. Biblioteca Apostolica Vaticana (BAV)
Reg. lat 1351

Printed Sources

Andrée, Alexander. "The Virtues of a Medieval Teacher: Ingenium and Memoria in the Twelfth Century." In Greti Dinkova-Bruun and Tristan Major, eds, *Teaching and Learning in Medieval Europe. Essays in Honour of Gernot R. Wieland.* Publications of the Journal of Medieval Latin. Turnhout: Brepols, 2017, 163–171.

Baudri de Bourgueil. *Baldricus Burgulianus Carmina.* Ed. Karlheinz Hilbert. Editiones Heidelbergenses 19. Heidelberg: C. Winter, 1979.

——. *Poèmes.* Ed. Jean-Yves Tilliette. Paris: Les Belles Lettres, 1998.

——. *The Historia Ierosolimitana of Baldric of Bourgueil.* Ed. Steven Biddlecombe. Woodbridge, UK: The Boydell Press, 2014.

——. *Baldric of Bourgueil "History of the Jerusalemites": A Translation of the "Historia Ierosolimitana".* Trans. Susan B. Edgington and Steven Biddlecombe. Crusading in Context, 2. Woodbridge, UK: The Boydell Press, 2020.

Benton, John F. "Consciousness of Self and Perceptions of Individuality." In Robert L Benson and Giles Constable, eds, *Renaissance and Renewal in the Twelfth Century.* Toronto: University of Toronto Press, 1999, 263–298.

Blänsdorf, Jürgen. "Ancient Genres in the Poem of a Medieval Humanist: Intertextual Aspects of the 'De Sufficientia Votorum Suorum' (c. 126 H.) of Baudri de Bourgueil (1046–1130)." *International Journal of the Classical Tradition* 2.2 (1995): 209–218.

Bond, Gerald A. *The Loving Subject: Desire, Eloquence, and Power in Romanesque France.* Philadelphia, PA: University of Pennsylvania Press, 1995.

Brower, Susannah Giulia. "Gender, Power, and Persona in the Poetry of Baudri of Bourgueil." PhD thesis. Toronto: University of Toronto, 2011.

Brown, Penelope and Stephen C. Levinson. *Politeness: Some Universals in Language Usage.* Cambridge, UK: Cambridge University Press, 1987.

Bullough, Vern L. "On Being a Male in the Middle Ages." In Clare A. Lees, Thelma S. Fenster, and Jo Ann McNamara, eds, *Medieval Masculinities: Regarding Men in the Middle Ages.* Minneapolis, MN: University of Minnesota Press, 1994, 31–46.

Burckhardt, Jakob. *The Civilization of the Renaissance in Italy: An Essay.* Oxford: Phaidon Press, 1981 (first German edition, 1860; first English edition, 1878).

Certeau, Michel de. *The Practice of Everyday Life.* Trans. Steven Rendall. Berkeley, CA: University of California Press, 2008.

Chartier, Roger. *Inscription and Erasure: Literature and Written Culture from the Eleventh to the Eighteenth Century.* Philadelphia, PA: University of Pennsylvania Press, 2008.

Connell, Raewyn. *Masculinities*. Cambridge, UK: Polity, 2014.
Constable, Giles. *Letters and Letter-Collections*. Turnhout: Brepols, 1976.
Currie, Elizabeth. *Fashion and Masculinity in Renaissance Florence*. London: Bloomsbury Publishing, 2016.
Curtius, Ernst Robert. *Essays on European Literature*. Trans. Michael Kowal. Princeton, NJ: Princeton University Press, 1973, 355–399.
Desmond, Marilynn. "Translatio in Wax: The Wax Tablet and the Composition of Benoît de Sainte-Maure's Roman de Troie." *Viator* 49.1 (2018): 51–76.
Dinshaw, Carolyn. *Chaucer's Sexual Poetics*. Madison, WI: University of Wisconsin Press, 1989.
Ferrante, Joan, trans. "A Poem from Baudri | Epistolae." *Epistolae: Medieval Women's Latin Letters*. Online https://epistolae.ctl.columbia.edu/letter/26117.html.
Haskins, Charles Homer. *The Renaissance of the Twelfth Century*. Cambridge, MA: Harvard University Press, 1927.
Jaeger, C. Stephen. *Scholars and Courtiers: Intellectuals and Society in the Medieval West*. Aldershot, UK: Ashgate, 2002.
——. *The Envy of Angels: Cathedral Schools and Social Ideals in Medieval Europe, 950-1200*. Philadelphia, PA: University of Pennsylvania Press, 1994.
——. *The Origins of Courtly Love: Civilizing Trends and the Formation of Courtly Ideals 939-1210*. Philadelphia, PA: University of Pennsylvania Press, 1985.
Kopaczyk, Joanna, and Andreas H. Jucker. *Communities of Practice in the History of English*. Amsterdam: John Benjamins Publishing Company, 2013.
McNamara, Jo Ann. "The *Herrenfrage*: The Restructuring of the Gender System, 1050-1150." In Clare A. Lees, Thelma S. Fenster, and Jo Ann McNamara eds, *Medieval Masculinities: Regarding Men in the Middle Ages*. Minneapolis, MN: University of Minnesota Press, 1994, 3–30.
Newman, Barbara. *Sister of Wisdom: St. Hildegard's Theology of the Feminine*. Berkeley, CA: University of California, 1998.
Newman, Jonathan M. "Ciceronian Ethos and Clerical Masculinity in the Regensburg Rhetorical Letters." *Florilegium* 34 (2017): 44–65.
Otter, Monika C. "Sufficientia: A Horatian Topos and the Boundaries of the Self in Three Twelfth-Century Poems." *Anglo-Norman Studies* 35 (2013): 245–258.
Prudentius Clemens, Aurelius. *The "Psychomachia" of Prudentius: Text, Commentary, and Glossary*. Ed. Aaron Pelttari. Norman, OK: University of Oklahoma Press, 2019.
Quaintance, Courtney. *Textual Masculinity and the Exchange of Women in Renaissance Venice*. Toronto: University of Toronto Press, 2015.
Tilliette, Jean-Yves. "Culture Classique et Humanisme Monastique: Les Poèmes de Baudri de Bourgueil." In *La Littérature Angevine Médiévale: Actes*. Paris: H. Champion, 1981, 77–88.
Wenger, Etienne. *Communities of Practice: Learning, Meaning, and Identity*. Cambridge, UK: Cambridge University Press, 1999.
Wilson, Anna. "Petrarch's Queer History." *Speculum* 95.3 (2020): 716–741.

2

MASCULINITY AS COMPETENCE

Thomas V. Cohen

In January 1557 in Rome, a notary of the governor's court deposed a young woman lying in bed sorely injured. After having lost her virginity amidst group sex to a soldier at her village of Santa Fiora (so she claims), Camilla had come to Rome and moved in with a Signora Margarita, and then made her living trading sex for income. Camilla said that, shortly before, she had fallen in with a Frenchman. Naming him she then tells what happened next.

> Mons. Basi, a Frenchman, brought me to the inn La Fortuna, where he stayed three nights, and two nights I slept with him, and one night I slept alone, and those nights he did it to me two times a night from in front. And, I don't know if it was three or four nights ago, the police came, along with Signora Margarita, a dry-goods seller, and they knocked on the door. And when I went to open it, that gentleman who was staying with me said to me, "Oh, you no-good whore, do you want me to be massacred instead of you." And so he made me climb up into a window sill, and he gave me a push, and I began to shout, "Help me! Help me!" and I fell [out the window]. And the police picked me up and they brought me here more dead than alive. And when I was here, Signora Margarita said that I was in terrible shape, and that I had broken my arms and legs and thighs.[1]

Camilla then adds that, with treatment, she is recovering.

This is clearly an ugly, tawdry story of unfeeling sex and callous harm. Rome's criminal records teem with such tales of cruelty, where men inflict

---

[1] Rome, ASR, Governatore, Tribunale Criminale [henceforth GTC], Atti di Cancelleria, busta 22, fol. 258[r–v]: "Mons. Basi franzese me menò al'Hostaria della fortuna dove stetti tre notti et due notti dormii seco, et una notte dormii sola, et in quella notte me le fece due volte per notte dinanzi, et non so se tre o quattro sere fa venne la corte insieme con la Signora Margarita pizzicarola, et battè alla porta, et volendo io aprire quello Signore quale stava con me mi disse oh puttana poltrona voi che io sia ammazzato per scambio tuo et così mi fece mi fece [sic] saglire su una fenestra et mi diede una spinta et così cominciai a gridare aggiutatime aggiutatime et cascai et la corte mi pigliò et mi portò qui più morta che viva et dopo che io sono stata qui la signora Margarita ha detto che io ero guasta et che havevo rotte le braccie et le gambe et le cosse."

harm on those weaker, be they women or other men who have less strength or social backing, or who just suffer momentary disadvantage. It would be easy, using records such as these, to depict masculinity as a toxic distillation, much unkind sex, and far more violence.[2] But we should not.

I propose here to take a different tack, to contend that, for being male and for proper manhood – as understood, assayed, performed, and felt, although sex did matter, and violence mattered a great deal more – those two things were hardly all that counted. To make this counter-case, I will restrict myself to the massive volume of papers of the criminal court of Rome's governor, suspecting that, if one can prove it there, one could easily do the same with documents that are less raw or harsh.

To begin, let us ponder what the just quoted passage is not. First off, it is not the event itself – poor Camilla falling, shoved out of a tavern window by a cowardly, thuggish lover, and perhaps breaking several limbs. It is instead a story, and that story is a not a dispassionate report, but a performance, staged by an injured woman of shabby reputation for a notary at her bedside. He, meanwhile, performs his profession, and, indeed, his very transcript would also soon perform its allotted task. Inquests were a genre known to witnesses and recorders alike. Their depositions and transcriptions had their familiar rhetoric, cadence, and role.

To push further, masculinity, like an inquest, was itself also a performance, or, better, a family of performances. If asked, Pierre Bourdieu almost certainly would, with reason, have preferred to call it a practice, or habitus, with his notion that practices are so instinctive, so stripped of pondered calculation and conscious choice that, as if unprompted, they just happen, just as Camilla simply unspooled, from her bed, her dire tale.[3]

But if masculinity was performance and practice, just what was it? This is a tricky question because the term is not theirs but ours. It is etic, not emic, a word we moderns lay on the past to help us think. My suggestion is that masculinity, best understood, is anywhere a competence befitting males in social roles that suit them well.[4]

---

[2] For a good overview of the literature on gender, violence, and the social setting of their intersection, see Rose, *A Renaissance of Violence*, 13–31. One implication useful for my argument here: much violence was not only martially but also socially competent. In Hunt, "Carriages, Violence and Masculinity in Early Modern Rome," we read how the carriage, at first a feminine conveyance, once masculinized became an instrument of confrontation; see especially 178–179. Note Simons, *The Sex of Men in Premodern Europe*, chap. 1, "How to be a Man in Early Modern Europe," 25–51; one sees there much sex, a good deal of violence, and nothing else at all.

[3] Bourdieu and Wacquant, *An Invitation to Reflexive Sociology*. For a canny sociology of practice applied to early modern Italy, see Judde de Larivière, *L'ordinaire des savoirs*.

[4] Competences were many and diverse. In this volume, Newman's "Work, Writing and Elite Masculinity in the Lyrics of Baudri of Bourgueil" explores the manly

Masculinity as Competence

To take masculinity in that sense untangles several problems. For one, it means that masculine and feminine are seldom polar opposites. Rather, they often overlap. Rather than seeing men as hard, women as soft, men as bellicose and assertive, women as pacific and accommodating, men as Mars-ruddy, women as Venus-pallid as in so many Italian paintings and so on, we can step back and catalogue the social skills the two sexes often had in common: tact, for instance, and a sense of timing, a generous spirit, loyalty, good sense, and many other canny virtues they either had or aspired to have as ideals. That duality of acts and values alerts us: masculinity and femininity were both practices and yardsticks that men and women used, instinctively for sure, to gauge both themselves and those around them.

Taking masculinity as competence solves a second problem: it lops off any mental shackles to the dominant male at his prime: the commander, prince, prelate, magistrate, master artisan, and so on. If masculinity was competence, then every social station and age had its standards of performance. Merchants, officials, clergy, artisans, peasants, and even beggars had their competences, as did children and old men.[5] Such folk were not less masculine, in their own or others' eyes; they were merely masculine, when competent, in a fashion suitable to their station. I come to this interpretation after having waded for four decades through the abundantly loquacious papers of Rome's criminal courts.

Now and again, one encounters in those records the privileged and the mighty, sometimes as witnesses, occasionally even as the accused, but most people who stood before the court were common folk of every station and almost every age. One meets even children of ten or eight. Any seasoned reader of rich trials from those lands where the conventions of Roman law fostered sedulous transcription of direct discourse (Portugal and Spain and their wide empires, and especially Italy) can claim to know that world in ways intimate, deep, and broad.

Yet, criminal records, as evidence, are incomplete. Let us tally what they are not. First, as we said of poor Camilla, they are not the social fact itself, like the actual tumble from a window. Rather, they are accounts of things

---

literary competence of a twelfth-century abbot; Doda's "Spurs and Negotiation of Masculinity" evokes mastery over horses, one metonymy for manhood; and Brizio's "Legal and Social Solutions," 127, points out skilled navigation of Sienese inheritance custom to preserve lineage capital. In other publications, Klaassen, in "Learning and Masculinity," cites, for young scholars, mastery of medieval student life. Neal, in "Suits Make the Man," 8–13, points to commercial probity and open dealing in fifteenth-century England, challenged by the common insult "thief"; Reinke-Williams, in "Manhood and Masculinity in Early Modern England," reviewing recent scholarship, picks up, for instance, masculine right conduct at feasts, and in sociable militia life; he sees in recent work a stress on self-control as manly. For striking Italian male incompetence and inept self-control, see Miedema, "The Sand Pot".

5 Shepard, "Anxious Patriarchs," 291, seeks a similar wide range of masculinities for England.

that happened elsewhere. And those accounts are hardly spontaneous. While any story is a performance, one performed in court is especially wary and strategic.[6] The tellers feel the stakes for themselves, their friends and allies, their foes, and also for the court and state. Moreover, the tellers dialogue with a court that both frames and shapes the subject and models a legal language. So, testimony is unfree speech, often both girt and guarded. There is a second incompleteness: what we have on paper are desiccated words, not lush speech. We cannot hear the speakers' voices, see their faces, behold their gestures, or sense their bodies. Third, the court itself, as theatre, as encounter's furnished space, is invisible on paper. True, when a witness sweats, trembles, sobs, or anxiously clutches the head, the scribe may note the action, but, by their rarity, such comments remind us of just how little we ever grasp of speech's rich fullness and complex setting. What we miss bore on a speaker's competence, both as witness and as person.

Despite these drawbacks, court records are rich, complex sources: they bear evidence of several kinds. It helps to count them.

First, these papers depict deeds done elsewhere, out in the world, as perceived, appraised, recalled, and recounted. The courtroom stories may be accurate or false, or a bit of both. To pin down what really happened, it helps vastly if accounts are many and witnesses diverge in goals and standpoint. But even a solitary, dodgy story swarms with clues. A lie, to be credible, must be plausible; its peripheral details must ring true. Even rank fabulations brim with hints to social codes and expectations. So, trials reveal a lot about what people either did or might have done – for instance, in cowardly, heartless rage push a poor sex worker out of an upstairs window.

Second, while they show the outer world though a glass darkly, trials also depict the immediate speakers far less dimly, or at least the speakers' "presentations of self," not in "everyday life," as Erving Goffman wrote,[7] but before a notary or judge. A deposition thus offers a double portrait, of the speakers themselves and of that world's denizens whose actions speakers both recounted and appraised. If masculinity was, to a great degree, in the beholders' eyes, then trials abound in faithful records of what beholders said they thought and showed they felt about the *personae* and actions of their fellows.[8]

Third, preciously for scholars, trial records are a very precise account by a notary, a trained observer, of a living social interaction – the trial itself – in real time, depicted in good order, move by countermove. A trial pitted witnesses against a powerful institution. Exchange, face to face, was often

---

[6] For a classic discussion of the artfulness of court documents, see Davis, *Fiction in the Archives*.

[7] Goffman, *The Presentation of Self in Everyday Life*.

[8] On masculinity as a social self, detectable in court records over insults, and viewed cannily by scholars as what people did, and what they were seen to do, and what they felt themselves to be doing, see Neal, "Suits Make the Man," 1–2 and passim.

adversarial; a court's purposes were seldom the speaker's own. Even when the court was an ally, it fell to the speaker to bend its routines and powers to heartfelt purposes. A speaker's risks were many. A court could punish. It could torture, and often did, not just suspects but even dodgy witnesses of low station. Any interrogation was thus a drama where the oral skills and social and moral capital of a witness were in play. We scholars can watch what happened there to appraise the competence a speaker brought to the fray. Meanwhile, the officials too engaged their own competence. One drawback for scholars, in Rome and elsewhere, is that, while the notary recorded witnesses in the vernacular, he veiled the court's own ploys behind formulaic Latin that masked its exact words.

Fourth, a thing extraordinarily important, is that the court's transcripts sometimes contain a second dialogue, not between witnesses and magistrates but rather between one witness and another. Here there is something altogether special.[9] For nowhere else, before the late nineteenth century, do we scholars possess clear, precise, immediate records of actual conversations. Plays, learned dialogues, *novelle*, and other genres do feature artful conversations sometimes roughly akin to actual practice, but these always hew to literary conventions that estrange them from the tumult of real talk. Meanwhile, conversations in court had conventions too: when it could not bend a witness, the tribunal would stage a *confrontatio*, bringing in a second witness who had told a different story and, in the presence of both, read the newcomer's earlier deposition in the hope, usually futile, of prying from one or the other speaker a cowed retraction. Usually, instead, each witness turned to the magistrate and performed indignation: "this fellow is lying through the throat!" After a spate of futile wrangling, with no one much the wiser, the magistrate would break the meeting off, send the newcomer away, and resume grilling his balky witness. Neither judge nor historian then gains much insight. But sometimes things go differently and become lively, one witness turning to the other, telling new stories, cajoling, blaming, and wheedling, while the other responds, dodging, bantering, and brandishing new information.[10] The magistrates then fade to black. Suddenly, we face such talk as went on in the tavern, by the well or washtub, at the fireside, and in the doorway. Although the courtroom is still there, this banter transports us, as nowhere else in the whole historical record, into the oral and moral world beyond the tribunal's forbidding walls. So what can we learn from these court papers about masculinity's contours?

---

[9] For this dynamic see Cohen, "Tracking Conversation in the Italian Courts."
[10] For a lively *confrontatio*, see Cohen, *Roman Tales*, 183–185. See also Cohen and Cohen, *Words and Deeds*, 110–115.

Thomas V. Cohen

EXCESS

If masculinity was competence, a mastery of the codes and practices defining a man's position, the Italian term, *eccesso*, echoing legal Latin's *excessus*, can help put sex and violence in their place. Both were often male; both, however, in eyes both social and legal, could be excessive and disorderly. Roman records are full of "excess" cases. What did that mean?[11]

Roman courts, like most tribunals elsewhere, understood violence to be a fact of life, sometimes even a convenience. Society largely regulated itself. Conflicts among men, and women too, although disruptive, were also a rough and ready regulator; the risk of violence often cowed and quelled bad behaviour.[12] Moreover, not only did men and women, singly or in concert, quarrel, fight, and wreak havoc; they also might intervene, mediate, arbitrate, and settle. The remedy and resolution of private war was private peace; the law strove less to impose peace than to coax the warring parties to settle and to guarantee a pact's observance. Thus, into the seventeenth century, in Rome as often elsewhere, the law was auxiliary, not central, to social regulation. Roman society was a self-help world, as it had been since the Ostrogoths arrived. But self-help, in the eyes of the law, had its rhythms, its proportions. When a man, or a woman too, retaliated beyond just measure, that action, in court, was called "excess." Thus, as the term implied, there was competent violence, well rationed, befitting, and then there was also ill-gauged violence, dubiously manly.

Take, for instance, Paolo di Grassi, whose *eccesso* trials Elizabeth Cohen and I once published.[13] Loud, boisterous, impulsive, and rough, Paolo crossed uncounted lines. He borrowed another man's courtesan, promising, if asked, to send her back, and contumeliously broke his word. With his men, he skirmished with the civic guards. When, amidst the tumult of Vacant See, his henchman was shot, Paolo blamed Rome's governor and thundered that his fellow Romans should burn his palace. When a courtesan jilted Paolo, he and his cronies attacked her doors with lewd doggerel, pulled off her shutters, and broke in, disrupting a domestic concert and threatening to beat her. This was "male behaviour" for sure, but ill-calibrated, out of line even in someone young and not yet married, and not competently manly. Well-born friends of the insulted courtesan lined up at court to denounce it. The court papers swarm with acts like Paolo's,

---

[11] For *excessus*, for Germany and Switzerland see Pohl, *Making Manslaughter*, 38–42. For English notions, less legal, more ethical, see Shepard, *Meanings of Manhood*, 140–143. For the importance of moderation, as ideal, in late medieval English household heads, see McSheffrey, "Men and Masculinity," 245, 257–262.

[12] Smail, *The Consumption of Justice*; For Iceland, see Miller, *Blood Taking and Peace Making*.

[13] Cohen and Cohen, *Works and Deeds*, 45–101.

Masculinity as Competence

by lords who purloined the village bells or snatched their vassals' wives. In one striking, awful incident, in his fief at Arignano, baron Onorio Savelli instigated a hideous charivari. A villager had moved in with a widow, breaking sexual codes. At the lord's instigation, villagers put the man's head in a bag and to beating drums marched his woman to the castle, where they laid a mattress on her head and, by dozens, raped her.[14] Male perhaps, but shocking excess. Italians had several words for this neglect of measure: *contumelia*, for instance, and *soverchiaria*. Such "insolence of office" was an overweening power they often called *prepotenza*.

CONDITIONS ON THE GROUND FOR MALE COMPETENCE

To be competent, males, and females too, had to master adversities fundamental to life – in Rome, and in Italy and Europe. They faced deep uncertainty in a world opaque, thoroughly hierarchic, and ridden by scarcity. They perforce conducted their lives, appraised themselves, and were assayed by others, with their world's fundamental nature much in mind. Let us survey this state of affairs.

Scarcity

First came material scarcity. Physical resources – food, fuel, materials, and shelter – were in short supply. Even land was scarce. As such resources were very unevenly shared, one mark of competence was plenitude. Scarcity of goods had parallels in shortages of power, information, honour, and trust. Such assets bundled, bolstering one another; whoever had one often enjoyed the others, too. Effective power was diffuse and blurry. At the apex of states, institutions, and social bodies sat decision-makers who set rules and enforced them, but institutional weakness rendered rulers and heads as inclined to co-opt as to command. Cajolery, bluff, blandishments, and complex exchanges binding others in hoops of steely obligation set the rules of polities, communities, and even families. In an opaque world running on rumour, the paucity of information compounded power's debilities. Accordingly, knowledge was both cause and consequence of power.

Honour, that intangible good rooted in others' estimation, stemmed from access to the other scarce resources and also from virtues that, as always, were expensive; to do right, often costly, thus bespoke access to deep reserves, to material and social strengths. This is capital, in its every sense. Thus, even where esteem came easily, honour in fact and in notion always seemed scarce. And it was contested, often won by stealing it from others. Locally, if not globally, honour was anthropology's "limited good": at a face-off, one snatched it. It felt precarious. Amidst myriad such contests big

---

[14] ASR, GTC, Processi, busta 116 (1566), case 3, fols. 645^r–647^r. For a published notice of this event, see Fosi, *Papal Justice*, 89.

and small, one crucial social competence was to win, at least often. Another, no less crucial, was to lose with grace. A third, also very handy, was to duck challenges unscathed.

Scarcity of trust pervaded life. This was Machiavelli's world; if it did not always read him, he of course read it. Mistrust was rife not because people were unduly bad, but because trust was often risky, thanks to the uncertain rule of law, the opacity of public knowledge, and the deep moral particularism and pervasive bargaining in a world that owed first loyalties to allies, not to public good. Under such circumstances, how was one to trust the quality of goods, the force of promises, the steady knees of services, or the character of a servant or a bride? Suspicion's antidote was faith, not in God and His celestial crew but in one's fellow men, in their words, undertakings, and support. *Fede* ("faith"): the word served for things both divine and human. In a man, *fede*, as a trait or notional possession, was a quintessential sign of manly competence. His word, promises, and proffered support were solid.[15] Accordingly, Romans persistently asked stalwart men, *uomini da bene*, to lend their reputations (their *publica fama*) and their material assets to guarantee the undertakings of others. The warrantor (*garante*), the faith-swearing *fideiussore*, staked his goods and honour, firming a promise, an assessment, an undertaking. There was no better gauge of masculine competence and moral capital than this action, be it legal, duly notarized, or informal: upon my oath, the steed is sound, the girl is as pure as snow. A competent man should merit the trust of others, embody that rare good, *fede*, and stake it, at a risk he could afford, to enable others to verify assertions and trust other men to carry out their proffered obligations.

Fede also stretched to threats – promises' unlikely close cousins. In this rambunctious, agonistic world, as Daniel Lord Smail has argued, "hatred" was indeed a social institution, and enemies in plenty signalled standing.[16] When a competent man threatened, he was believed. To warrant *fede*, he must carry through. Both allies and enemies prized the certainty this male competence afforded. The fool who uttered rash threats beyond his means soon lost both face and *fede*.

---

[15] See Bernardino, music teacher and abductor, strike a moral stance, in Cohen and Cohen, *Words and Deeds*, 114: "When a person makes me a part of her affairs, she obligates me to put my life upon the line." Shepard, *Meanings of Manhood*, 185–214, examines male and female "credit," an expression of economic and social competence, and one facet, in Italy and England both, of the broader *fede* complex. She treats credit as a social fact; we might instead view it as performed, in situ. For England's term "true," a current mark of a man's credit, and the term's resonance and range, see Neal, "Suits Make the Man," 12–16.

[16] Smail, "Hatred as a Social Institution."

Masculinity as Competence

We should keep in mind that women, too, had access to both honour and *fede*, but played them less intensely and less often, in the tumultuous politics of daily life, than did men. Female honour went well beyond chastity; the same virtues of steadiness and straight dealing, the same willingness to fight back when slighted, attached to females as it did to males. Here, as elsewhere, the genders differed in style, but were hardly polar opposites.

Opacity

Despite the spread of writing and rise of print, sixteenth-century Italy remained profoundly oral. Most information that counted went by mouth, not by script. The weakness of a public sphere, aggravated by social fragmentation into tight alliances, amidst a climate of discretion and mistrust, made the world opaque. Moreover, a culture of secrecy prized privy knowledge. Every craft had its secrets, seldom entrusted to print. And each family kept its counsel, while princes schemed discreetly. In Rome, the papacy moved by stealth; many an arrest took its victim unawares. The great, blithely oblivious to their fates, often fell swiftly without an inkling. See, for instance, the clamorous fall of Cardinal Carlo Carafa (1517–1561), carousing among the courtesans the night before his dire swift tumble from grace to arrest, trial, and execution.[17] At princely courts, a culture of dissimulation made decoding hard. In the merchant classes, guile was widely prized and practiced; see Ronald F. E. Weissman's brilliant chapter "Judas the Florentine."[18] Machiavelli's half-wily devil Belfagor, as witless merchant buffaloed by his in-laws, is only partly fantasy.[19] In such a world, one key competence was the capacity to decode and appraise. How to weigh the prince's word? How to apprise a distant agent's sales in foreign markets? How to assess this velvet's quality, this vessel's seaworthiness, a servant's loyalty, the menace in a swagger, the value of a vineyard, the portent blowing on a *scirocco*: is a hard rain about to fall? Amidst such opacity, experience, practical knowledge, swift judgment, a good eye, ear, nose, and tongue, and a judicious hand were precious assets, anchors of competences both professional and social. Amidst this swarm of doubts, Romans often turned to others, to appraise things. The "appraiser" (*stimatore*) was a crucial figure. He brought his skill and staked his honour and social credit, easing transactions by squelching doubt. Such figures abounded. Their competence reflected not only professional skills but also social reputation. Such men

---

[17] See too the sudden fall of prosecutor Alessandro Pallantieri in 1557 in Cohen, *Love and Death*, 129–130; for Carafa's fall, see Pattenden, *Pius IV and the Fall of the Carafa*, 58.
[18] Weissman, *Ritual Brotherhood*, 26–41.
[19] Machiavelli, "La favola di Belfagor arcidiavolo." Any edition.

assayed because *fidedegni*, worthy of the *fede* that lubricated all transactions. It was a manly trait, a competence assessors cashed in on.[20]

Uncertainty and Risk

"Risk" began as an Italian word linked to estimates in contracts; Italians were the first to devise a calculus to gauge it, inventing insurance to palliate the harm risk might inflict. Insurance cushioned the commercial shock of shipwreck or war but could not parry the many other looming dangers Roman life was prone to. Apocalypse: pick your horseman. Famine: the food supply was often wobbly; crops could fail. Pestilence: the plague aside, so many other ills; malaria was rampant. War: from 1494 to 1557, and then again in the 1630s–1640s, Italy suffered wars big and small. Alongside the great rivalries of France, Spain, the Ottomans, and the Holy Roman Empire there were simmering baronial feuds and factious urban tumults. The later sixteenth century saw banditry so massive that it felt like warfare. Amidst these Apocalyptic blights, Death rode right behind. Romans met it everywhere. They lost children in a blink and shed wives at childbirth.[21] The violence of the streets and honour's prickly mayhem cut down many a man in the bloom of health, cut or cudgeled with scant warning. Against these many plagues, public offices were of small avail. The police were weak, the courts chaotic and often slow. Indeed, the law, in its zeal for good, could sometimes seem a force for bad. Often, Romans languished in prison, as debtors, as jailed witnesses, or as suspects locked up for imputed fraud, violence, heresy, or mutterings against the pope. So, risk was everywhere; a competent man had to gauge it, dodge what he could, and confront it resourcefully with steady nerves and canny wits. A life skill, altogether central.

Hierarchy

Before the French Revolution with the "isms" its age later spawned – liberalism, socialism, communism, each, even fascism, egalitarian in its own way – inequality seemed natural, like the morning dew. The great chain of beings, replicated in state, church, community, family, and all the natural world, sorted and aligned all things. Accordingly, among Romans, power, wealth, prestige, health, safety, knowledge, clothing, diet, language, posture, gait, contentment, and agility of mind were unequally deployed. Only blessedness broke this sweeping rule: God cherished everybody equally, or loved the lowly more. Accordingly, everyone, even the ruler, looked both up and down a scale. There was one competence in ruling, another in being ruled. Those below – that is everyone, because even the

---

[20] For the function of *stimatore*, see Meneghin, *The Social Fabric*, 111–124; Cohen, *Roman Tales*, 142–162.

[21] Hanlon, *Death Control in the West*, stresses high mortality and also widespread prudential infanticide.

prince looked up to God – had to manage exchanges with superiors so as to offer them satisfaction, dodge their huff or scorn, and snatch what boons came down. Courtiers and men of state with princes, officials with their superiors, domestics with their masters, workers with the shop *padrone*, soldiers with their captains, children with their elders, all knew how to avoid friction, win approval, accomplish tasks, and fit in among their peers. When they did this well, in their own eyes and their betters', nothing in their actions, when done with proper ease, rendered them less male; they were merely male according to their station, as several essays in this collection illustrate.[22] Similar codes also held true down the scale, where poets seldom sang, but loyal servants still claimed the regard of others: "I have eaten my master's bread," so call me loyal.[23]

So far, this argument has remained blithely free of its own facts. How to prove, or at least defend, its contentions? How indeed to document a sense of masculinity, an idea diffuse, often inarticulate, and weakly labeled? How, especially, to capture appraisals of others and self-assessments expressed less in words than in posture, breath, movements of eye and limb, and darting feelings so swift and furtive that minds seldom fished them onto the tossing deck of speech? Perhaps it is best to tell some stories, parsing them for manliness in its immediate setting, as enacted, sensed, gauged, and eventually recounted.

YOUTH: A BOY TELLS TOO WELL

I once wrote a mournful story: the struggle of three young women, a lute-maker's daughters, against the thuggish sexual predations of an overweening state prosecutor, Alessandro Pallantieri.[24] I tried to awaken compassion and awe for the dogged courage with which they faced their tormentor and finally told their tale in court. Some years later, I returned to a different trial I had seen early in my Roman work, as a detail there had long ago once caught my eye. It was a policeman's description of how a boy of ten had recounted some tawdry sexual exploitation on which he stumbled when a jailer's mistress sent him upstairs in prison to fetch a towel. In October 1557, the lad, Cencione, had observed Flaminio Ruffo, a judge he knew by sight, atop a female prisoner, his

---

[22] For examples of condign good war services by elite men, see: Ross "The Many Faces," on faithful soldiery in an epic adopted by the Golden Gorde, see Wilk, "Military Masculinities," on the wondrously ever-true Bertrand de Guescelin and loyal French captains, where masculinity attached easily to such high-ranked underlings; see Lukas, "From the Knightly Bayard." See also Elbl, "A 'Great Man,'" for the loyal, patient *varonia*, the warrior manliness, of Prince Henry the Navigator.

[23] Cohen and Cohen, *Words and Deeds*, "The Abbot's Assassins," 35–43, for "I have eaten the bread" of my master, and servants' asserted loyalties.

[24] Cohen, *Love and Death*, 127–128, 137–168.

hose about his ankles. His report soon oozed around the prison and began to leak beyond its walls. But only five months later, in March 1558, did Rome's governor learn what his judge had done. Alarmed, he summoned the boy, two chief jailers, and the female victims. Judge Ruffo, no longer in Rome, seemingly eluded interrogation. The two jailers tried to deny knowing much and each vied to finger the other as derelict. Listen here to the jail chief, Captain Michelangelo:

> I was sick in bed after I came back to my job, and it was the month of November, staying with Ser Alvaro, who came to find me there, and he talked to me, discreetly [*a l'orecchia*] and asked me if I knew about this thing we were talking about here just now, about Messer Flaminio [Judge Ruffo], and how things stood.
>
> I told him that I was not there [i.e., not then employed], and that I knew nothing about it.
>
> He answered: "This lad of Horazio [the other chief jailer] who is staying with you knows the whole of it."
>
> And I told him, "Talk to the boy. He knows."
>
> He talked to him off to the side, and then Messer Alvaro told me that it was true, and that the boy told the story in a very spirited fashion [*molto gagliardamente*].[25]

Gagliardamente: odd expression. My memory of that nearly untranslatable adverb drew me back to this half-forgotten case. *Gagliardo* is tricky; modern English has nothing like it. Florio's 1598 dictionary, *A Worlde of Words*, translates *gagliardo* as "strong, lustie, brave, gallant, valiant, disposed, stout, frolike, blith."[26] The range was wide, the flavour decidedly male. So why attach it to a youngster's description of a shabby sexual act? Perhaps because he displayed a spirited, precocious competence that was striking and rather fun? Cannily for a boy so young, Cencione had laid out the scene with admirable precision, impressing and amusing the adults. As he again did when the governor called him in. Cencione described both the act and its perpetrator,

---

[25] "Essendo io amalato in lecto doppo che io ce ero rintrato che fu del mese del 9.bre ad Ser Alvaro quale me venne ad trovare illi et me parlò a l'orecchia et me domandò se io sapevo questa materia dicta di sopra di messer Flaminio et como stava. Li resposi che io non ce ero et che io non sapevo niente. Me respose questo putto di Horatio che sta con voi sa il tutto. Et io li dissi parlate al putto esso lo sa. Lui li parlo da banda et disse messer Alvaro poi a me che era vero che il putto lo raccontava gagliardamente.": ASR, GTC, Processi, busta 38 (1558), case 3, fol. 42[r.]

[26] Florio, *A Worlde of Words*, 261. The French range was similar to the Italian, but a dictionary of 1690 adds, pertinently, sauciness, "on le dit aussi des choses qui sont licentieuses, hardies, incroyables. Ce conte est un peu gaillard, le trait est gaillard": Furetière, *Dictionnaire universel*, 2:137. I thank Jane Couchman for this reference.

glimpsed briefly through a doorway, before he had retreated, flustered, when the judge, glancing sideways, caught him spying.

> I don't know what his name was, but he had a black beard, not too short, not too long, and he was a big man.
> *And to a question from me the notary he said*: He was a man as big as Monsignor Governor here, and he was not old, and he was not too thin, but if I were to see him I would not recognize him. And he was wearing a long, black cloak [*zimarra*] and he was wearing the cloth cap in the fashion of a priest like the one the Governor is wearing, and he was white of face.[27]

Child that he is, Cencione twice uses the governor as a yardstick or prop, for comparisons. In court, adults of simple culture sometimes did the same, but his gambit shows youthful naivety. Nonetheless, Cencione's powers of description are indeed spirited, admirable, and, given the sexual subject, decidedly male. He has worldly wisdom, a competence beyond his years: he is *gagliardo*. His story merits *fede*.

Returning to this forgotten trial, I was startled and dismayed. I knew those young women. The very ones, the lute-maker's daughters, poor things, while courageously recounting their sexual exploitation, facing down their vile tormentor, the dismissed, arrested prosecutor, who harried them with his own fierce and skilled defence, back in their cells were suffering similar abuse by another magistrate. Worse, long before the governor knew of it, the imprisoned prosecutor's family, alerted to these prison misdeeds, haunted Cencione to worm out details, aiming to disgrace the women and scupper their testimony. That, most likely, is why the governor was so keen to plumb the whole mess. Incompetence all around – an errant judge, slipshod jailors, compromised witnesses – his case against prosecutor Pallantieri at risk. Besides the lad, few here come off well.

YOUTH AGAIN: A BOY STEALS GOLD

Francesco, a boy of ten, adroitly stole his master's money – twenty-eight gold pieces – and then for weeks squandered them until, one day, coins toppled from his shirt, the maid saw them, his mistress caught on, and the law pounced.[28] The tale of how Francesco, erratically competent, quirkily male, used his new ill-gotten wealth suggests how swiftly Roman youngsters

---

[27] "Io non so come havesse nome ma haveva la barba negra non troppo corta ne troppo lunga, et era homo grande et ad interogationem mei notarii dixit era homo grande come qui monsignore gubernatore et non era vecchio et non era troppo magro ma se io lo vedessi non lo recognosceria et era vestito di una zimarra longa negra et portava una barretta da prete como porta il gubernatore et era bianco in viso.": ASR, GTC, Processi, busta 38, case 3, fol. 36^v.

[28] On this case, see Cohen, *Roman Tales*, 189–199.

sponged up the ways of men. A nimble thief, Francesco sneaked a key, twice unlatched his master's money box, and filched three extras from a purse. Twenty-eight gold scudi was more than many a workman's annual income. But gold was awkward, too big to spend. So, four times Francesco tapped a banker who, despite the rascal's youth, changed his gold, no questions asked, for silver. Francesco then hired a worker to do chores he owed his master. Meanwhile, like any man of honour, he played the patron; largess, both gifts and loans, rained on other boys. And, open-handed, big-hearted, he lent a worker money to buy shoes. And, like Roman males of every age, and females too, he very often played. Francesco gambled at games, *bocce* for instance, and often lost. His boldest exploit was hosting. Four times he brought a band of friends to the Inn of the Sun, near where he worked and stole, regaling them at table with Sunday pigeon, veal, cakes, and more wine than he or they could hold. Once, he even once paid in gold; change for his glittering *scudo* nearly stripped the till of silver. Francesco's competence had limits; he was too drunk that day to track the change. This we know because the waiter who had brought the food and drink was hauled to court to explain where that bright coin had gone; Francesco's master, at the end-game, was chasing as best he could all his missing bullion.

In court, Francesco lied almost as competently as many an older suspect, as did Nicola, twelve, accomplice not in theft but in the enjoyment of its fruits. But Francesco, charmingly, revealed the limits to his mastery of law's mysteries. He was truthful, he insisted, because his father had warned him:

> Today my father talked to me when I was in prison and he asked me if I had been examined.
> I told him no.
> And he said to me, "Be sure that, if they examine you, you tell the truth. Otherwise they will beat you." That is all he said to me.[29]

Roman courts were often cruel to suspects. They had several modes of torture and were quick to use them. There were thumb-screws, mostly for women, and the painful *veglia*, hours perching on a cruel point, and even, rarely, fire to the feet. Most common, though, was the *corda*, the hoisting rope, used on two of the lute-maker's daughters to test their denunciations of the prosecutor who had abused them. But courts never thrashed a witness the way a father did his sons.

---

[29] "Signor si che hoggi me parlò 'l mio padre quando ero in pregione e me dimandò se io era stato essaminato che gli dissi di non e lui me disse guarda se te essaminaranno che tu dichi la verità altramente te piccaranno et altro non me disse.": ASR, GTC, Costituti, busta 143 (1567), fol. 288ᵛ.

Masculinity as Competence

AGE: AN ELDER TELLS STORIES

In the spring of 1557, a judge hauled to Rome men from Rocca Sinibalda, a village that one year earlier had first rebelled against its lord and then attended an inquest held at their behest by a roving judge, Anselmo. But now a less friendly magistrate inquired: who went to Anselmo's village hearings; how full had the room been? One witness, having striven to name no names, finally proffered this spare vignette:

> I was there too, and not only I but that room was always almost full of people when they took testimony [...] Those who came to prison with me will know better than I because they were almost always there [...]
> And his lordship asked if he remembers the witnesses who were examined in his own presence.
> He answered: I would have to think carefully because I did not commit it to memory but I remember now that I was there when he examined Carosio di Spirillo. Then it was so full that it could not hold more persons, and Messer Anselmo was examining him about the conduct of Signor Giuliano [the deposed lord], and about his other ancient things, and about many other things of great moment because the fellow was around ninety years old, and he was informed about everything.[30]

A mountain village had no written history; whatever ancient memory it possessed dwelt in elders' heads. This vignette is highly informative. When, at Anselmo's prompting, elderly Carosio reeled out tales from days long gone, everyone came to hear. The man was a local treasure. When he spoke, he spoke the community's story; villagers, who may have heard these things time and again already, gathered to drink in both the performance and the awesome transcription of village words into solemn script on official paper. Here the world of speech met the realm of writing. Old Carosio, likely himself illiterate, was crucial to this solemn alchemy. His was a competence that sat well with age; it required long life, crisp memories, and ready speech. Was this manly? It surely was.

---

[30] "Respondit io ci stevo presente anch'io qualche volte et non solamente io ma era quasi piena quella stanza di gente sempre quando si esaminava. [...] questi che sonno venuti pregioni insieme con me la sapranno megio di me che ci stavano quasi sempre [...] dicente domino an ipse memorie habeat de testibus qui fuerunt examinati in presentia ipsius constituti. Respondit bisogneria che io ci pensassi bene perche io non m'e comesso a mente ma mi ricordi adesso che ero presente quando esaminava Carusio de Sperillo che allhora era piena che non ce ne poteva capir più et messer Anselmo lo esaminava sopra delle portamenti del signor Giuliano et delli sui antichi et di molte altre cose grande perche costui havea circa 90 anni, et era informato de ogni cosa."; ASR, GTC, Processi, busta 34 (1557), fol. 62^{r-v}.

Thomas V. Cohen

ARTE

In early modern Italy, *arte* had a wide semantic range, covering not only today's museum-worthy "fine arts," but also almost any other craft or action, from hoeing ground to waging war. In trials peasants aver firmly that theirs is the *arte de zappare* [the occupation of hoeing] or, more generally, *l'arte de fora* [outdoors] or *della terra*.[31] The expression is striking and instructive. To claim an *arte*, as those peasants did, elevated their work to a calling. Artisans embraced the term more often; *arte* was what they called their guilds, whether they were humble shoemakers or the rich wool merchants of Florence's *Arte della Lana*.[32] The term was competence's proud blazon. In truth, the lowly *arte della terra*, though scorned by those higher, demanded countless strengths and skills; they who practiced it surely assessed their fellows and respected mastery. Note, however, the word's general absence from the female sphere. Women, in their work and social lives, had many competences, often complex, seldom shared by men, but rarely could these skills claim the male label of *arte*. Of the mother, housemaid, wet nurse, washerwoman, embroiderer, lace-maker, and midwife, skilled all, none could easily boast an *arte*. The rare exceptions: the actress, the poetess, the rare painter, and the courtesan, a transgressive figure who might dress male and caterwaul with men under the windows of her rivals.

As for the artists, in our modern sense, a Roman trial of 1603, well known to art historians, adjudged a suit by the painter Giovanni Baglioni, defamed, said he, by Caravaggio, who then testified in self-defence.[33] At stake: what painter dared call himself a *valent'huomo*. Caravaggio named those who made the grade and explained:

> To me, that word, *valent'huomo*, means that he knows how to do well, that is that he knows how to do his art well. So a *valent'huomo* knows how to paint well and imitate well natural things.[34]

---

[31] Rome, ASR, GTC, Processi, busta 8, case 7 (1542), fol. 339ᵛ: "Io fo l'arte del campo et lavoro colli bovi et colli bovi mei et del lavoriccio"; fol. 341ʳ: "fa l'arte de fora che veniva da sementar."

[32] For instance: ASR, GTC, Processi, busta 116 (1566), case 3, fol. 787ᵛ: "Interrogatus ut dicat quam artem exerceat dictus Matheus Respondit se li dice Matteo scarpellino, ma non so che arte si faccia"; ASR, GTC, Processi, busta 34 (1557), fol. 1ᵛ: "zappando e fa l'arte de fora."

[33] I saw this trial in Roman archive when Elizabeth Cohen worked through it. For the excerpt with this text see "Il processo del 1603" online. For the story of the entire quarrel and trial, see Langdon, *Caravaggio*, 267–269.

[34] "Quella parola, valent'huomo, appresso di me vuol dire che sappi far bene, cioè sappi far bene dell'arte sua, così un pittore valent'huomo, che sappi depinger bene et imitar bene le cose naturali." "Il processo del 1603" online.

Masculinity as Competence

Implicitly, then, in the eyes of these disputing artists, a competent painter has a kind of valour. The term is conventionally attached to combat, but as in battle so in craft an agonistic streak produced the habits of challenge and response so familiar from the tall-but-telling tales of Benvenuto Cellini, whose alleged spun-out contest for a fatter commission than the one due to *quel valente* goldsmith Lucagnolo ended, as he recounted with gusto, in a splendid confrontation before the entire shop, a symbolic battle much like a joust.[35]

MASTER AND SERVANT: MUTUAL FAITH, MUTUAL SUPPORT

Filippo della Valle was a young civic noble descended via bastardy from a grandfather, brother of cardinal Andrea della Valle.[36] Filippo dwelt in the palace complex tracing to the cardinal's grand building projects. He lived the life of a noble youth, visiting courtesans, gambling, buying fine clothes and paying late, if ever. In the summer of 1550, Francisco de Avila, a Spaniard and solid clothier running commerce with his father on a major street, took Filippo's debts to court, winning an excommunication and an order: pay up now or suffer consequences. Francisco posted this official decree by the shop door.

In Filippo's palace there lived a servant, Lorenzo de Olevano. The two men were milk brothers, no rare thing when the wealthy routinely hired peasant women to nurse the children. The two had probably played together, as toddlers, back at Olevano, in the mountains east of Rome. As well-born nurslings returned when weaned, milk-brotherhood suggests that, of the two, Lorenzo was the elder, but probably, given continuity of mother's milk, by little. However spaced in age, master and servant were close and fiercely loyal.

When Francisco posted that warrant, Filippo was in Florence. Returning, as the merchant surely hoped, he saw the notice on the wall. He threatened the Spaniards, son and father, to their faces; they shrugged him off. He then went to his lawyer to have it removed, but to no avail. A few days later, Filippo passed again and ordered his milk-brother Lorenzo to tear the notice down and shred it. At once, Lorenzo did as he was told. Not at all deterred, the Spaniards swiftly re-posted. Filippo returned, saw the second paper, fumed, and commanded. Lorenzo swiftly complied.

What we have here is a duel across social lines: a noble and his milk-brother peasant servant, high and lowly, against a solid merchant, middling. Francisco, keen on honour, soon posted his warrant a third time, defiantly out of reach, high above the door. Filippo saw the saucy warrant and, stymied, rode back and forth repeatedly. Filippo, a dodgy witness,

---

[35] Cellini, *Vita*, chs xix–xxi, 37–43.
[36] I thank Kathleen Christian for help on Filippo Della Valle, his family, and their palaces.

later told the court that he then spoke with Francisco's father, promising to pay up, and the taunting notice at last came down. End of story, one would think; a minor victory for the Spaniards should their money really come. But, if it really happened, this truce (only Filippo reports it) was flimsy.' Some three weeks later, Filippo rode past, with Lorenzo in escort on foot. When he reached the Spaniards' shop, Lorenzo stopped to piss against a wall. His urine likely sent a pungent message. His master rode on around the gentle curve that today still coaxes Via del Pellegrino towards the ancient bridge across the Tiber. Spying Lorenzo, a Spaniard at the shop door rasped scornfully in his throat.

> And Lorenzo went over and asked him if he had made that rattling sound for him. And they told him, "We did not do it for you." [*per te*] And then they said, "And if we had done it to you, who would care?" And Lorenzo said, "It would make no difference." And then that Spaniard said, "And wait and I will show you."[37]

Lorenzo and these Spaniards knew instinctively just where this was heading: the inevitable fight. Men poured out of the Spaniards' shop, halberds in hand. When Filippo, alerted by racket, rode back to the scene, Lorenzo, badly outnumbered, despite his sword was down and so sorely wounded that, come evening, back at the palace, the della Valle called a priest lest, before dawn, the servant should die unshriven. But Lorenzo survived and, healing, soon demanded compensation. The Spaniards proffered peace terms; scorning their offer, the servant refused unless they returned his sword and covered his medication expenses. Filippo, seeking a settlement, reached out to noble allies, even to Portugal's ambassador, to no avail. Eventually, with a peace accord out of reach, says Filippo, fearing further violence the Della Valle expelled the servant. Lorenzo then sheltered among old cronies in the civic palace on the Capitoline hill, plotting the ambush that, in February 1551, dealt Francisco the wounds that soon killed him.

The attack shocked Rome. The assassins struck Francisco and his armed escort at the porch of remote Santa Balbina, on the church's Lenten Station Day (then as today Lent's second Tuesday), a moment of seasonal high liturgy that made annual rounds, on long-fixed days, among traditional churches. As the assassins must have known, Santa Balbina's patron was a Spanish cardinal, perhaps a motive for Francisco to attend services.

---

[37] "Lorenzo andò lì et li domandò se haveva fatto quel raschiare per lui, et che loro li dissero non che non l'havemo fatto per te, et poi che dissero et ben l'havessemo fatto per te che cosa saria. Disse Lorenzo non saria altro et che alhora quel spagnolo disse et aspecta che te lo farò vedere": ASR, GTC, Processi, busta 16, case 4 (1550); Busta 20, case 10 (1555); Costituti 50 (1555), fols 74^v–77^v, 189^v–192^v. The exchange is recounted by a partner in killing Francisco, not present at this brawl, but who knows the story well.

When, assaulted at the door, the merchant fled in-doors, Lorenzo and his henchmen followed, hewing their victim inside the doorway and again, shockingly, before the high altar. Lorenzo then fled Rome, but crept back for visits and was eventually caught, jailed, tried, and tortured for a confession that implicated Filippo. But he then broke out of prison and fled again, probably forever. In Lorenzo's spates of rural exile, Filippo and his family housed and supported the fugitive, smuggling out money and clothing and warning him of a planned arrest. The lesson here is *fede*, in this case faithful hostility: the iron will with which all parties pursued this quarrel, move by trenchant move. And also faithful service. Lorenzo served his master well, running risks for him. But *fede*'s bargain ran both ways: if Lorenzo was a faithful servant, Filippo was a faithful master. The court inquired: was killing Francisco just one more loyal service and, if so, for whose satisfaction? They even tortured Filippo, a nobleman, not a thing this court did lightly, but he never bent. The story illustrates vertical honour affairs, less common than the horizontal spats where the honour ethic figured more often. As for masculine gestures, they abound, in the posturing and ripostes: the postings, tearings, fights, and the master's laments, regret, and anger. The peace-negotiations, killing, and staunch protection all were manly. Utterly scripted, well performed – a deep wrong done right.

CONCLUSION

This chapter began by positing that masculinity need not be toxic yet, despite contrarian intention, it ends with the usual mayhem. To palliate this tale of sacrilege and gore, we might note the strong affection: Filippo's for his wounded man; Lorenzo's for his offended master.

In conclusion, then, as scholars often say, sex and violence indeed were masculine, even if women also engaged in both, but, we add, so was competence: competent sex and competent violence, suitably aligned with the social codes, were better than excess in either. But, we argue here, there was far more to masculinity, as understood then, than merely sex or violence; masculinity figured in many other realms of action, wherever codes of conduct, social practices, and plain habit expected males to act – in work, in play, indeed in sex or combat, and in personal exchanges of all sorts – surfacing as competence in accomplishing tasks or fulfilling roles. This wider view of masculinity subverts the usual male–female dipole and allows ample ways of being male to the weak, the poor, the lowly, the young, the old, and the many outsiders, as well as to the elite in the prime of life.

York University

Thomas V. Cohen

ABBREVIATIONS

ASR   Archivio di Stato di Roma
GTC   Govenatore, Tribunale Criminale (in ASR)

CITED WORKS

Manuscript Sources

Rome, Archivio di Stato di Roma (ASR), Fondo: Governatore, Tribunale Criminale (GTC)
Atti di Cancelleria, 22.
Processi, buste 8, 16, 20, 34, 38, 116.
Costitutiti, buste 50, 143.

Printed Sources

Brizio, Elena, "'If My Sons will have no Male Heir'. Legal and Social Solutions to a Sienese Patriarchal Dread." In Jacqueline Murray, ed., *The Male Body and Social Masculinity in Premodern Europe*. Toronto: Centre for Renaissance and Reformation Studies, 2022, 113–132.

Bourdieu, Pierre and Loïc J. D. Wacquant. *An Invitation to Reflexive Sociology*. Chicago, IL: The University of Chicago Press, 1992.

Cellini, Benvenuto. *Vita*. Turin: Einaudi, 1975.

Cohen, Elizabeth S. and Thomas V. Cohen. *Words and Deeds in Renaissance Rome*. Toronto: University of Toronto Press, 1993.

Cohen, Thomas V. *Roman Tales: A Reader's Guide to Microhistory*. London: Routledge, 2019.

——. "Tracking Conversation in the Italian Courts." In Thomas V. Cohen and Lesley Twomey, eds, *Spoken Word and Social Practice: Orality in Europe (1400–1700)*. Leiden: Brill, 2015, 139–181.

Davis, Natalie Zemon. *Fiction in the Archives. Pardon Tales and their Tellers in Sixteenth-Century France*. Stanford, CA: Stanford University Press, 1987.

Elbl, Ivana. "A 'Great Man' Who Became a Virgin. The Masculinity of Prince Henry the Navigator." In Jacqueline Murray, ed., *The Male Body and Social Masculinity in Premodern Europe*. Toronto: Centre for Renaissance and Reformation Studies, 2022, 133–158.

Florio, John. *A Worlde of Words. A Critical Edition [1598 edition]*. Toronto: University of Toronto Press, 2013.

Fosi, Irene. *Papal Justice, Subjects and Courts in the Papal State, 1500–1750*. Trans. Thomas V. Cohen. Washington, DC: Catholic University of America Press, 2011.

Furetière, Antoine. *Dictionnaire universel, contenant généralement tous les mots François, tant vieux que modernes, et les termes de toutes les sciences et des arts, divisé en trois tomes*, Vol. 2. Paris: Arnout et Rainier, 1690.

Goffman, Erving. *The Presentation of Self in Everyday Life*. Edinburgh: University of Edinburgh Social Sciences Research Centre, 1956.

Hanlon, Gregory. *Death Control in the West 1500–1800. Sex Ratios at Baptism in Italy, France and England*. Abingdon, UK and New York: Routledge, 2023.

Hunt, John. "Carriages, Violence and Masculinity in Early Modern Rome." *I Tatti Studies* 17 (2014): 175–196.

Judde de Larivière, Claire. *L'ordinaire des savoirs, Une histoire pragmatique de la société vénitienne*. Paris: EHESS, 2023.

Klaassen, Frank. "Learning and Masculinity in Manuscripts of Ritual Magic of the Later Middle Ages and Renaissance." *Sixteenth Century Journal* 38.1 (2007): 49–76.

Langdon, Helen. *Caravaggio. A Life*. New York: Farrar, Strauss and Giroux, 1999.

Lukas, Benjamin. "From the Knightly Bayard to Captain Monluc: Representations of Masculinity in Sixteenth-Century French Military Literature." In Konrad Eisenbichler and Jacqueline Murray, eds, *Premodern Masculinities in Transition*. Woodbridge, UK: The Boydell Press, 2024.

McSheffrey, Shannon. "Men and Masculinity in Late Medieval London Civic Culture. Governance, Patriarchy and Reputation." In Jacqueline Murray, ed., *Conflicting Identities and Multiple Masculinities: Men in the Middle Ages*. New York: Garland Press, 1999, 243–278.

Meneghin, Alessia. *The Social Fabric of Fifteenth-Century Florence: Identities and Change in the World of Second-Hand Dealers*. London: Routledge, 2019.

Miedema, Aaron. "The Sand Pot: the Politics of the Uomo da Bene in Rural Latium." In Jacqueline Murray, ed., *Patriarchy, Honour, and Violence: Masculinities in Pre-modern Europe*. Toronto: Centre for Renaissance and Reformation Studies, 2022, 49–70.

Miller, William Ian. *Blood Taking and Peace Making: Feud, Law, and Society in Saga Iceland*. Chicago, IL: The University of Chicago Press, 1990.

Neal, Derek. "Suits Make the Man: Masculinity in Two English Law Courts, ca. 1500." *Canadian Journal of History* 37 (April 2002): 1–2.

Newman, Jonathan M. "Work, Writing, and Elite Masculinity in the Lyrics of Baudri of Bourgueil." In Konrad Eisenbichler and Jacqueline Murray, eds, *Masculinities in Transition in Premodern Europe*. Woodbridge, UK: The Boydell Press, 2024.

Pattenden, Miles. *Pius IV and the Fall of the Carafa: Nepotism and Papal Authority in Counter-Reformation Rome*. Oxford: Oxford University Press, 2013.

Pohl, Susanne. *Making Manslaughter: Process, Punishment and Restitution in Württemberg and Zurich, 1376–1700*. Leiden: Brill, 2018.

Rose, Colin. *A Renaissance of Violence: Homicide in Early Modern Italy*. Cambridge, UK: Cambridge University Press, 2019.

Ross, Danielle. "The Many Faces of Qahramān: A Medieval Persianate Romance as a Window on Mongol and Muslim Masculinities in the Volga-Ural Region (1400s–1700s)." In Konrad Eisenbichler and Jacqueline Murray, eds, *Premodern Masculinities in Transition*. Woodbridge, UK: The Boydell Press, 2024.

Shepard, Alexandra. "Anxious Patriarchs to Refined Gentlemen? Manhood in Britain, circa 1500–1700." *Journal of British Studies* 44.2 (2005): 281–295.

——. *Meanings of Manhood in Early Modern England*. Oxford: Oxford University Press, 2003.

Simons, Patricia. *The Sex of Men in Premodern Europe: A Cultural History*. Cambridge, UK: Cambridge University Press, 2011.

Smail, Daniel Lord. "Hatred as a Social Institution in Late Medieval Society." *Speculum* 76 (2001): 90–126.

——. *The Consumption of Justice, Emotions, Publicity and Legal Culture in Marseille, 1264–1423*. Ithaca, NY: Cornell University Press, 2003.

Weissman, Ronald F. E. *Ritual Brotherhood in Renaissance Florence*. New York: Academic Press, 1982.

Wilk, Sarah. "Military Masculinities in La Chanson de Bertrand du Guesclin." In Konrad Eisenbichler and Jacqueline Murray, eds, *Premodern Masculinities in Transition*. Woodbridge, UK: The Boydell Press, 2024.

Electronic Sources

"Il processo del 1603." https://archiviodistatoroma.beniculturali.it/it/237/il-processo-del-1603

3

THE MANY FACES OF QAHRAMĀN: A MEDIEVAL PERSIANATE ROMANCE AS A WINDOW ON MONGOL AND MUSLIM MASCULINITIES IN THE VOLGA-URAL REGION (1400s–1700s)

Danielle Ross

Upon succeeding his brother as king of Iran, Hirasıp gives his son, Qahtarān, the following advice:

> Never stop being a champion. Never take an interest in kingship. Be a friend to your friends and an enemy to your enemies. Do not oppose a necessary and just king. Serve him and never go against his wishes. Being a champion is a greater thing than being a king, because a king becomes a king only through the deeds of his champions.[1]

Hirasıp's advice neatly encapsulates the overarching message of the *Qahramān-nāma* / *Qahramān-i Qātil*, a medieval Persian romance that, in Turkish translation, circulated in Russia's Volga-Ural Muslim communities from the time of the Golden Horde until the early twentieth century. Central to *Qahramān*'s enduring popularity were its portrayals of masculine conduct in times of conflict and heroic submission to a higher authority. These models were clearly defined but also proved flexible enough to be adapted and reinterpreted as the political, social, and cultural landscape of the Volga-Ural region changed from the fourteenth century to the eighteenth century. In the political world of the Golden Horde and its successor states, *Qahramān* offered a template for warrior-aristocratic masculinity that reinforced views on cooperation, submission, and service expressed in Chinggisid literature and histories. After the mid-sixteenth century, as the Volga-Ural region's Chinggisid-Muslim political culture was gradually replaced by a Russian Christian one, the titular hero of the *Qahramān* romance was embraced as an

---

[1] *Kaharman katil*, 21. Henceforth, simple page references to this work will be incorporated parenthetically into the text.

ideal for Muslim masculine self-discipline in a society in which Islam was no longer the politically dominant faith.

Qahramān offers a glimpse of the complexities of masculinity in a medieval and early modern Inner Asian society. In examining these complexities, this essay approaches masculinity as something that individuals were expected to achieve and demonstrate rather than as an inborn trait.[2] The character arcs of *Qahramān*'s male characters and, especially, of the titular hero, center around the achievement of full membership in a warrior-aristocratic elite and the continuing display of the characteristics valued by that elite. At the same time, both the specific masculinity to which *Qahramān*'s men aspire and the aspects of that masculinity that readers of *Qahramān* emphasized at different historical moments were determined in relation to social class, the political order, and other co-existing masculinities. Masculinity in *Qahramān* is perhaps best understood through the lens of hegemonic masculinity. In both the world depicted in *Qahramān* and the historical Inner Asian societies inhabited by its readers, masculinities were hierarchical. Only a few powerful men were able to fully perform their society's model of "strong" masculinity, while other men reaped benefits by supporting that model and its practitioners.[3] Such support took the form of constructing and adhering to forms of masculinity that did not challenge one's superiors. As political conditions shifted (from Mongol rule to Russian rule), so too, did the specifics of these subordinate masculinities.

One of the greatest challenges facing historians studying the Volga Basin before the eighteenth century is the paucity (and, sometimes, total absence) of surviving written sources. Many causes of this situation have been posited: (1) oral tradition rather than written documents as the main mode of disseminating and preserving information;[4] (2) the widespread destruction of written records by fire, natural disaster, and foreign conquest;[5] (3) indigenous patterns of document preservation and recopying that did not privilege the genres of documents that would have provided historians with detailed information about political, social, and cultural life.[6] One substantial body of extant written sources – Turkic-language literary works composed between the thirteenth and the eighteenth centuries – presents historians with several interpretive challenges. First, these sources are literary works rather than egodocuments or historical accounts. Second, many of them were

---

[2] Gilmore, *Manhood in the Making*, 10–12.
[3] Connell and Messerschmidt, "Hegemonic Masculinity," 832, 846–848.
[4] Halperin, "The Missing Golden Horde Chronicles," 1–15; See also the discussions of the interactions between oral and written sources throughout DeWeese, *Islamization and Native Religion*, 65–81.
[5] Keenan, "Muscovy and Kazan," 1, 4; Äkhmätjanov, "Tatar ädäbiyatı tarikhın öyränüdä chıganak bularak kul'yazma kitap," 46–47.
[6] Paul, "Archival Practices in the Muslim World," 339–360.

written outside the Volga-Ural region. Third, most of them are translations or reworkings of older literary works and storylines from Arabic and Persian into Turkish rather than wholly original indigenous compositions.

Despite these difficulties, even the literary texts that migrated to the Volga-Ural region from elsewhere can be made to yield information on local Muslim values and culture in the 1700s and earlier, especially if the inquiry begins with the assumption that the adoption of these texts into the Volga-Ural literary canon was not inevitable. The existence of a text in the Persian language did not guarantee its translation into Turkish, nor did the popularity of a Turkish-language text in Anatolia or Central Asia guarantee its popularity in the Volga-Ural region. The literary works that were read and reproduced by many generations of Volga-Ural Muslims were embraced in the first place because they resonated in some way with regional audiences. Similarly, literary works that maintained their popularity across major political-cultural ruptures (such as the Russian conquest of the Kazan Khanate in 1552), did so because they remained meaningful to their readers. Interrogating why and how specific literary texts fit into the broader value systems of Volga-Ural audiences allows researchers to consider the position of that work in the region's cultural world, and, also, to focus on the values and anxieties of its readers.

The life of the medieval romance *Qahramān the Slayer* (*Qahramān-i Qātil*) in the Volga-Ural region offers a view into the circulation of Persian-derived literature in a less-studied frontier of the Persianate world[7] and an example of how regional ideals of masculinity were refracted through a specific literary work at various historical moments. *Qahramān*'s presentation of masculinity played a significant role in the romance's spread through the lands of the Golden Horde. Its tale of a charismatic general leading an army of men and women of diverse ethnic, religious, and social backgrounds in world conquest dovetailed neatly with the Mongol ruling elite's own origin story. At the same time, *Qahramān*'s origins in the Persianate Islamic world made it well-suited to serve as a bridge between Muslim and Chinggisid identities and values as the Golden Horde ruling class embraced Islam. *Qahramān*'s portrayals of masculinity was equally important in its survival as a Volga-Ural text in the 1550s–1750s as the Chinggisid nobility's influence declined under Russian rule, when readers and teachers chose to emphasize the spiritual aspects of the poem's hero's masculinity rather than the martial and aristocratic ones. Through a study of *Qahramān* in the Volga-Ural region, one gains a view of how local ideals of Muslim masculinity shifted over four hundred years.

---

[7] On the Persianate cultural-linguistic world and its boundaries, see Green, "Introduction," 1–71; Amanat, "Remembering the Persianate," 15–62; Spooner and Hanaway, "Introduction," 1–69.

Danielle Ross

THE HISTORY OF THE TEXT

The plot and characters of *Qahramān-i Qātil* derive from a much longer Persian-language work, the *Qahramān-nāma*. This longer work has been attributed to Abū Ṭāhir Muḥammad b. Ḥasan b. ʿAlī b. Mūsā Ṭarsūsī, an author of the 900s–1000s who has been credited with writing a number of medieval Persian-language romances, including the *Dārāb-nāma* and the *Qirān-i Ḥabashī*.[8] Like Persian romances such as *Dārāb-nāma* and *Samak-e ʿayyār*, the *Qahramān-nāma* was drawn from Persian oral tradition, was meant to be recited to a popular audience, and was composed in such a manner as to simultaneously serve as entertainment and didactic material.[9] Featuring a blend of royal, warrior-aristocratic, and commoner characters, the Persian romances offered readers and listeners class-based models for proper behaviour. At the same time, through their characters' interactions, these works presented an idealized vision of society in which good kings and their subjects of various classes worked together to preserve the political and moral order.[10]

The Persian-language *Qahramān-nāma* relates the deeds of Qahramān, the champion of Hūshang Shāh, a mythical ruler of ancient Iran who appears as one of the rulers in Abul-Qasem Ferdowsi's *Shāhnāma* and as the central figure of the epic romance *Hūshangnāma*.[11] Qahramān features in the latter work as an administrator to Hūshang Shāh.[12] Despite the ancient setting, Hūshang Shāh and his followers are clearly identified as Muslims and his military campaigns are as much about spreading Islam as about world conquest. His war against Rā-i Hind, the infidel king of India, has been interpreted as a confrontation between Islam and the pre-Islamic Zoroastrians ("fire-worshipers"),[13] but it also bears a resemblance to the raids carried out against the non-Muslim polities in India in the 1000s–1100s by Sultan Maḥmūd of Ghaznī (971–1030) of the Persianized Turkic Ghaznavid dynasty, in whose court Ṭarsūsī served as a storyteller.[14]

The *Qahramān-nāma* begins with the kidnapping of the child Qahramān by demons (*diular*). After Qahramān grows up and leaves the demon kingdom, he encounters Hūshang Shāh's army. He initially confronts Hūshang Shāh as a foe, but later joins the *shah*'s forces and becomes a defender of Islam and the husband of the warrior princess Sarwi Khoraman. Qahramān interacts with

---

[8] Gaillard, "Abū Ṭāhir al-Ṭarsūsī"; de Bruijn, "Ḳahramān-nāma"; Massé, "Abū Ṭāhir al-Ṭarsūsī," 1:152; Hanaway, "Darab-name."
[9] Hanaway, "Persian Popular Romances," 178–195.
[10] Hanaway, "Darab-name."
[11] de Bruijn, "Ḳahramān-nāma," 4:444–445; Massé, "Hūshāng."
[12] de Bruijn, "Ḳahramān-nāma," 4:444–445.
[13] Menzel, "Ḳahramān-nāma."
[14] Eaton, *India in the Persianate Age*, 19–22; Gaillard, "Abū Ṭāhir al-Ṭarsūsī."

The Many Faces of Qahramān

numerous secondary characters, including other warriors, the fairies (*peri*) and their king, the demons, and the cunning *ʿayyār*-sorcerer Gerden-Keshān.[15]

Starting in the Middle Ages, the *Qahramān-nāma* underwent translations and adaptations into other languages. The work found especial popularity in the Turkic-speaking world. A full Ottoman translation of the *Qahramān-nāma* was produced in the sixteenth century.[16] Shorter Turkic-language versions of the *Qahramān* story (variously titled *Qahramān-nāma*, *Qahramān kitābı*, *Qahramān-i Qātil*, and *Dāstān-i Qahramān*) were composed and circulated in the Ottoman Empire, Central Asia, and the Kazakh steppe from the fourteenth century onward.[17]

Marsel' Äkhmätjanov dates the *Qahramān* tradition that circulated in the Volga-Ural region back to the Golden Horde era (1242–1502), though the oldest surviving manuscript produced in the region was copied in Kazan in the 1700s.[18] The language of this manuscript shows significant Ottoman influence, suggesting that it may be a copy of a version of the *Qahramān-i Qātil* originally composed in the Ottoman Empire. Despite the relatively late dates of the surviving manuscripts, Äkhmätjanov has argued that the *Qahramān* story and the broader canon of Persianate romances to which it belongs had become part of the cultural milieu of Turkic-speaking Volga-Ural region in the fourteenth and fifteenth centuries.[19] A comparison of Sahīb Girāy Khan (1501–1551), *khan* of Kazan and, later, Crimea, with the Qahramān who appears in the sixteenth-century chronicle *Tarīkh-i Sahīb-girāy* suggests that *Qahramān* made its way into the territory of the Golden Horde and its successor states no later than the 1500s.[20] This article uses Äkhmätjanov's published edition of the written version of *Qahramān* most prevalent in the Volga-Ural region.[21] However, it proceeds with the understanding that many Turkic versions of *Qahramān* likely existed and were circulated throughout the 1300s–1700s, both in written texts that have not been preserved in the regional archives and though oral tradition.[22]

---

[15] Menzel, "Ḳahramān-nāma."

[16] de Bruijn, "Ḳahramān-nāma," 4:445.

[17] Parsatalab, Moazzeni and Hadi, "Muʿarrafī nash nawyafat-e *Qahramānnāma*," 202–208; Akhmetzianov, "Kakharman kitaby," 268.

[18] "Kaharman kitabı" IIaLI, Fond 39 Opis 1 Delo 3497.

[19] Äkhmätjanov, "'Kaharman katil' dastanı" in *Kaharman katil*, 9–11.

[20] Abduzhemilev, "Remmal Khodja. Khronika "Tarikh-i Sakhib Gerai khan," 152.

[21] Äkhmätjanov's edition was assembled based on the version of *Qaharmān kitābı* published in Kazan in 1879 and several manuscript versions produced in Kazan in the eighteenth and nineteenth centuries; Äkhmätjanov, "'Kaharman katil' dastanı," 12–13.

[22] On the differences among the manuscript versions recovered in the Kazan region and the discrepancies between them and the published versions of the late

Danielle Ross

READING *QAHRAMĀN* IN THE CHINGGISID WORLD

As *Qahramān* migrated from eleventh-century Ghaznavid society to fourteenth- and fifteenth-century steppe society (with possible stopovers in Anatolia and/ or Chagatay Central Asia), the story changed cultural contexts. The characters of the original *Qahramān-nama* – the wise king, the superhumanly strong, but also loyal and honourable, the fairies and demons, the warrior princess, the wily, and the mischievous *'ayyār* – were recognizable archetypes found across Persianate romances and would have been assigned specific roles and significances by writers and audiences living in the Persianate world before the Mongol conquests.[23] Once *Qahramān* (or, rather, its translations) reached Turkic-speaking societies in the steppe (after the Mongol conquests), its plots, characters, and tropes entered a different political and cultural world. Characters such as Geshen-Kerdān the *'ayyār*, a representative of the social organizations formed by working-class men and women in early medieval Persianate urban centres, would have had no known equivalents in the culture of the Volga-Ural region.[24] Similarly, as the *Qahramān-nāma* moved into the steppe and the Volga Basin, it was removed from the complex web of written and oral romances within which it was originally situated and, at the same time, distanced from the Persian cultural constructs of just kingship and loyal subjecthood underpinning those romances.

When the *Qahramān* tales reached the Turkic-speaking communities of the steppe and Volga-Ural region, they encountered the cultural-literary tradition and political ideology that had taken shape in the wake of the Mongol conquests. Starting in the thirteenth century, writers across the Mongol commonwealth wove existing cosmological and political motifs from the steppe, royal genealogies, and the history of the conquests into new narratives legitimating the rule of Chinggis Khan and his descendants over their vast Eurasian empire. This narrative was constructed in and disseminated through extensive histories such as Rashīd al-Dīn's *Compendium of Chronicles* (*Jāmi' al-Tawārīkh*) and Juvaynī's *History of the World Conqueror* (*Tarīkh-i Jahān-gushā*), as well as through texts focused on the lineage and biography of Chinggis Khan and his descendants, such as *The Secret History of the Mongols* and various oral epics and genealogies. As later generations of Chinggisid elites converted to Islam (in the Golden Horde, the Il-Khanate, and the Chagataid Ulus) and Buddhism (in China and Mongolia), regional histories

---

nineteenth and early twentieth centuries, see Äkhmätjanov, "'Kaharman katil' dastanı," 12.

[23] For a full analysis of these elements, see Hanaway, "Persian Popular Romances."
[24] On the *'ayyārun* in medieval Islamic history, see Mottahedeh, *Loyalty and Leadership* and Goshgarian, "Beyond the Social and the Spiritual." On the role and depiction of the *'ayyārun* in medieval Persian romances, see Hanaway, "Persian Popular Romances," 129–177.

The Many Faces of Qahramān

such the *Daftar-e Chinggis-nāma* and *The Jewel Translucent Sūtra*, reconciled Chinggisid narratives of dynastic legitimacy with the morals and cosmologies of these religions.[25]

The *Qahramān* story was especially well-suited to the new Chinggisid-Muslim cultural milieu of the Golden Horde. Its overarching narrative of world conquest echoed the story of the Mongols' own rise to power and the Chinggisids' political ideology that all peoples were destined to be brought together under their rule.[26] Additionally, the overlay of Islam onto the pre-Islamic story of Hūshang Shāh's conquests offered a narrative that brought together the Juchid Mongols' history as conquerors and their conversion to Islam as mutually reinforcing. Most importantly for the present study, *Qahramān* offered a model of warrior-aristocratic masculinity that benefited both conquered local elites and their Chinggisid conquerors and that could serve as a blueprint for a functional relationship between the rulers and their subjects.

STRONGER TOGETHER: BUILDING THE COOPERATIVE CHINGGISID MAN

According to the *Secret History of the Mongols*, Alan Gua, a female ancestor of the future Chinggis Khan, gathers her five sons together and shows them a group of arrows. First, she breaks one arrow between her hands. Then, she gathers a bundle of arrows and tries to break them. This time, the arrows, supported by one another, do not snap. She uses this demonstration to teach her children that they must always act together, for individually they will easily be defeated by their adversaries.[27] The message communicated in this parable – solidarity and mutual aid in the face of adversity – was a pillar of Turco-Mongol political ideology.[28] Temujin and Jamuqa rise to prominence as warriors through their cooperation in raids.[29] On many occasions Temujin succeeds thanks to the assistance of others: Sorkhan Shira, who hides him during his escape from captivity among the Tayichigud; Bogorchu, who helps him recapture his family's stolen horses; and Dei-Sechen, who honours the marriage agreement brokered with Temujin's late father and becomes a constant ally.[30] The moral of these stories is clear: those who act together and support one another are capable of much more than they could accomplish

---

[25] *Däftäre Chınggız-namä*; Elverskog, *The Jewel Translucent Sūtra*; Atwood, "Titles, Appanages, Marriage and Officials," 2:611, 624–625.
[26] de Rachewiltz, "Some Remarks," 165–173.
[27] Kahn, *The Secret History of the Mongols*, 5.
[28] Welsford, *Four Types of Loyalty in Early Modern Central Asia*, 115.
[29] Kahn, *The Secret History of the Mongols*, 36–48; Rogers, *The Golden Summary of Činggis Qayan*, 69–70.
[30] Kahn, *The Secret History of the Mongols*, 24–25, 28–29, 30–31.

alone. Indeed, in the harsh environment of the steppe, a man cannot survive alone, regardless of his strength, intelligence, or martial skill. It is repeated, if more briefly, in the Volga-Ural region's *Daftar-i Chinggis-nāma*, in which Alan Gua, while discussing the family's wealth, exhorts her sons not to work against one another.[31]

Qahramān-i Qātil offers this same lesson through two of its male characters: Qahramān and Bahrām Jebelī. Each of these characters is introduced as a formidable warrior. Their respective character arcs are not built around their improvement as fighters, but, rather, their transformation from proud loners into productive members of Hūshang Shāh's army.

Qahramān is by far the most formidable warrior in *Qahramān-i Qātil*. As a small child, he is kidnapped and raised by demons. Initially, these demons train him and equip him for war, but they become so terrified by his brute strength and his penchant for violence that they ultimately decide to send him back to his own people (18, 24–26). On his way to find his birth family, Qahramān encounters an army. Uncertain of who they are or how he should interact with them, Qahramān mounts his *karkadann*[32] and rides into their midst. The warriors ask what he is doing and warn him that he should fear their king, Hūshang Shāh. In response, Qahramān promises them that he will show them and their king exactly who he is; he then starts bludgeoning them with his giant mace (29). Hūshang Shāh's prime minister, Bahrām Jebelī, again asks who Qahramān is and why he is behaving in such a villainous manner. As Qahramān begins to explain himself, Bahrām realizes that Qahramān had made an error out of ignorance. However, when he recommends that Qahramān apologize for his bad behaviour, Qahramān becomes enraged. He calls Bahrām a fool and demands that Hūshang Shāh apologize to him (30). He continues his attack. Qahtarān, Hūshang Shāh's champion, asks Qahramān why he insists on being so prideful, but this appeal also has no effect on Qahramān (32). He defeats all Hūshang Shāh's best fighters and then rides off into the mountains (35).

At this point in the story, Qahramān has two defining characteristics: he is a skilled fighter and a proud loner. The second characteristic wholly negates the benefits of the first. Qahramān's pride in his own strength, his sense of superiority, and his refusal to acknowledge when he has made a mistake make him a menace to all humanity. Outside the context of the human relationships

---

[31] *Däftäre Chınggız-namä*, 12–13.

[32] A *karkadann* is a mythical creature found in Persian folklore. It has black, scaly skin, a dewlap under its chin, and yellow hooves. A single horn extending from its nose. *Karkadann*s are noted for their ferocity, although they could be tamed and ridden and could be deferent to virginal women. The *karkadann* is thought to have been inspired by the rhinoceros and to have been one of the sources of inspiration for the unicorn. Suhr, "An Interpretation of the Unicorn," 93, 106 and Lavers, "Origin of Myth," 104–105.

The Many Faces of Qahramān

of friendship, marriage, and vassalage, his skills as a fighter serve no higher purpose. He commits pointless violence and creates disorder.

Before taking up service with Hūshang Shāh, Bahrām Jebelī also spends the first part of his life committing pointless violence. The son of the fairy king Shāhbal and the warrior princess Qamarrukh, Bahrām is born in the dungeon of his father's enemy, the demon king Akhwāl, who had previously captured Qamarrukh. Bahrām is subsequently sent as a foster-son to another demon prince. Bahrām's identity and allegiances become the cause of a brutal and, ultimately, futile war between the fairy and demon kingdoms (49). When neither side prevails, both finally agree to let Bahrām choose which side he will join. Bahrām chooses neither, opting instead to take over his foster-father's island kingdom and to lead the island's demon army in a war of conquest in China (50–51). At first, fending for himself seems to work well enough for Bahrām. He conquers China and marries the daughter of the Chinese emperor (51–52). But his fate takes a turn for the worse. The defeated Chinese emperor appeals to a sorcerer, who sets a hailstorm on the capital city that kills Bahrām's demon soldiers (52–54). Bahrām is taken captive and transformed into a stone statue (56). With no friends or allies to aid him, Bahrām remains trapped in this statue form for twelve years until Hūshang Shāh happens by and frees him (57, 70–71).

Qahramān's pride in his strength and his insistence on independence render him a ruthless killer; the same qualities render Bahrām powerless. At first, fighting only for himself frees him from his obligations to his father and his foster family, but by refusing these obligations he also gives up the mutual protection and support that might have come with them. As a result, his conquest of China proves not only violent, but ephemeral. He captures the empire but loses it again as soon as his enemies mobilize their network of allies and vassals.

Bahrām's conversion from loner to useful ally is accomplished relatively quickly. After Hūshang Shāh and Gerden-Keshān release him from his curse, he willingly becomes Hūshang Shāh's vizir. By contrast, Qahramān's transformation is longer and more nuanced, taking up most of the narrative of *Qahramān*. The first step in this transformation is set in motion by Gerden-Keshān and Qahtarān's hunt for Qahramān through the mountains, a search that ends with Qahtarān revealing Qahramān's parentage and identity and offering him a place in Hūshang Shāh's army (37–39). Through this act, Qahramān is offered both a community and a purpose. He becomes Hūshang Shāh's champion in the war against India. His strength is channeled into fighting and defeating those of his lord's enemies that no one else can.

The progress of Qahramān's conversion from chaotic destroyer to noble champion is marked by his adoption of a new riding animal, a six-legged, fiery-eyed, horned beast that emerges from the Gulf of Oman and begins to wreak havoc among Hūshang Shāh's troops (73). The rest of the army sees the beast as a threat to be neutralized; Qahramān alone sees its potential usefulness (74). He climbs onto it, harnesses it, and trains it (74–75). By the end of the story, the beast is so tame that it can be tied up outside Qahramān's tent and looked after by his wife (76, 179). Qahramān's acquisition of a larger riding animal signifies how his status has increased through his service to Hūshang Shāh. The taming of the sea beast also parallels Qahramān's own taming. Both man and beast are transformed from destructive forces to allies through their submission to a new master.

Qahramān takes another step in his transformation during the quest to save Bahrām's mother, Qamarrūkh. In this specific case, Qahramān possesses unique skills and qualities that make him the only one able to complete the mission. The heroes discover that the secret entrance to the demonic fortress on Muḥīṭ Mountain has been constructed explicitly for Qahramān. According to its architect's prophecy, Qahramān is the only one who can resolve all the challenges to open the series of gates and passages that leads to the throne room of the mountain's demon prince, Shaʿbān (182–183). At the same time, Qahramān is still not able to succeed in the quest alone. He is assisted first by the inscriptions left by the fortress's architect Qārūn, then by his fiancée Sarwi Khoraman, who reveals to him how to keep Shaʿbān from reanimating, and, finally, by the flying demon Suhmān, who carries Qahramān and Sarwi-Khoraman back to their companions (182, 185, 191, 193–195). By the end of the quest on Muḥīṭ Mountain, Qahramān has demonstrated not only that he is able to submit to a king, but also that he can listen to others, accept their advice, and show mercy and restraint.

This final step in the evolution of Qahramān's masculinity is marked by another change of riding animals. In the last stage of the quest to rescue Qamarrūkh, Qahramān must ascend Ballūr Mountain, whose sides are covered with stone as smooth as glass, to reach the fortress of the demon king, Akhwāl. No man or beast can climb Ballūr Mountain and no bird, save the *simurgh*, lord of birds, can fly high enough to reach the top (201–202). Unlike the sea beast, the *simurgh* is an intelligent being and cannot simply be harnessed and tamed. Upon the advice of the reformed demon Suhmān, Qahramān hides inside an elephant carcass and tricks the *simurgh* into carrying him to her nest. While the *simurgh* is away hunting, a dragon comes to eat her young. Qahramān slays the dragon and saves the baby *simurgh*s (203–204). The *simurgh* is so grateful that she is willing to fulfill Qahramān's request to fly to the top of Ballūr Mountain, so long as Qahramān provides her with food along the way (204–208).

Through his interactions with the *simurgh*, Qahramān shows that he has finally learned how to use his brute strength appropriately. He kills not out of anger or for his own glory or even for the glory of his king, but in defence of his allies. Qahramān's deeds solidify the bonds of friendship among the members of Hūshang Shāh's retinue. They also bring together the forces of good/order (the Muslim kingdom of Hūshang Shāh, the fairy kingdom, and the *simurgh*) against the forces of evil/chaos (the demon kingdoms, the

The Many Faces of Qahramān

non-Muslim king of India, and the sorcerer Dizid Afsar). By the end of the tale, Qahramān has demonstrated Hirasıp's Persianate lesson to Qahtarān: a champion becomes the best version of himself through selfless service to his lord. Simultaneously, Qahramān's actions demonstrate Alan Gua's lesson to her sons that men are strongest when they band together.

REHABILITATING THE DEFEATED: SUBMISSION WITHOUT THE LOSS OF MASCULINE HONOUR

Another facet of the warrior-aristocratic masculinity on display in *Qahramān* that fits well with Mongol political culture can be seen in the tale's depiction of defeated men. A distinguishing feature of the Mongol commonwealth was the integration of diverse outsiders into the army, government, and economy. As the Mongols carried out their conquests, they built upon pre-existing steppe cultural concepts of blood brotherhood and fictive kinship as tools for integrating outsiders into their social world and expressing relationships among political leaders.[33] In Mongol army camps, cities, and administrative institutions, Chinese, Persians, Mongols, Turks, Arabs, Franks, Slavs, and numerous others met, mingled, and, in some cases, established multi-generational familial dynasties in the service of their Chinggisid lords.[34]

The diversity of the Mongol commonwealth and its successor states in the steppe is echoed in *Qahramān*. Hūshang Shāh's closest retainers include a diverse group of men: Qahramān the demon-raised warrior, Qahtarān, the son of the Iranian ruler who preceded Hūshang, Bahrām the half-fairy prince, and Gerden-Keshān, a mischievous sorcerer of uncertain origins. In addition, *Qahramān* has numerous instances of former enemies coming over to Hūshang Shāh's side and becoming important members of his army. Among these enemies-turned-loyal subjects are Kiwān the king of Balkh, the warrior Sahrap, and the demon Suhmān.

The case of Kiwān illustrates a path by which aristocratic men might be reintegrated as the political fortunes of their lords changed. Kiwān, although an in-law to Hūshang Shāh, lives as an exile in Rā-i Hind's court (92). As the war between Iran and India progresses, Gerden-Keshān sneaks into the Indian camp and approaches Kiwān. The sorcerer scolds Kiwān for siding against his kin and convinces him to appeal to Hūshang Shāh for forgiveness (112–113). Hūshang Shāh chides Kiwān for his lapse in loyalty, but, after Kiwān apologizes for his actions, Hūshang Shāh welcomes him back into his court (122).

---

[33] Kennedy, "The Juchids of Muscovy," 194–223; Atwood, "Titles, Appanages, Marriage and Officials," 2:620–621.

[34] To gain a sense of the diversity among the Mongols servitors, courtiers, and military officers, see *Along the Silk Roads*.

Kiwān's story does not stray far from the biographies of some Mongol military officers and administrators who, driven by ties of kinship and ethnic-cultural affinity, changed sides, sometimes many times, during the Mongol conquests and their aftermath.[35] What is important to note is that neither Kiwān's social status nor his masculinity are diminished by his defection or by his apology. In fact, his admission before his lord of his own wrongdoing is a necessary step in his reintegration into Hūshang Shāh's army and his restoration from exile to nobleman. In this aspect, Kiwān stands as a foil to Qahramān, who initially refuses to apologize for his unprovoked attack on Hūshang Shāh's army. In this instance, Kiwān proves himself a better man than Qahramān because he is able to admit his faults.

Sahrap the warrior presents a second model of masculine transformation from enemy to ally. When Sahrap first appears in the story, he is the champion of Rā-i Hind (110–114). The greatest among Rā-i Hind's warriors, he is undefeated until Bahrām takes to the battlefield (119). Sahrap and Bahrām fight a long, brutal bout of single combat while the Muslim and Indian armies watch (119–121). In the end, Bahrām seizes hold of Sahrap, raises him over his head and prepares to dash him against the ground. At the last second, Sahrap surrenders and begs Bahrām to "have mercy and lower him slowly" (121). When Sahrap is brought before Hūshang Shāh, he requests to be allowed to convert to Islam and join Hūshang Shāh's army (121). Hūshang Shāh grants this request and a banquet is held in honour of Sahrap's conversion (121–122). The next day, he fights on the battlefield as one of Hūshang Shāh's champions (122–123).

As with Kiwān's apology, Sahrap's defeat at the hands of Bahrām did not diminish his reputation as a man or a warrior. Rather, his admission that he was outmatched and his request for mercy begin the process by which he can continue to serve with honour in a new army under a new lord. His embrace of Islam also signals his worth as a man by showing that he is perceptive and honourable enough to recognize which side holds the moral high ground. In the case of Sahrap, it is possible to see how Mongol and Muslim practices of inclusivity interacted with one another. Both service to the conquering ruler and conversion to the ruler's faith provided paths for warrior-aristocratic men to change their political allegiances without sacrificing their status or their lives. Finally, when Sahrap's fate is placed in contrast with that of Rā-i Hind's other champion, Kahal, who was chopped in half by Qahramān (101), *Qahramān*'s views on masculinity become even clearer: being strong or good with a sword is not enough to make a man. A true man possesses a strong moral compass and the grace to acknowledge when he has been bested.

Suhmān's case represents a third path by which a man might change allegiances while preserving or, indeed, enhancing his masculinity. Suhmān

---

[35] For an excellent example of such changing allegiances, see Amir Mazor, "Sayf al-Dīn Qipchaq al-Manṣūrī: Defection and Ethnicity between Mongols and Mamluks," *Along the Silk Roads*, 102–119.

starts his process of transformation at a greater disadvantage than either Kiwān or Sahrap. As a demon, he is inherently an enemy of God-fearing human beings and, indeed, of God himself. Initially, Qahramān trusts Suhmān only because an inscription left behind by the architect Qarun instructs him to do so (192–193). Suhmān repeatedly proves his usefulness and loyalty, first by bearing Qahramān and his allies to Gulistān-Irām to aid the besieged fairy kingdom against the demon armies, then by instructing Qahramān on how to reach the fortress atop Ballūr Mountain where Qamarrūkh is held prisoner, and, finally, by accompanying Qahramān there to slay the demon king Akhwāl (193–195, 197–199, 202–203, 207). In return, Suhmān is rewarded with gold and fine clothes by King Shāhbal and, more importantly, he is accepted by Qahramān and his companions as one of their own; he returns with them to Shāhbal's court (212–213).

Suhmān's transformation is more than a lateral shift from one court to another. As he transfers his allegiance from the demons to the Muslim ruler Hūshang Shāh, he is elevated from a "monstrous" demon to a human being. This transformation is marked by Suhmān being awarded clothes, but also by the amputation of his tail at the end of the story. As the sorcerer tells him, "Hey, Beast, you want to go among humans, you want to be a human. And once you are a human, what do you need the tail for?" (213). This changing of outer trappings mirrors the process by which non-Mongols who demonstrated loyalty and useful skills entered Mongol administrative and military service and, in the process, shed their pre-conquest identities and loyalties to become part of the Mongol body politic.[36]

The understanding of the relationship among honour, loyal service, and submission communicated in *Qahramān*, if only by coincidence, reinforced the narrative of empire that Chinggisid elites expressed through their political ideology, dynastic literature, and actions. Defeat by the Mongols did not have to spell either the end of a man's career or honour. Conquered elites (and non-elites) could regain and even increase their masculine honour through submission to their Chinggisid conquerors and service on their behalf. *Qahramān* offers an example of how pre-Mongol notions of warrior-aristocratic masculinity could (and did) retain their relevance in the new Chinggisid order.

PIOUS MASCULINITY IN A POST-CHINGGISID WORLD

In the fifteenth century, the Golden Horde declined in power and fragmented. By the early sixteenth century, a constellation of new, smaller states had emerged in its place: the khanates of Astrakhan, Crimea, Kazan, and Siberia, the Noghay Horde, and Principality of Muscovy. Through the fifteenth and early sixteenth

---

[36] Morgan, *The Mongols*, 91–96, 108–111.

century, these states vied with one another. By the end of the sixteenth century, Muscovy emerged victorious, conquering Kazan in 1552, Astrakhan in 1556, and Siberia by 1598. These conquests did not bring about the immediate demise of Chinggisid literary and political culture in the conquered khanates. The *Compendium of Qādr-ʿAlī Bek*, composed in 1602 at the court of the Qāsim khanate, a Muslim buffer state of Muscovy, included summations of parts of *Compendium of Chronicles* and epic poems describing the lives and deeds of regional Chinggisid leaders.[37] The *Daftar-i Chinggis-nāma*, a local history in circulation in the Volga-Ural region in the seventeenth and early eighteenth century, still included a section on the lineage and life of Chinggis Khan.[38] From 1552 to the 1670s, the warrior-aristocratic families of the Golden Horde's successor states were still employed as military servitors under their new Russian Christian rulers.[39] However, by the 1680s, Moscow relied less on its Turkic-Muslim servitors to guard its frontiers and placed increasing pressure on these servitors to convert to Christianity or risk losing their lands and status.[40] This policy eventually led to the decline of the Golden Horde-era Muslim aristocracy as the shapers of the culture and politics in the Volga-Ural region; local Chinggisid political ideology declined with them.[41] At the same time, the new wave of calls for Muslims to convert to Christianity led Volga-Ural Islamic jurists to question whether the Russian conquest had removed their region from the House of Islam and placed it in the House of War.[42]

As Chinggisid political culture receded from the Volga-Ural region, *Qahramān* migrated from now-liquidated Chinggisid courtly society to the Muslim villages and frontier settlements that gradually became the new centres of Muslim culture under Russian rule. The preservation, transmission, and production of historical, literary, and religious texts was assumed by teachers, Islamic jurists, Sufi *shaykh*s, and their students in their rural *madrasa*s and *khanaqah*s. In this new context, *Qahramān* was read alongside works such as the *Baṭṭalnāma / Seyyid Baṭṭal Ghazī*, *The Song of Sayf al-Mulūk* (*Qiṣṣa-i Sayf al-Mulūk*), and

---

[37] Usmanov, *Tatarskie istoricheskie istochniki*, 38–39; Frank, *Islamic Historiography*, 13.
[38] *Däftäre Chınggız-namä*, 5–22; Frank, *Islamic Historiography*, 15–17; Usmanov, *Tatarskie istoricheskie istochniki*, 97–133.
[39] Romaneillo, *The Elusive Empire*, 117–128. Gabdullin, *Ot sluzhilykh Tatar k tatarskomu dvorianstvu*, 17–31.
[40] Romaneillo, *The Elusive Empire*, 177–205.
[41] Frank, *Islamic Historiography*, 17.
[42] This question is the subject of a written exchange in the late seventeenth century between two Islamic scholars of Kazan district, a copy of which has been preserved in the Kazan University Library's manuscript and rare book collection; see KFU–ORRK, 399T, "Yūnus al-Qazānīdan ʿAbd al-Karīm al-Shirdānīga tarjīḥ." On the debate over whether Volga-Ural Muslims cold still consider their land part of the House of Islam, see Bustanov, "The Bulghar Region," 183–204.

The Many Faces of Qahramān

The Book of Joseph (*Yūsuf kitābı* / *Qiṣṣa-i Yūsuf*). Many of these works were not of local origin, but they shared key characteristics. All were composed in some form of Turkic, making them accessible to readers not trained in Persian or Arabic. All were narrative sources, describing the deeds of one or a small number of characters and most included some elements of adventure or wonder tales. Finally, all placed their Muslim heroes in direct confrontation with non-believers, either through their participation in a jihad (*Qahramān-i Qātil, Baṭṭalnāma*) or by their involuntary entry into a non-Muslim society (*The Book of Joseph, The Song of Sayf al-Mulūk*). During these confrontations, the stories' heroes resisted temptations to abandon Islam. They also took on the role of bringing non-believers into the faith. Their triumph was defined not only (or at all, in some cases) by their feats of arms, but by their steadfastness in their faith and/or in their expanding the boundaries of the Islamic world (*Dar al-Islam*).[43]

This new social-intellectual context led to a reshuffling of the masculine virtues of the *Qahramān* heroes. For Rammāl Khwaja, writing in the sixteenth century, Qahramān was synonymous with daring shows of courage, strength, and skill on the battlefield. By contrast, a version of *Qahramān kitābı* copied in Kazan in the eighteenth century starts out by emphasizing Qahramān's inner personal qualities such as being just and devoted to his king.[44] This same emphasis is evident in descriptions of actual Turkic-Muslim military men in Russian service in the eighteenth century. Raḥīmqūl Abubakr-uh's untitled praise poem (Arabic: *maddaḥ*) to ʿAbd al-Mannān bin Muslīm, a military servitor on the South Urals frontier, opens with the following description of its subject:

> His name was ʿAbd al-Mannān, son of Muslīm, and he was a heroic man,
> He came from a line of distinguished people and he himself was a champion.
> And he was of generous people and clever and well-spoken,
> He was mercy and perfection and justice of this epoch.[45]

Raḥīmqūl goes on to compare ʿAbd al-Mannān's feats in battle to those of Rustam, the hero of the *Shahnāma*, who shares many characteristics with Qahramān.[46] However, this description of ʿAbd al-Mannān's military accomplishments appears only later in the poem. First and foremost, the reader/listener's attention is called to ʿAbd al-Mannān's virtuous moral character.

---

[43] For an example of such readings of some of these texts in the Volga-Ural region in a slightly later period, see Kefeli, "The Tale of Joseph and Zulaykha," 373–398.
[44] "Kaharman kitabı" IIaLI Fond 39, Opis 1, Delo 3497, List 1.
[45] Räkhimkol Äbübäker-ugh, "Dıngagız, i ähle mäjläs," 1:216.
[46] Räkhimkol Äbübäker-ugh, "Dıngagız, i ähle mäjläs," 1:217; On the relationship between Rustam and Qahramān, see de Bruijn, "Ḳahramān-nāma," 4:445.

Danielle Ross

This emphasis on Qahramān as a model for inner virtue and self-discipline was reinforced by the reading/reciting of other didactic moral texts alongside the *Qahramān* tales. In his account of his education at Rasūliyya Madrasa in the 1890s, author ʿAbd al-Majīd al-Gafūrī recalls reading *Qahramān kitābı* together with the *Baṭṭalnāma* and *The Book of the Severed Head (Kisekbash kitābı)*.[47] He may well have read them from locally produced copies of all these works that survive from the seventeenth and eighteenth centuries. The *Baṭṭalnāma and The Book of the Severed Head* are among those known to have been used in the 1700s–1800s as didactic stories for educating Volga-Ural Muslims about Islamic morality, so it is almost certain that Gafūrī's encounter with *Qahramān* reflected educational practices that had been in place for at least two centuries by the time he described it.[48] The placement of *Qahramān* beside other wonder tales used to teach students and non-*madrasa*-educated Muslims about Islam suggests the rise of a metaphorical understanding of *Qahramān* in the Volga-Ural region. As *Qahramān*'s heroes fought to subdue actual demons and infidels to make the world a safer place for Islam, so too did Volga-Ural Muslims fight daily internal battles of resistance against the corrupting influences of the Christian society that surrounded them, rejecting forbidden food and drink, sexual immorality, and excessive or inappropriate contacts with non-Muslims. Unlike the warrior-aristocratic masculinity of the Chinggisid era, this new masculinity based on inner virtue and self-discipline was open to men of all classes who wished to master their desires, reject temptation, and devote themselves to keeping the laws of Islam.

CONCLUSION

The plot, characters, and motifs of the *Qahramān* romance did not originate in the Volga-Ural region. However, in its Turkic-language translations, the *Qahramān* stories found a stable audience in the Volga-Ural region and, more broadly, on the territory of the Golden Horde, from the fourteenth century to the modern era. Integral to *Qahramān*'s continued popularity was its flexibility. As the political culture of the Volga-Ural region shifted, readers were able to emphasize different aspects of the story and its characters. This flexibility can be seen in the various models of masculinity that were reflected in and extrapolated from the romance's male characters and, especially, from its titular hero, Qahramān, whose personal development and struggles were used to represent both masculine conduct on a literal battlefield and men's internal striving to become better Muslims.

Utah State University

---

[47] Gafuri, "Tärjemäi khälem," 4:455.
[48] Kefeli, *Becoming Muslim in Imperial Russia*, 60–116, especially 75–76.

The Many Faces of Qahramān

ABBREVIATIONS

IIaLI Institut Iazyka, Literatura i Iskusstva imeni G. Ibragimova, Tatarstan, Russian Federation.

KFU-ORRK Kazanskii Federal'nyi Universitet-Otdel' Rukopise i Redkikh Knig, Tatarstan, Russian Federation.

CITED WORKS

Manuscript Sources

Institut Iazyka, Literatura i Iskusstva imeni G. Ibragimova (IIaLI)
 Fond 39. Opis 1. Delo 3497, "Kaharman kitabı."
Kazanskii Federal'nyi Universitet – Otdel' Rukopise i Redkikh Knig (KFU-ORRK)
 No. 399T. List 168ob –175, "Yūnus al-Qazānīdan ʿAbd al-Karīm al-Shirdānīga tarjīḥ."

Printed Sources

Abduzhemilev, Refat. "Remmal Khodja. Khronika "Tarikh-i Sakhib Gerai khan" ("Istoriia o khane Sakhib Gerae"). Chast 3." *Krimskoe istoricheskoe obozrenie* 1 (2019): 147–174.

Äkhmätjanov, M. I. "Tatar ädäbiyatı tarikhın öyränüdä chıganak bularak kul'yazma kitap." In R. G. Izmailova, ed., *Kitapka khitab / Slovo o knige*. Kazan: Tatarstan kitap näshriyatı, 1994, 46–60.

Akhmetzianov, M. I. "Kakharman kitaby." In M. Kh. Khasanov, ed., *Tatarskaia entsiklopediia*. 7 vols. Kazan: Institut Tatarskoi entsiklopedii, 2006, 3:268.

Amanat, Abbas. "Remembering the Persianate." In Abbas Amanat and Assef Ashraf, ed., *The Persianate World: Rethinking a Shared Space*. Leiden: Brill, 2019, 15–62.

Atwood, Christopher. "Titles, Appanages, Marriage and Officials: A Comparison of Political Forms in the Züngar and Thirteenth-Century Mongol Empires." In David Sneath and Christopher Kaplonski, eds, *History of Mongolia*. 3 vols. Leiden: Brill, 2010, 2:610–634.

Biran, Michal, Jonathan Brack and Francesca Fiachetti, ed. *Along the Silk Roads in Mongol Eurasia: Generals, Merchants, and Intellectuals*. Oakland, CA: University of California Press, 2020.

de Bruijn, J. T. P. "Ḳahramān-nāma." In H. A. R. Gibb et al., eds, *Encyclopaedia of Islam*, 2nd edn, 12 vols. Leiden: Brill, 1960, 4:444–445.

Bustanov, Alfrid. "The Bulghar Region as a 'Land of Ignorance': Anti-Colonial Discourse in Khvārazmian Connectivity." *Journal of Persianate Studies* 9.2 (2016): 183–204.

Däftäre Chınggız-namä. Kazan: Iman, 2000.

Connell, R. W. and James W. Messerschmidt. "Hegemonic Masculinity: Rethinking the Concept." *Gender and Society* 19.6 (2005): 829–859.

DeWeese, Devin. *Islamization and Native Religion in the Golden Horde: Baba Tükles and Conversion to Islam in Historical and Epic Tradition*. University Park, PA: The Pennsylvania University Press, 1994.

Eaton, Richard M. *India in the Persianate Age, 1000–1765*. London: Penguin, 2019.

Elverskog, Johan. *The Jewel Translucent Sūtra: Altan Khan and the Mongols in the Sixteenth Century*. Leiden: Brill, 2003.

Frank, Allen J. *Islamic Historiography and 'Bulghar' Identity Among the Tatars and Bashkirs of Russia*. Leiden: Brill, 1998.

Gabdullin, I. R. *Ot sluzhilykh Tatar k tatarskomu dvorianstvu*. Moscow: [no publisher], 2006.

Gafuri, Mäjit. "Tärjemäi khälem." In *Mäjit Gafuri: Äsärlär*. 4 vols. Kazan: Tatarstan kitap näshriyatı, 1981, 4:352–456.

Gilmore, Davd D. *Manhood in the Making: Cultural Concepts of Masculinity*. New Haven, CT: Yale University Press, 1981.

Goshgarian, Rachel. "Beyond the Social and the Spiritual: Redefining the Urban Confraternities of Late Medieval Anatolia," PhD thesis, Harvard University, 2007.

Green, Nile. "Introduction: The Frontiers of the Persianate World, (ca. 800–1900)." In Nile Green, ed., *The Persianate World: The Frontiers of a Eurasian Lingua Franca*. Oakland, CA: University of California Press, 2019, 1–71.

Halperin, Charles. "The Missing Golden Horde Chronicles and Historiography in the Mongol Empire." *Mongolian Studies* 23 (2000): 1–15.

Hanaway, William L. "Persian Popular Romances before the Safavid Period," PhD diss. Columbia University, 1970.

Kaharman katil. Dastan. ed. Marsel' Äkhmätjanov. Kazan: Tatarstan kitap näshriyatı, 1998.

Kahn, Paul. *The Secret History of the Mongols: The Origin of Chingis Khan*. San Francisco, CA: North Point Press, 1984.

Keenan, Edward Louis. "Muscovy and Kazan', 1445–1552: A Study in Steppe Politics," PhD diss. Harvard University, 1965.

Kefeli, Agnés Nilüfer. *Becoming Muslim in Imperial Russia: Conversion, Apostasy and Literacy*. Ithaca, NY: Cornell University Press, 2014.

——. "The Tale of Joseph and Zulaykha on the Volga Frontier: The Struggle for Gender, Religious and National Identity in Imperial and Post-Revolutionary Russia." *Slavic Review* 70.2 (2011): 373–398.

Kennedy, Craig Gayen. "The Juchids of Muscovy: A Study of Personal Ties between Émigré Tatar Dynasts and the Muscovite Grand Princes in the Fifteenth and Sixteen Centuries." PhD thesis, Harvard University, 1994.

Lavers, Chris. "Origin of Myth Related to Curative, Antidotal and Other Medicinal Properties of Animal 'Horns' in the Middle Ages." In Philip Wexler, ed., *Toxicology in the Middle Ages and Renaissance*. London: Academic Press, 2017, 101–114.

Massé, H. "Abū Ṭāhir al-Ṭārsūsī." In H. A. R. Gibb et al., eds, *Encyclopaedia of Islam*, 2nd edn, 12 vols. Leiden: Brill, 1960, 1:152.

Morgan, David. *The Mongols*. Cambridge, MA: Blackwell, 1990.

Mottahedeh, Roy P. *Loyalty and Leadership in an Early Islamic Society*. Princeton, NJ: Princeton University Press, 1980.
Paul, Jürgen. "Archival Practices in the Muslim World prior to 1500." In Alessandro Bausi et al., eds, *Manuscripts and Archives: Comparative Views on Record-Keeping*. Berlin: De Gruyter, 2018, 339–360.
de Rachewiltz, Igor. "Some Remarks on the Ideological Foundations of Chingis Khan's Empire." In David Sneath and Christopher Kaplonski, eds, *The History of Mongolia*. 3 vols. Leiden: Brill, 2010, 1:165–173.
Räkhimkol Äbübäker-ughı, "Dıngagız, i ähle mäjläs …" In Gäräy Räkhim, ed., *Tatar poeziiase antologiiase*. 2 vols. Kazan: Tatarstan kitap näshriyatı, 1992, 1:215–217.
Rogers, Leland Liu. *The Golden Summary of Činggis Qayan*. Wiesbaden: Harrassowitz Verlag, 2009.
Romaneillo, Matthew. *The Elusive Empire: Kazan and the Creation of Russia, 1552–1671*. Madison, WI: University of Wisconsin Press, 2012.
Spooner, Brian and William L. Hanaway. "Introduction: Persian as Koine: Written Persian in a World Historical Perspective." In Brian Spooner and William L. Hanaway, eds, *Literacy in the Persianate World: Writing and the Social Order*. Philadelphia, PA: University of Pennsylvania Museum of Archaeology and Anthropology, 2012, 1–69.
Suhr, Elmer G. "An Interpretation of the Unicorn." *Folklore* 75.2 (1975): 91–109.
Usmanov, M. A. *Tatarskie istoricheskie istochniki XVII–XVIII vv*. Kazan: Izdatel'stvo Kazanskogo universiteta, 1972.
Welsford, Thomas. *Four Types of Loyalty in Early Modern Central Asia: The Tūqāy-Tīmūrid Takeover of Greater Mā Warā al-Nahr, 1598–1605*. Leiden: Brill, 2013.

Electronic Sources

Gaillard, Mariana. "Abū Ṭāhir al-Ṭārsūsī." In *Encyclopedia of Islam*, 3rd edn. https://referenceworks.brillonline.com/entries/encyclopaedia-of-islam-3/abu-tahir-tarsusi-SIM_0034?s.num=365&s.start=360.
Hanaway, William L. "Darab-name." In *Encyclopaedia Iranica*, www.iranicaonline.org/articles/darab-nama.
Menzel, Th. "Ḳahramān-nāma." In *Encyclopaedia of Islam*, 1st edn, https://referenceworks.brillonline.com/entries/encyclopaedia-of-islam-1/kahraman-nama-SIM_3804.
Parsatalab, ʿAbbās, ʿAlī Mohammad Moazzeni and Ruhollah Hadi. "Muʿarrafī nasḥ nawyafat-e *Qahramānnāma* (*Dāstān-e Qahramān-e Qātil*) wa muʿarrafī shaṣiyat-e Qahramān." *CFL* 8.32 (2020): 201–226. https://cfl.modares.ac.ir/browse.php?a_id=39323&sid=11&slc_lang=en.

FLUID MASCULINITIES

4

MARKED DIFFERENCES: BEARDS IN RENAISSANCE EUROPE

Patricia Simons

Seemingly incidental, men's facial hair signaled a variety of significant differences and masculinities during the Renaissance. In medical, legal, and social terms, the ability to grow a beard was considered a distinctive, exclusive marker of the adult male reproductive body. But that normative structure did not always mean that men did not shave. There were shifts in the practice over time: on the whole, men shaved in the fifteenth century but began to grow beards by the second decade of the sixteenth century, and that habit was maintained until facial hair was replaced by false, sometimes ludicrously abundant, wigs in the late seventeenth century. In some examples of fifteenth-century portraits, stubble or morning shadow was subtly represented in portraits in order to assert the sitter's full masculine virility and identity. By the sixteenth century, for a variety of reasons, groomed beards became fashionable and remained so for some time thereafter. This chapter offers an overview of the meaning of certain differences between facial hair and examines reasons for the adoption of beards, thereby bringing to the fore a consideration of how such personal yet socially recognizable habits resonated with power differences between men.

The visual shift in self-presentation from shaved to fully bearded faces was partly due to the mere vagaries of fashion, which usually cycle back and forth. However, a fashionable trend is more about popularity than change; that is, description of a vogue is not the same as an analytical explanation of its initial cause and subsequent acceptance. Studies that focus on the different styles of beards – as is also done with contemporary beards today – similarly reduce the mode to no more than personal taste and neglect social meanings. I argue, instead, that differences in facial hair were not about styles for their own sake and did not merely indicate the wearer's choice or character, which are modern, superficial criteria about fashion. Today and in yesteryears, facial hair and its meaning depend on such factors as genetics and physiology, health, age, wealth, origin, the pressure of ethnic and national norms, religion, and, at times, occupation, status, or desirability and sexuality.

Patricia Simons

The perception and categorization of race and ethnicity were of growing interest over the course of the Renaissance. In an etching of the head of an Ottoman, his geographical origin, ethnic and religious difference, and visual interest are immediately apparent by means of his turban, and his moustache (Fig. 4.1). According to inscriptions, the artist Wenceslaus Hollar observed the Turkish man first-hand in London in 1637 and that memory resulted in the print produced eight years later. It was not a portrait of the anonymous man, however, but part of a series of heads and ethnic types, including the presentation of a twenty-three-year-old Native American that was also based on the artist's eye-witness experience of a captive put on display in Amsterdam and Antwerp.[1] In the latter case, alongside the ornamentation of necklace, earrings, headband, and facial markings, shaving is a key feature. Whether or not the young man needed to shave his face, a sharp implement had been used to shave much of his head, producing a memorable image that Hollar recorded for a broad print-buying clientele.

The point to be drawn from this is that in these and all other portraits of the fifteenth and sixteenth centuries, what is being analyzed is appearance rather than actuality. What personal particulars the artist really saw cannot be absolutely known for sure. For example, how utterly shaved was the Native American's head after he had spent at least several weeks away from his homeland and its tools? And the Ottoman gentleman may have had more of a beard but Hollar reduced the facial hair to the typical moustache because he was meeting viewer's expectations and following convention. This chapter will thus discuss visual choices made for public, and often widely disseminated, images that appeared plausible and thus in accord with overall social patterns or that betray departures from convention. Art historians look for cultural patterns and visual exceptions rather than claiming that the art is no more than a straightforward reflection of actual appearances.

Distinctly Turkish features were already well-known to Europeans because what we now call a handlebar moustache had come to be a stereotypical marker of Ottomans. In particular, a certain representation of the Ottoman Sultan Suleiman the Magnificent spread via prints, first issued in 1526, and European paintings produced thereafter on the basis of those prints.[2] He is sometimes shown with a beard too, but the striking moustache was the stock attribute of a Turk, readily

---

[1] London, British Museum (hereafter, BM) 1852,0612.165 (first state), 1875,0710.742 (second state). In the interest of brevity, notes are kept to a minimum. Using the accession number of objects, readers can find basic bibliography and information on the webpage of the museum or repository.

[2] The woodcut by Jan Swart depicting Suleiman on horseback includes the date of 1526 (BM 1904,0519.13) but is probably later than the engraving of his head in profile by the Italian monogrammist A.A., also dated 1526 (Vienna, Albertina DG1962 / 1175).

Figure 4.1. Wenceslaus Hollar, *Head and Shoulders of a Turk, with a Moustache and a Large Turban*, 1645, etching (third state of three), 3 3/16 × 2 7/16 in. (8.1 × 6.2 cm). Metropolitan Museum of Art, New York (17.3.3117).

Figure 4.2. Albrecht Dürer (after Gentile Bellini), *Three Turks*, 1496–97, pen and black and brown ink with watercolour, 30.6 x 19.7 cm. British Museum, London (1895,0915.974).

recognizable as though the turban and the moustache sufficiently indicated any Ottoman for European viewers. In fact, the distinctive fashioning had already been observed in the later fifteenth century, possibly in lost drawings made by the Venetian painter Gentile Bellini during his visit to Istanbul in 1480 and certainly preserved in drawings produced by the German artist Albrecht Dürer when he visited Venice in the mid-1490s (Fig. 4.2).[3]

Over several centuries, then, European artists and their audience thought they knew that turbans, when depicted in conjunction with the extravagant moustache, visually documented an entire empire. Thus, to signify the defeat of the Ottoman army by the European Hapsburg empire at the decisive Battle of Lepanto in October 1571, Titian personified the vanquished enemy in the form of a nearly naked warrior, his clothing stripped from his body, and his turban fallen from his head, yet still he sports the distinct moustache.[4] But this impression of uniform difference between Europeans and Ottomans was wrong. Many Ottomans wore a full beard as well as the wide, thick moustache and some inhabitants of the empire were beardless. As one sees in Dürer's drawing there is a third figure, a black African attendant, either free or, more likely, enslaved, standing at a respectful distance, wearing a turban but simpler, shorter garb and without any facial hair, as though he is not only of lower status but also less of a virile man and, possibly, a eunuch. That absence probably puzzled a later artist, whose woodcut from the drawing turned the figure into a much younger man, of an age before facial hair was expected, though he still registers as dark-skinned.[5] In both drawing and woodcut, the lack of visible facial hair adds to the impression of subservience and marked difference.

Abundant facial hair instead conveyed power and sagacity. Lengthy beards denoted the age, wisdom, seniority, and virility of men of authority, including some military commanders of antiquity or senior gods such as Jupiter and Neptune. In a religious context, long and seemingly ungroomed beards similarly marked venerable men, saints, and martyrs, and other wise men and prophets were also endowed with the long, usually hoary beard connoting august, learned personages of considerable experience. Thus, they are a standard marker of holiness in such images as a miracle-working icon from medieval Russia, a famous image disseminated by variants like one painted in Bulgaria between 1570 and 1650 (Fig. 4.3).[6] The only hairless faces are those of the sole woman, that is, the Virgin Mary, two secular but haloed figures regarded as sanctified patrons, and various angels who, according to theologians, are sexless characters conventionally pictured by artists as androgynous figures approximating beardless adolescent youths.

[3] BM 1895,0915.974.
[4] Madrid, Museo del Prado, P000431.
[5] BM 1895,0122.786.
[6] BM 1895,0915.974.

Inherited from the image of ancient Greek philosophers, the lengthy beard of priests and hallowed figures in the Byzantine and then Greek Orthodox church created a theological, political, gendered, and sexual divide that was too far to cross when attempts were made to join the Latin and Greek Christian churches. The hierarch Symeon, Archbishop of Thessalonica from 1416 until his death in 1429, was dismayed by the deceptive, elaborate attempts at realism in the plays of the Western church, presumably staged by Venetians while they controlled the city for seven years in 1423–1430. Because Latins shaved, for performances they donned fake beards of white hair in order to simulate the appearance of authoritative figures like God the Father. He opined that shaving was effeminizing and "contrary to natural law," whereas his church's habit of growing long hair and beards was "in honor of nature and according to what God intended."[7]

Later in the fifteenth century, when the Greek churchman Bessarion, who had switched allegiances and was made a cardinal in the Latin church at the end of 1439, became a possible candidate for the papacy in 1455, objections included the fact that he had kept his Greek beard, taken as a sign of incomplete conversion. We have a contemporary account of his appearance in Gentile Bellini's painting commissioned around 1472 for the door of the tabernacle housing Bessarion's precious gift to a Venetian confraternity.[8] Unlike the clean-shaven faces and closely cropped heads of two younger, local members of the confraternity, the cardinal sports a grey, wavy, and carefully groomed beard that extends well beyond his chin, covers his upper lip and all of the lower cheeks.

Presenting the confraternity members in full-face but Bessarion in profile signified that he was the donor, painted in the typical side-view of the key devotee who has commissioned a painting. But the profile against a dark background and his somber black clothing may also indicate that the portrait is posthumous, for he died in November 1472. Admired as a scholar, he was one of the few contemporaries honoured by inclusion in the Famous Men cycle of panels painted by Justus van Ghent for Duke Federico da Montefeltro's *studiolo* in Urbino (c. 1476).[9] That depiction in three-quarter view probably derives from Bellini's panel or preparatory drawings for it, and shows a slightly forked, whiter, and less neatly trimmed beard, following more closely the conventional type of long-bearded, revered philosopher. Most of the ancient men in the Urbino cycle, including Moses, Hippocrates, Plato, and Aristotle, are pictured with beards, but Bessarion is the *only* bearded Christian.

In life as in death, Bessarion's iconographic attribute was considered by some to be the essence of the man. According to the eye-witness report of the humanist Aeneas Silvius Piccolomini (later Pope Pius II), Bessarion's chance to be elected to the papacy was derailed by the insidious murmurings of Alain

---

[7] White, "What the Archbishop Saw," 33. White was unable to date the text.
[8] London, National Gallery NG6590.
[9] Paris, Musée du Louvre, MI 646.

Figure 4.3. Bulgarian, *Icon of the Bogolyubovo Virgin*, c. 1570–1650, tempera on wood, 63.2 x 50.5 x 2.2 cm. Royal Ontario Museum, Toronto (978.353.12.A).

de Coëtivy, cardinal of Avignon. The Frenchman went around the room, whispering in one ear, then the next: "So we'll give the Latin Church to a Greek pope, will we? We'll put a neophyte at the head of the book? Bessarion hasn't even shaved his beard, and he's going to be our head? How do we know his conversion is sincere? [...] I, and those who think with me, will never accept a Greek as pope."[10] His rhetorical emphasis on *caput* (head) more than once, in the symbolic sense of head of the church, further drew attention to the literal as well as emblematic otherness of Bessarion's visage.

The story fits the fierce debates of the time regarding ecclesiastical reintegration and Alain's clever ploy relied on long-standing beliefs that beards were outward signs of inner convictions. Far from merely exotic fashion, Greek beards were read as vital political and religious signs. Such experiences and images of foreign beards generated awareness of facial hair as a cultural rather than purely personal phenomenon, signifying allegiance, faith, and wisdom. They also demonstrated that beards could encapsulate virility *and* virtue, an idea that came to fruition during the sixteenth century.

So, diverse religions disagreed about facial hair. For different reasons, adult male Jews, Muslims, and members of the Greek church were all bearded. But considerable historical variation characterized rules regarding the Latin church. In the New Testament, St Paul decried long hair on men as shamefully effeminate, while praising it as a glory on women, acting like a veil, and resorted to "natura" as the reason for this difference (I Cor. 11: 14–15). He did not specifically opine on beards though, unlike some early Church Fathers who argued for the Greek value of manly beards against Roman shaving and depilation practices that were considered effeminate. The beard was the crucial sign of a man. In the last decade of the second century Clement of Alexandria wrote that the beard was "the badge of a man [that] shows him unmistakably to be a man" and "the symbol of manhood."[11] The Latin authority St Augustine opined that, by definition, "a man is bearded (*barbatus homo est*)."[12]

A fifth-century Latin canon credited to a church council at Carthage laid down the simple rule that "clerics neither grow their hair nor shave their beards" but sometime before the ninth century the wording was changed so that short hair was to be accompanied by facial shaving.[13] That disavowal of hirsuteness remained the general rule for centuries, though it was not always followed in practice. Temporary beards were allowed at times of fasting, mourning, or penance, for example, signifying a state of non-worldly preoccupation. Some high officials, including popes, occasionally adopted permanent beards, probably according to secular practice of the time, especially in order to

---

[10] Pius II, *Commentaries*, 1:141 (2.28.5).
[11] Clement of Alexandria, *Christ the Educator*, 214–215.
[12] Augustine, *Enarratio in Psalmos*, 132.7, from Constable, "Introduction," 60.
[13] Constable, "Introduction," 103–107.

appear as august and powerful as kings. Beards were also more permissible in cases of older age and senior rank.

The core purpose of regulating facial hair among the Latin clergy was either to distinguish certain clerical groups, like monks, from the laity or to allow them to be more integrated, which was often the case for priests. When, in the sixteenth century, secular men in western Europe were almost universally bearded, the Catholic church dithered with its precepts. The fifth-century canon against shaving was first printed in 1538, but the crucial word *radat* (shave) was dropped in the volume's second edition of 1551.[14] That mid-century return to disallowing clerical beards when most secular men were growing them nevertheless swam against the tide, for Pope Clement VII had made them optional for all priests in January 1531.[15]

In the meantime, the Protestant Reformation introduced a radically different religious perspective. One of the ways in which leading reformers distinguished themselves from Catholics was to adopt the long beard that signified wise, venerable elders. Numerous propaganda images, both printed and painted, showed them gathered around a table, nearly all of them bearded, but always with the notable exception of their founder, Martin Luther (Fig. 4.4).[16] Why did Luther continue to shave? Only once, due to particular circumstances, was he represented with a beard, and this exception proved the rule, for his disguise as Junker George in 1521 was about deception and hiding.[17] When he came out of seclusion, woodcuts designed by Lucas Cranach of a stylishly whiskered Luther were circulated, dispelling rumors of his death. The imagery aligned his visage, albeit briefly, with other bearded reformers and also with the type of facial hair displayed by his protector Frederick III, Elector of Saxony (who died

---

[14] Crabbe, *Concilia Omnia*, fol. 258ʳ, no. 44: "Clericus nec comam nutria, nec barbam radat"; the second edition of 1551 has "Clericus nec comam nutria, nec barbam," col. 439. See also Constable, "Introduction," 103–104.

[15] Rodocanachi, *La Première Renaissance*, 47, no. 5, published the brief notation from an anonymous French diary in the Vatican Library (Cod. Barb. Lat. 3552, fol. 51v): "En moy de janvier 1531, pape Clèment VII fit une bulle que tous presbiters puissent porter la barbe." I have checked the passage, digitized from a poor microfilm, at https://digi.vatlib.it/view/MSS_Barb.lat.3552.

[16] Surviving prints date from the late 1620s on: see, for example, 1877,1208.325 (1682), 1907,0326.31 (c. 1640), 1907,0326.32 and O,3.197 (c. 1647–1648); Jones, *The Print in Early Modern England*, 162–163. The inspiration was probably Lucas Cranach the Younger's *Last Supper* (1565) in Dessau, in which the apostles are portrayed as reformers, many of whom are bearded: Koerner, *The Reformation of the Image*, 379–385 passim, pl. 130.

[17] When seen again in Wittenberg in January 1522 letters reported that Luther had a "long beard (*langen bart*)," a "thick beard over all his mouth and cheeks, so that at first his damned friends did not know him (*ein dicken partt vber all sein mundt vnd wangen, das in erstlich seine allergehammeste freundt nicht kandt haben*)": Müller, *Die Wittenberger Bewegung*, 159, 170.

Figure 4.4. Cornelis Danckertsz. the Younger (attrib.), *The candle is lighted, we cannot put it out*, c. 1640, etching, 26 × 37.3 cm. British Museum, London (1907,0326.31).

Marked Differences: Beards in Renaissance Europe

Figure 4.5. Hans Baldung Grien, *Martin Luther as an Augustinian Friar*, woodcut, 15.5 x 11.4 cm. Albertina, Vienna (DG1929/429).

in 1525), adding a certain elite authority and audacity to Luther's countenance.[18] In actuality, his facial hair was much thicker, and after his short period of concealment his always clean-shaven face implied that he was unafraid, open, and independent of political machinations. His anachronistic visage was also distinctive, separating him out from that crowd at the figurative table.

Another reason for his choice, I suggest, was that as a former Augustinian friar who bore the tonsure Luther was aware of fervent arguments against facial hair (Fig. 4.5). Many Catholics believed that beards marked men as akin to uncontrolled, lusty goats, whereas shaving was a visible sign of self-management and of a more purified, sexless state, closer to that of angels. For instance, in the early twelfth century the Benedictine chronicler of English history Orderic Vitalis explained that long beards were normally the sign of penitents, prisoners, and pilgrims because they "publicly proclaimed their condition."[19] These three roles continued to be marked by conspicuous beards in the visual culture of early modern Europe. All were rueful, humbling signs of sin being expelled by

---

[18] BM O,3.190 and 1895,0122.279, both dated 1522 but with different inscriptions. Posthumous images of him occasionally followed this bearded prototype.
[19] Vitalis, *The Ecclesiastical History*, 189.

acts of penitence, punishment, or pilgrimage. Just as it was believed that bodily humours and masculine heat expelled more hair from the male body, so were sinful excesses emitted from that body by means of lengthening the hair.

But, as Orderic went on, "those who, in the sight of God, are bristling with sins and unkempt within may walk outwardly bristling and unshorn before men, and proclaim by their outward disgrace the baseness of the inner man. Long beards give them the look of he-goats, whose filthy viciousness is shamefully imitated by the degradations of fornicators and sodomites, and they are rightly abominated by decent men for the foulness of their vile lusts."[20] Luther's shaved countenance avowed that he was unlike "stinking goats" and lusty satyrs, thus obstructing potential polemic that could be cast against him for leaving the Augustinian Order and for marrying.

A certain type of long, messy beard was long-described as goat-like. In 1611, a French dictionary listed *Barbasse*, "a filthie great, or goat-like, beard," and an Italian one similarly translating into English defined the word *Barbariccia* as "a grim, shagged, Goatish beard. Also fraud, guile, or cheating."[21] That is, beards could also be regarded as deceitful disguises, as Luther knew. Notably, the disheveled beard continues today to connote belligerent, untrammeled masculinity, whereas most military and police forces insist instead on the extreme cropping of hair on the face and head, continuing the assumption that virtue and self-control are marked by shaving.

Artists depicting Luther chose much subtler ways to remind viewers of his regulated but powerful masculinity, including endowing him with monumental size and occasionally depicting stubble (Fig. 4.5). Hans Baldung Grien's woodcut of Luther as an inspired friar adds the naturalistic touch of stubble because, in fact, tonsuring and shaving in the cloister took place only every several weeks, and the clean-shaven, smooth faces seen in countless images and portraits of monks and friars are idealizations of them in their most purified, freshly shaven form. Combining the everyday detail of prickly hair with the blessing of the Holy Spirit in the form of a dove, which creates a halo-like aura around Luther, cleverly creates the visual impression that this is indeed a life-like representation of a truly divinely sanctioned theologian.

St Francis was a religious figure with a variable countenance, fully tonsured and shaved in some images, but shown as an ascetic bearded hermit in the earliest known representation of him, probably painted during his lifetime.[22] To some extent, the variation in his iconography pointed to divisions within the Franciscan Order, but it was also due to the degree to which an artist's

---

[20] Vitalis, *The Ecclesiastical History*, 64–65.
[21] Cotgrave, *A Dictionarie*, s.v.; Florio, *Queen Anna's New World of Words*, 54 (the second sentence was not in the 1598 edition).
[22] In the Benedictine abbey of Subiaco, perhaps within two or three years of his demise in 1226, though other scholars date the painting to the 1240s: Cook, *Images of St Francis of Assisi*, 221–222.

Marked Differences: Beards in Renaissance Europe

Figure 4.6. Petrus Christus, *Portrait of a Young Man*, c. 1450–60, oil on oak, 35.4 x 26 cm. National Gallery, London (NG2593).

close observation of the actual effect of tonsure was deemed important. When freshly shaved, a tonsured man not only had what was described as a "crown" or circle of bare scalp but also a fully beardless face and hair shaved well above his ears. During the fifteenth century, many secular men adopted the half-tonsure, omitting the "crown" but ensuring that they were portrayed with the high razor shave that extended above the ears (Fig. 4.6). Thereby, their outward appearance declared that they were upright citizens who followed monastic exemplars in their virtuous piety. When Florence was in the grip of the extreme religious reformer Girolamo Savonarola during the 1490s, one of his supporters described the positive effect he had on the city's youths, whose turn from vices like gambling and lascivious poetry was evident in their removal of codpieces and their adoption of new haircuts. They disavowed the newer fashion for long hair and instead were seen "with their hair cut short up

Patricia Simons

Figure 4.7. Albrecht Dürer, *Self-Portrait*, detail, 1493, oil on linen (transferred from vellum), 56 x 44 cm. Musée du Louvre, Paris (R.F. 2382).

above the ear."[23] That is, they were returning to an older, strict style of shaving, publicly and visibly declaring their newfound purification by way of haircuts that were akin to those of the friars who were mobilizing them.

Shaved faces of any style that were displayed in fifteenth-century portraits demonstrated masculinity that was contained, controlled, normative, honourable, and seemingly asexual. But close inspection reveals many cases in which stubble was painstakingly rendered, white in the case of old men who were by that means

[23] "taglisi e' capelli corti insino che scopra l'orecchio"; Burlamacchi, *La Vita del Beato Ieronimo Savonarola*, 121–122.

bestowed with ongoing vigour and authority, and whose portraits are given a subtle, compelling texture and naturalistic presence even if, as in some cases such as Piero di Cosimo's portrait of Francesco Giamberti da Sangallo (1482–1485), the family ancestor was actually already deceased.[24] In other cases, dark stubble proclaims that the sitter is very much alive, with a sexual, virile nature, even cheeky willingness to stretch the limits of convention in the case of Antonello da Messina's *Portrait of a man* now in Cefalù, where gleaming eyes, engaging gaze, smiling face, and strong stubble convey the striking sense of presence.[25]

Most often, facial hair is barely evident, emerging above the lips and, sometimes, on the chin, as is visible in Dürer's self-portrait of 1493 painted when he was aged twenty-two (Fig. 4.7).[26] He holds a plant that traditionally connoted courtship and this self-presentation is plausibly related to his marriage less than one year later. I argue that his budding facial hair is a vital aspect of his formal staging, proclaiming that he is now of legal age, capable of reproduction and of offering complete sexual pleasure. We need to remember that beards came in much later than they tend to now, often in the early twenties. Rembrandt, for instance, was twenty-three before the first traces of his facial hair were recorded.[27] When the twenty-three-year-old goldsmith and later sculptor Benvenuto Cellini had to disguise himself to flee from the Florentine police in 1523, he asked a friend "to pull out a few hairs that were on my chin, the first sign of my beard" and then he dressed as a friar; once clear, "I immediately unfrocked myself and became a man once more."[28]

Thus, different modes of facial hair conveyed political, imperial, sexual, and religious notions of masculinity according to various factors including ethnicity and race, occupation, age, and faith. Such customs were neither just personal nor merely fashion trends of no significance. And they shifted over the decades. In what follows I will briefly sketch out why beards were understood as such fundamental and "natural" declarations of masculinity and then consider the question of why they became normative from the early sixteenth century.

Medical thinking, in both the Arabic and ancient Greek and Roman traditions (each of which were influential in European culture for millennia), regarded

---

[24] Geronimus, *Piero di Cosimo*, 34, 40, 42–45.
[25] Lucco et al., *Antonello da Messina*, 162–163 no. 14. For further examples of noticeable stubble in Antonello's portraits, see pp. 174–175, 194–195, 242–245, nos 20, 26, 38, and for works by other artists, see pp. 296–297 no. 52 (Jan van Eyck's *Portrait of a man with a blue chaperon, holding a ring*, c. 1430) and pp. 330–331 no. 67 (Alvise Vivarini's *Portrait of a man with a cap*, c. 1494).
[26] Panofsky, *The Life and Art of Albrecht Dürer*, 6.
[27] See Rembrandt's *Self-portrait* of c. 1629 in Nuremberg's Germanisches Nationalmuseum (Gm391). Slightly more facial hair is evident in the copy by one of his pupils, probably Gerrit Dou, in the Mauritshuis, The Hague, 148.
[28] "subito mi sfratai, e ritornato uomo"; Cellini, *Vita*, 118 (1.18); *The Autobiography of Benvenuto Cellini*, 39.

Figure 4.8. The Mint of Pesaro, *Medal of Giovanni Sforza*, 1503, cast bronze, 5.4 cm diameter. British Museum, London (1922,0709.3).

facial hair as emblematic of masculine vigour.[29] Medically, legally, and socially, the onset of a beard was believed to signal a man's ability to reproduce. In the 1490s, relaying the succinct words of a Greek peasant who was well aware of bearded men in his Orthodox church, the Venetian surgeon Alessandro Benedetti noted that the beard "is contained in the testicles."[30] That is, the production of reproductive semen was thought to be directly related to the male body's ability to produce hair, including on the chin. It was a gendered and genital distinction.[31]

[29] Simons, *The Sex of Men*, 29–30, 35, 38, 140, 167, 186, 214.
[30] "quoniam testibus continetur, atque ita mentum graeca maiestate barba cohonestari"; Benedetti, *Historia corporis humani*, 240; translated in Lind, *Studies in Pre-Vesalian Anatomy*, 113–114.
[31] Thus I disagree with the fundamental argument in Fisher, "The Renaissance Beard"; see Simons, *Sex of Men*, 30.

Marked Differences: Beards in Renaissance Europe

Benedetti also reported the standard chronology: "pubic hair grows first, then the hair in the armpits, lastly the beard," meaning that only with the advent of facial hair is the transition to male adulthood complete. The fundamental law code of the Holy Roman Empire gave legal weight to that medical precept, decreeing that a man came of legal age once he grew hair in all three of those areas of his body.[32] Since it was common for facial hair to emerge only when a man was in his early twenties, the understanding of a male body's sexual charge differed from that of more modern times. Poetry in ancient Greek, Latin, Arabic, and various vernaculars proclaimed a youth's advent from homoeroticized appeal to marriageable status once hair began to appear on the beloved's face.

Already by the last decades of the fifteenth century and the early years of the sixteenth century, some men flaunted social expectations about shaving. One such example was Giovanni Sforza, who subsequently issued a medal portraying him with a heavy beard and thick mane of hair (Fig. 4.8).[33] Lord of Pesaro and an illegitimate member of the powerful Milanese ruling family, he faces right with a fierce gaze, a stern set to his mouth. Rivulets of long curling hair run down from his head and the beard is a thriving mass of curls extending high up the cheeks and to a trimmed degree below the jaw. The medal emphatically presents a determined, hirsute soldier clad in armour and mail. A detailed inscription runs around the entire rim: "Giovanni Sforza. Son of Costanzo. [Lord of] Pesaro. Aged thirty-seven. 1503." The medal commemorates his retaking of the city after a hiatus under Cesare Borgia during the years 1501–1503, a restoration emphasized on the reverse, which bears the inscription "Received Home" and a broken yoke (symbolizing victory over Borgia's heavy rule). Coins first struck in April 1498 display a similar beard, and his later medal slightly changes that design, probably both produced by the mint in Pesaro.[34]

It was unusually early for a European man's visage to be represented with such a full beard, so it may primarily indicate that the condottiere was a tough soldier. But the facial distinction also answers rumours about impotence that had circulated since at least early 1497.[35] After his first wife died, in 1492 Giovanni married by proxy the thirteen-year-old Lucrezia Borgia, illegitimate daughter of Pope Alexander VI, though the marriage was not celebrated until June 1493. However, the ambitious pope soon wanted to use Lucrezia to forge more prestigious political ties and pressured Giovanni to admit to impotence so that the marriage could be dissolved. After much resistance from Giovanni lasting most of the year, the union was annulled in December 1497. A considerable

---

[32] Bartlett, "The Symbolic Meanings of Hair," 44.
[33] Hill, *A Corpus of Italian Medals*, 1:74–75 no. 302, vol. 2, pl. 47.
[34] Olivieri degli Abati, "Della Zecca di Pesaro," 234–235, pl. III. Earlier coins did not carry a portrait.
[35] Bradford, *Lucrezia Borgia*, 59–60, 64–67; Ambrogiani, *Vita di Giovanni Sforza*, 218–253.

dowry was also at issue, but Giovanni's unwillingness stemmed chiefly from concerns about his honour.

In the end, Lucrezia's statement that she did not know whether their marriage had been consummated moderated the outright charge of impotence against Giovanni. But the implication was damning. Lucrezia officially remained a virgin, whereas his virility and honour were impugned. Subsequent coins and medals bearing images of his bearded face, first issued four months later, resoundingly publicized the man's hirsute virility. Easy to disseminate, they were capable of spreading the assertive message far abroad, responding to scandalous gossip regarding the notorious Borgia pope, his daughter, and a princeling from the powerful Sforza clan. Within months of Alexander VI's death in August 1503, Giovanni was back in charge of Pesaro; the medal announced the renewal, presenting him as a strong soldier, patriotic ruler, and virile man.

Within a decade Sforza's countenance would have looked less exceptional because more and more men were exhibiting full beards. Besides the generic, dismissive explanation that the degree of shaving simply cycled in and out of fashion, a second explanation for such a widespread swing toward bearded countenances is that an important ruler such as Francis I of France adopted the fashion and thereafter so did his courtiers and then the habit quickly spread. This account resorts once more to an individual element, though with an acknowledgement of power, but it too tends to be descriptive and begs the question as to *why* that ruler changed and why his new practice became so widespread.

The earliest portrait of Francis was painted around the very time that he married in May 1514 and became king on 1 January 1515.[36] As with Dürer (Fig. 4.7) and many others, the first portrait of the French prince is an instance of an unnoticed trend, the commissioning of portraits that proclaim that young men are now marriageable because their incipient facial hair demonstrates their physiological status as new adults who could father children, were sexually capable, and independent legally and financially. Facial hair was thus a charged, communicative assertion of masculine authority, social standing, and sexual potency.

The early portrait of Francis is in that vein, though the artist shows the beard beginning to fill out at the chin. Later portraits of the king show a thicker, darker beard (possibly, in later years, augmented with hair dye). So, the question is not why did a man grow his beard but why did he *keep* it and groom it? Francis I, whose proud display of the beard balanced his oversized nose, was one of several younger rulers of the early sixteenth century who permanently adopted a beard, competing with each other in their overt declaration of masculine prowess and power. In some cases, including Cosimo I de' Medici and Emperor Charles V von Habsburg, their facial hair

---

[36] The portrait in the Musée Condé, Chantilly may be an early work by Jean Clouet: Jollet, *Jean & Francois Clouet*, 164–165.

Figure 4.9. Jan Cornelisz. Vermeyen (manner of), *Portrait of Emperor Charles V*, c. 1530, oil on wood, 26.4 x 14 cm. Rijksmuseum, Amsterdam (SK–A–164).

was developed with some difficulty. Thin, patchy, and irregular (though it depended on the artist's interest in veracity), Cosimo's beard was accompanied by frequent depiction in hefty armour. Although Charles' beard is usually explained as a device to disguise his jutting Hapsburg jaw, the family was proud of its distinctive "brand," as it were, which connoted strength and unity. Indeed, the projecting points of his still-developing beard, especially evident in a painting of around 1530 when the sitter was thirty, exaggerated the genetic deformity and affirmed his Hapsburg lineage (Fig. 4.9). His reasons for cultivating a beard were again public more than personal, involving the avowal of power (he ascended to the throne of Spain at the age of sixteen and became Holy Roman Emperor at the age of nineteen), and virility (he was engaged at the age of twenty-five once he became keen to father children and continue the dynasty).

Overall, while the adoption of beards by rulers was widely known and possibly influential in the early decades of the sixteenth century, that practice was nevertheless coterminous with the widespread growth of facial hair at the time. No one man was a trend setter. What is notable is that a cluster of four soon-bearded rulers – Henry VIII, Francis I, Suleiman, and Charles V – were all born within a decade of each other, on or before the year 1500, became rulers at a relatively young age, and married around the same time, often at a younger age than had been true for earlier rulers. These men adopted permanent beards in order to assert their adulthood, authority, and virility at a time when many lesser men were also ceasing to shave.

Another explanation was published in 2015: "Why the shift to beards? [...] What propelled the change in fashion [...] was *insecurity*, the feeling on the part of so many Italians belonging to the elite or aspiring to be part of it that, despite all the colossal capital and urban planning and civic pride [...] Italy was as weak and vulnerable as ever."[37] However, on a factual basis alone there are many problems with this claim. Invasions of the Italian peninsula by French forces began in the 1490s, and the Kingdom of Naples fell to Spain in 1503, for instance, several years or even decades before the cultivation of beards became widespread. The chronological problem is matched by a geographical one: beards were neither confined to Italy nor started there.

More fundamentally, the association of beards with a crisis in masculinity participates in a trend in historical as well as contemporary studies to situate and explain masculinity in relation to anxiety and crisis. But that is about rhetoric rather than reality. Recent studies have begun to analyze the assumptions and flaws in notions that link masculinity with crisis.[38] The problematic model reinforces the practices of masculinity rather than

---

[37] Biow, *On the Importance*, 187.
[38] Simons, *Sex of Men*, 4, 17–18, 26, 48, 64–78; Roberts, "Beyond 'Crisis' in Understanding Gender Transformation"; Dupuis-Déri, *La Crise de la masculinité*; Bryce, "Academic Viagra."

analyzes them. When investigated, many of these "crises" of the sixteenth century are about age, authority and power in an increasingly imperial, hierarchical period, so such supposed emergencies and insecurities are about political and social shifts more than psychic ones. Whereas "crisis" has been considered by some scholars to be a sufficient explanation, I find it merely an after-effect and an artificial construct.

A confluence of numerous factors helps to explain the onset of what became, for more than a century, the conventional practice of not shaving: awareness of and by a new, younger generation of leaders in charge of territories with increased imperial might; the importance of dynastic succession centred more on genetic offspring than adoption or overthrow, especially by the Hapsburgs, ensuring stable centralized and longer-lived regimes; growing knowledge by other men of the medical, social, and sexual import of the age of maturity; the rise in militarized status; more travel and trade across the Mediterranean forging a degree of integration as well as competition; claims by different faiths to be virile and venerable; the understanding that beards signified healthy male bodies that were potent and syphilis-free (a disease that first became noticeable around 1495).

Another factor was a loosening of sexual restrictions among the upper class and thus a greater interest in sexual pleasure. In keeping with ideas about goatish beards, the ancient Greek natural philosopher Aristotle believed that "Men that are hairy are more prone to sexual intercourse and have more semen than men that are smooth."[39] After citing that passage, in 1610 the physician Jacques Ferrand opined that indeed "our ladies hate men with scant beards, not only because they are frequently cold and sexually feeble, but also because they, like eunuchs, are inclined to cruelty and cheating."[40] The cultivation of beards suited a greater focus on the eroticization and virility of classicized, powerful male bodies. About to marry and with facial hair starting to grow, in 1538 Cosimo I de' Medici was portrayed by Bronzino as Orpheus seductively charming the animals.[41] About a decade earlier, Giulio Romano's frescoes in the pleasure palace of Duke Federico Gonzaga of Mantua included an image of genitally aroused Jupiter about to adulterously father Alexander the Great with the king of Macedonia's wife, and the supreme god Jupiter bears some resemblance to Duke Federico.[42] In the 1550s, Emperor Charles V, in his fifties, was represented by Leone Leoni with removal armour, enabling display of the ruler as an alternatively armoured and classically nude conqueror, victoriously subjugating the figure of Fury and thereby sustaining order and

---

[39] Aristotle, *Generation of Animals*, 455 (774a35).
[40] Ferrand, *A Treatise on Lovesickness*, 284.
[41] Philadelphia Museum of Art, 1950–86–1.
[42] Simons, *Sex of Men*, 92–94, fig. 15.

Figure 4.10. Agnolo Bronzino, *Portrait of Andrea Doria*, c. 1545–46, oil on canvas, 149 x 199.5 cm. Pinacoteca Brera, Milan (1206).

peace.[43] In each case, legendary personas join with *all'antica* musculature and grandeur, further enhanced by manly beards.

The same is true of Bronzino's portrait of Andrea Doria, Charles V's admiral from Genoa, pictured like the semi-naked god Neptune (Fig. 4.10). One crucial element of the imposing effect is the long beard, similar to what is seen in other representations of ancient, idealized leaders and mature divinities. Doria's beard retains some dark colour amidst the silvery grey tones and the tendrils curve in seemingly continuous motion, visually affirming the sense of an energetic body and alert mind. However, we have an earlier impression of the man, recorded around 1529 by the eye-witness Christoph Weiditz, a German artist. He saw the beard very differently, as a longer, undifferentiated

---

[43] Madrid, Museo del Prado, E000273.

mass of mostly white, with touches of grey.[44] The German drawing is likely to be more "accurate" as to literal appearance seen by the artist who produced a silver medal of the man, in which the beard is still bushy but granted the classicizing tendrils that are absent in the drawing and exaggerated even more in Bronzino's painting. The latter more effectively captures the imperious air of the persona and, more importantly, the office-holder of a high military rank in Europe's major fleet.

When displayed in Paolo Giovio's portrait collection soon after its production, Bronzino's canvas was accompanied by a Latin poem. In the English translation published recently the opening lines read: "This is Doria / with disheveled beard and fierce trident / he holds dominion over the great sea."[45] Notably, the beard is considered as important as the trident, underlining the implied comparison with Neptune, god of the seas, and accentuating dominion over that realm. However, "barba horrentem" is rendered in English as "disheveled beard," whereas neither the poetic nor the pictorial context is descriptive. The Latin phrase that immediately follows refers to a fierce or furious trident not a sharp or spiky one, and the two attributes convey the sense of imperial control. Furthermore, untidiness is not worthy of a commander. Rather, the phrase means dreadful, fearful, horrible beard, akin to the use of the word *terribilità* by contemporaries for Michelangelo, referring to the quality of arousing awe and terror.[46] Such is the effect provoked by the beard of Michelangelo's *Moses*, one of the sculptures carved for the tomb of Pope Julius II, a work inducing dreadful respect, of the commanding figure and of its sculptor. Beards such as these were assertions of ongoing patriarchal might, aristocratic privilege and artistic imagination. Facial hair in Early Modern Europe was not all the same, but it was readable in social, medical, sexual, legal, and religious terms, being one way in which differences between men were visibly and proudly proclaimed.

University of Michigan

CITED WORKS

Ambrogiani, Francesco. *Vita di Giovanni Sforza: (1466-1510)*. Pesaro: Società pesarese di studi storici, 2009.
Aristotle. *Generation of Animals*. Trans. A. L. Peck. Cambridge, MA: Harvard University Press, 1942.
Bartlett, Robert. "The Symbolic Meanings of Hair in the Middle Ages." *Transactions of the Royal Historical Society* 4 (1994): 43–60.

---

[44] Weiditz, *Authentic Everyday Dress of the Renaissance*.
[45] Eliav, "Trident and Oar in Bronzino's Portrait of Andrea Doria," 796, 814.
[46] Summers, *Michelangelo and the Language of Art*, 234–241.

Benedetti, Alessandro. *Historia corporis humani sive Anatomice*. Ed. Giovanna Ferrari. Florence: Giunti, 1998.

Biow, Douglas. *On the Importance of Being an Individual in Renaissance Italy. Men, their Professions, and their Beards*. Philadelphia, PA: University of Pennsylvania Press, 2015.

Bradford, Sarah. *Lucrezia Borgia. Life, Love and Death in Renaissance Italy*. New York: Viking, 2004.

Bryce, Traister. "Academic Viagra: The Rise of American Masculinity Studies." *American Quarterly* 52 (2020): 274–304.

Burlamacchi, Pacifico. *La Vita del Beato Ieronimo Savonarola*. Ed. Piero Ginori Conti. Florence: Leo S. Olschki, 1937.

Cellini, Benvenuto. *The Autobiography of Benvenuto Cellini*. Trans. George Bull. Harmondsworth: Penguin, 1956.

——. *Vita*. Ed. Ettore Camesasca. Milan: B.U.R., 1985.

Clement of Alexandria. *Christ the Educator*. Trans. Simon Wood. New York: Fathers of the Church, 1954.

Constable, Giles. "Introduction." In *Apologiae duae: Gozechini Epistola ad Walcherum; Burchardi, ut videtur, abbatis Bellevallis Apologia de barbis*. Ed. R. B. C. Huygen. Turnhout: Brepols, 1985, 47–150.

Cook, William. *Images of St Francis of Assisi in Painting, Stone and Glass from the Earliest Images to ca. 1320 in Italy*. Florence: Leo S. Olschki, 1999.

Cotgrave, Randle. *A Dictionarie of the French and English Tongues*. London: Adam Islip, 1611.

Crabbe, Pierre. *Concilia Omnia*. Cologne: Peter Quentel, 1538.

Dupuis-Déri, Francis. *La Crise de la masculinité: autopsie d'un myth tenace*. Montreal: Remue-ménage, 2018.

Eliav, Joseph. "Trident and Oar in Bronzino's Portrait of Andrea Doria." *Renaissance Quarterly* 73 (2020): 775–820.

Ferrand, Jacques. *A Treatise on Lovesickness*. Trans. and ed. Donald A. Beecher and Massimo Ciavolella. Syracuse, NY: Syracuse University Press, 1990.

Fisher, Will. "The Renaissance Beard: Masculinity in Early Modern England." *Renaissance Quarterly* 54 (2001): 155–187.

Florio, John. *Queen Anna's New World of Words*. London: Bradwood, 1611.

Geronimus, Dennis. *Piero di Cosimo: Visions Beautiful and Strange*. New Haven, CT: Yale University Press, 2006.

Hill, George Francis. *A Corpus of Italian Medals of the Renaissance before Cellini*. 2 vols. London: British Museum, 1930.

Jollet, Étienne. *Jean & Francois Clouet*. Paris: Editions de la Lagune, 1997.

Jones, Malcolm. *The Print in Early Modern England*. New Haven, CT: Yale University Press, 2010.

Koerner, Joseph Leo. *The Reformation of the Image*. Chicago, IL: The University of Chicago Press, 2004.

Lind, L. R. *Studies in Pre-Vesalian Anatomy*. Philadelphia, PA: American Philosophical Society, 1975.

Lucco, Mauro et al., *Antonello da Messina: L'opera completa*. Milan: Silvana, 2006.
Müller, Nikolaus. *Die Wittenberger Bewegung 1521 und 1522*. Leipzig: Nachfolger, 1911.
Olivieri degli Abati, Annibale. "Della zecca di Pesaro e delle monete pesaresi dei secoli bassi." In G. A. Zanetti, *Nuova raccolta delle monete e zecche d'Italia*. Vol. 1. Bologna, 1775, 179–246.
Panofsky, Erwin. *The Life and Art of Albrecht Dürer*, 4th edn. Princeton, NJ: Princeton University Press, 1955.
Pius II. *Commentaries*. Ed. Margaret Meserve and Marcello Simonetta. 3 vols. Cambridge, MA: Harvard University Press, 2003.
Roberts, Mary Louise. "Beyond 'Crisis' in Understanding Gender Transformation." *Gender & History* 28 (2016): 358–366.
Rodocanachi, Emmanuel. *La Première Renaissance, Rome au temps de Jules II et de Léon X*. Paris: Hachette, 1912.
Simons, Patricia. *The Sex of Men in Premodern Europe: A Cultural History*. Cambridge, UK: Cambridge University Press, 2011.
Summers, David. *Michelangelo and the Language of Art*. Princeton, NJ: Princeton University Press, 1981.
Vitalis, Orderic. *The Ecclesiastical History*. Ed. and trans. Marjorie Chibnall. Vol. 4. Oxford: Clarendon, 1973.
Weiditz, Christoph. *Authentic Everyday Dress of the Renaissance*. New York: Dover, 1994.
White, Andrew W. "What the Archbishop Saw: A Byzantine Christian Watches Catholic Sacred Plays." *Ecumenica* 4 (2011): 27–38.

5

SPURS AND NEGOTIATIONS OF MASCULINITY IN EARLY MODERN ENGLAND

Hilary Doda[1]

The simple spur is an often described but rarely analyzed item of armorial dress. It was a minor riding accessory: a handful of pieces of metal and leather strapped to the foot used to apply pressure and guide the animal's movements. An iron tool in its earliest forms, the medieval spur – now cast in copper alloy, gilded and tinned – became intrinsically connected with knightly status and chivalric masculinity. Ambiguity followed, as negotiations of masculinity changed in the fifteenth and sixteenth centuries, and the semiotic resonance of spurs declined. In the late sixteenth and early seventeenth centuries they became a highly symbolic article of dress as they moved into the contemporary fashion system, bringing with them an embodiment of the masculine ideal now distilled into portable form. This change in the way spurs were perceived and used was an expression of the rising anxieties about gender and the body that rippled through this period.

This research project began with a question, one about significance and symbolism, and about performances of masculine display in an early modern colonial setting. The Acadians, French colonists who arrived in modern-day Nova Scotia in the 1630s, have historically been represented as isolated peasantry and farmers. Archaeological investigations of Acadian homesteads and villages in the mid-to-late twentieth century, on the other hand, unearthed counterexamples to this archetype of poverty. The Melanson settlement, across the Annapolis River from the English Fort Anne, was first excavated in the summer of 1984.[2] Among the finds was a partial copper-alloy spur buckle cast with floral designs, curling leaves, and a pair of fleur-de-lys (Fig. 5.1). Far fancier in design than the other known Acadian spur – a rowel spur of plain metal, likely iron, found at the Roma site on Prince Edward Island – this

---

[1] With deep and abiding thanks to Thomas V. Cohen, Martha Hollander, and Lisa Toms, for the tea-time conversations and comments that heavily informed the edits and rewrites of this chapter.

[2] See site reports by primary investigator Andrée Crépeau, "Lot Summaries, Melanson 17B: 17B2"; and Crépeau and Dunn, "The Melanson Settlement."

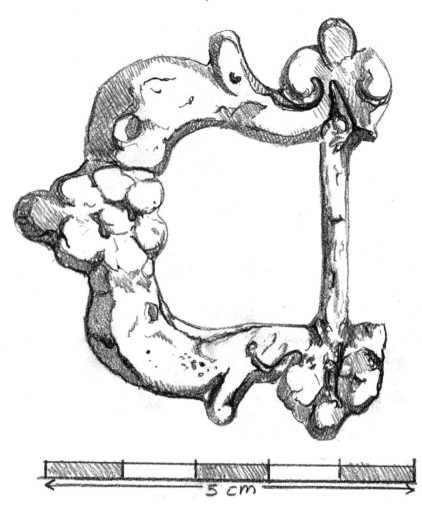

Figure 5.1. Partial spur buckle found at the Melanson site, Nova Scotia. Illustration by Richard Morris, 2023. In the collections of Parks Canada, Object #17B7L3.1.

decorated buckle seemed incongruous.³ Why would one of the Melanson men have worn a fancy pair of spurs on a small farming settlement in the early eighteenth century? They had horses, certainly, but the predominant forms of riding gear in the region were cruder iron and pewter. The answer seems to

3   Korvemaker, "Archaeological Excavations at the Roma Site," 126–127; spur buckle from the Melanson site, artifact 17B7L3.1, Woodside Parks Canada Archaeology Lab.

lie in the symbolic resonance of the decorative spur and the status it accrued over time, even in a small colonial outpost far from France.

We might ask, if decorative spurs had meaning even in Acadia, what is the larger picture? How did they fit into the fashion systems on the European continent? Archaeological data is available in quantity for English spurs, portraits and engravings included images of boots and spurs, and early modern English literature includes widespread use of spurs as metaphor. Our answer can begin here, with the Atlantic empire that held Acadia in the eighteenth century.

Nailing down the nature of the historical resonance of the spur, however, is not as easy as it might first appear. Spurs have appeared in histories of dress and military equipment predominantly as one armour piece among many.[4] In archaeological literature spurs are referenced in descriptions of artifact assemblages and have been the focus of detailed chronological typologies. Literary analysis has engaged with the metaphor of the spur in chivalric literature and in references from authors like Chaucer when they evoke the image of the knight. Meanwhile, little work has engaged both with the material qualities of the spurs and the ways in which the venues and styles of their usage have shaped concepts of gendered behaviours over time. Work by Mary Ellen Roach-Higgins and Joanne B. Eicher in the later twentieth century on dress and adornment developed a framework with which to examine the material culture of clothing, and its use in the performance of social identities, both contemporary and historical.[5] Operating on the assumption that dress functions as a dialect, a form of visual language, their works have suggested multiple strategies for how dress could be "read" as a text, explaining not only the body inside the garment, but also the socio-cultural, economic, and gendered contexts of the world around the wearer. The notion of gender and gendered bodies as a form of performance was famously articulated by Judith Butler in 1988.[6] In her wake, later authors have engaged with a variety of dress objects and styles of bodily adornment as means of discussing and resolving the tension of the gendered form.

The predominant focus in early dress studies on female costume has been balanced out more recently by scholars exploring the significance of male dress. David Kuchta's work on men's wear draws direct connections between the seventeenth-century creation of the three-piece suit and the emergence of modern forms of masculinity.[7] Will Fisher's examination of beards as a construction of masculinity in the early modern posited dress as a gendered extension of the body, with the beard functioning as a prosthetic or phallic

---

[4] See for example, de Lacy, *The History of the Spur*; Rivers-Cofield, "A Guide to Spurs"; Mathias, "Bootspurs"; and especially Ellis, "Spurs and Spur Fittings."
[5] See Roach-Higgins and Eicher, "Dress and Identity."
[6] Butler, "Performative Acts," 520.
[7] Kuchta, *Three-Piece Suit*.

replacement, and in this volume, Patricia Simons explores changing fashions surrounding beards in Renaissance Europe as an articulation of social structure and power differentials around race, age, and status.[8] Cynthia Herrup found that in the early modern period masculinity was closely tied with concepts of self-control as a counterpoint to the excesses of emotion expected from women, and earlier in this volume Thomas V. Cohen examined self-control in masculine behaviour, finding that Italian law made the important distinction between acceptable exuberance and criminal excess when it came to men, sex, and violence.[9] Tim Reinke-Williams concurred, adding that it was not enough to have self-control; to prove manliness, one needed to manifest it.[10] As Ruth Mazo Karras has pointed out, that need to prove oneself in homosocial competition pervaded medieval masculinity, and Benjamin Lukas has identified the link between chivalric masculinity and nobility in the period as a structure that reinforced the socioeconomic status-quo.[11] A need for dominance over others can be added to that notion of self-control. Clare Backhouse picked up these conversations about the male body and argued that the concept of the body was becoming more concrete during the seventeenth century, therefore less able to be molded by its coverings. This change in the concept of malleability provoked further anxiety about gendered presentation and alertness to the different ways clothing could be both a formative shell and a display of internal identity.[12]

Control over bodies – both one's own and those of others – was a part of a performance of masculinity that was connected, both literally and metaphorically, to the spur. It was itself a form of gendered performance, acting as a visible symbol of power and who might have it.[13] If masculinity was the ability to maintain control over self and others, then the spur was the ideal ornament to outwardly display that internal manliness.

THE SYMBOLISM OF MEDIEVAL ENGLISH SPURS

Spurs have a long history in the British Isles. Very basic forms of spurs have been recovered dated as early as the first century CE in England, around the time of the Roman conquest.[14] Some of these early spurs were decorative, others very simple. Then, for a while they vanish almost entirely from the British archaeological record. By the ninth century spurs become more

---

[8] Fisher, "The Renaissance Beard," 157. See also Simons' article "Marked Differences" in this volume.
[9] Herrup, "The King's Two Genders," 499–500; Cohen, "Masculinity as Competence."
[10] Reinke-Williams, *Manhood and Masculinity*, 690.
[11] Karras, *From Boys to Men*, 10; Benjamin Lukas, "From the Knightly Bayard," p. 178.
[12] Backhouse, *Fashion and Popular Print*.
[13] Karras, *From Boys to Men*, 21; Underdown, "The Taming of the Scold," 116–136.
[14] The Portable Antiquities Scheme, "Late Iron Age or early Roman spurs."

Spurs and Negotiations of Masculinity in Early Modern England

1. Prick Spur, 11th - 12th Century.

2. Rowel Spur, late 13th - early 14th Century.

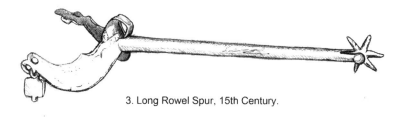

3. Long Rowel Spur, 15th Century.

Figure 5.2. English spur types. Illustration by Richard Morris, 2020.

common again; surviving examples have been found cast from iron, as well as copper alloy.[15] This early medieval spur was a prick spur, a solid piece of metal that had been cast as one with the terminals that wrapped the foot and strapped to the boot. Many of these had decorations. Well-preserved examples of these have come from sites along the Thames.[16] In the thirteenth century the prick spur was replaced by the rowel spur, a type of spur where the solid goad was replaced by a split neck on to which was mounted a rotating disk with five to ten points or "teeth." The rowel spur quickly became the dominant form of the accessory, almost entirely replacing the prick spur (Fig. 5.2 and Graph 5.1). The late medieval and early modern spur was this rowel spur, the

---

[15] The Portable Antiquities Scheme, "9th century spurs."
[16] Ellis, "Spurs and Spur Fittings," 124.

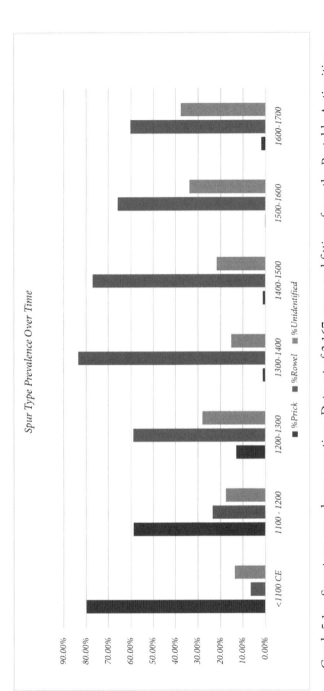

Graph 5.1. Spur type prevalence over time. Data set of 2,167 spurs and fittings from the Portable Antiquities Scheme. Finds.uk.org.

Spurs and Negotiations of Masculinity in Early Modern England

U-shaped metal bracket fastening around the boot with a leather strap that closed with a buckle at the side.

In the high medieval period spurs were certainly not immune to fashion trends, so much so that in some cases they were clearly part of a high-fashion wardrobe. In the fourteenth century, long spurs appeared, consistent with the trend toward elongation in clothing in general (Fig. 5.2). References to these elongated versions of the spur appear in text, as in the fourteenth-century political poem "On the Times" that describes greedy and pretentious men gallivanting about in their fashionable clothes and with "Longe spores on the hele."[17] Intriguingly, despite – or perhaps because of – their occasional notoriety, the fashionable long spurs appear to have been less popular than the shorter variations. Illustrations from the period show people wearing poulaines (shoes or boots with extremely elongated pointed toes), but the images generally do not include spurs unless the wearer is also armoured. We can see this trend in the archaeology, as only a few examples of the long versions have been found to date.[18] Other shapes may have been just as decorative; the rowels of some surviving spurs were fairly large, with particular examples made in shapes and of materials that appeared to value form over function. Examples from France and Spain from the fourteenth and fifteenth centuries include extremely elaborate design elements, including embossing, moulded decorations and punched work that in some cases resembles fine filigree (Fig. 5.3). Still, as with the extra-long-necked spurs that visually balanced the poulaines' long toe-boxes, the impractical spurs were in the minority.[19]

Spur use was not confined to the cavalry. In England, spurs were a commodity, in the reach of many. By necessity spurs were worn with boots, and buckle styles ranged from very simple iron trapezoids to molded, stamped, and plated copper.[20] Most English spurs were likely made in London, where by the fourteenth century there was a concentration of spur-making workshops on the west side of the city – including along Creed Lane near Ludgate which, in the Middle Ages, was known as "Spurrier Row."[21] Cheaper

---

[17] "On the Times," cited in Dean, *Medieval English Political Writings*, 141–142.
[18] Data from Portable Antiquities Scheme database and the collection of the British Museum (Museum numbers 1915,1208.189 and OA.4796, for example). The PAS is a venture of the British Museum and Amgueddfa Cymru – National Museum Wales to record small finds discovered by detectorists and other members of the public in England and Wales. The finds are subject to a certain amount of survival bias, as well as irregularities which come from the voluntary nature of the reporting. It does, however, provide a sizable dataset for non-elite items, as well as a general provenience for same.
[19] Ellis, "Spurs and Spur Fittings," 128–129.
[20] Rivers-Cofield, *A Guide to Spurs*, 46; White, "Constructing Identities," 419.
[21] Ellis, "Spurs and Spur Fittings," 124–125.

Figure 5.3. "Pair of Rowel Spurs" (ca. 1350) of French or Italian origin. Metropolitan Museum of Art. Gift of Amory S. Carhart, in memory of his father, Amory S. Carhart, 1926. Accession Number: 26.80.1–2. Image in the public domain.

iron spurs were also part of the ironmongery sold by chapmen and peddlers alongside scissors, thimbles, whistles, and knives, while more expensive ones, made of or plated in precious metals, could be custom-made or purchased at the jeweller.[22] These less-expensive spurs were available to anyone; there are references in both literature and later in court cases to serving men and city-dwellers owning sets.[23]

The specifics of spurs' physicality set them apart from other items of dress. The metals from which spurriers crafted them guaranteed better survival rates than the boots to which they were attached. While the body shaped materials like leather, the heat of the foot creating space for itself inside the boot or shoe, spurs in their turn restricted the foot's movement, the types of clothing that could be worn with them, and the ways in which the wearers could move through space. The processes of tinning or gilding, coating the iron or copper alloy with another metal, acted as a preservative on the core metals, preventing corrosion or rust. The gilding and tinning wore off with time, but more of this decoration survived than the leather that decayed much more quickly. The majority of spurs found from the medieval and early modern period were designed to be worn with boots, though some samples have survived of spurs with fittings made to hook over the heel of a low-cut shoe.

The medieval period laid a symbolic weight on the spur that connected it to the notions of knighthood and the incorporation of spurs as part of official regalia. A knight was known by his accessories, the decorations on his armour, and the heraldry on his horse's barding announcing his rank and status. To become a knight signalled a movement from subordination to domination – a squire in service, became a leader of men.[24] To a boy, "earning his spurs" both literally and figuratively moved him into a kind of manhood that granted him power and control. This was not, as might be expected, restricted to the sons of the elite; as Ruth Mazo Karras has observed, the chivalric ethos provided the template for masculinity to young men not only of the aristocracy but down to sons of smaller landowners who could access spurs of their own through the city's spurriers and smiths.[25]

---

[22] Spufford, *The Great Reclothing*, 64; Rivers-Cofield, *A Guide to Spurs*, 59.

[23] Two pairs of spurs appear in the inventory from the St Scholastica's Day Riot in 1355. My thanks to Andrew Larsen for this reference. A single iron spur valued at 4d was in a list of items stolen and recovered from Andrew Fryer in Essex, along with gold rings, holland sheets, and other items of luxury and value. Old Bailey Proceedings: Accounts of Criminal Trials. Harvard University Library, LL ref: t16910422-41.

[24] Karras, *From Boys to Men*, 29.

[25] Karras, *From Boys to Men*, 21.

Spurs in the medieval period were associated variously with humility and service, arrogance and power, and always with manhood.[26] There was a danger in doting on the visual design of the spurs and embracing the attention they attracted, however, in that flashiness and display could imply a level of femininity in the wearer. Already in the early twelfth century Bernard of Clairvaux, a highly influential Cistercian, was speaking out against what he saw as decadent pompousness among knights, railing against knights who "adorn[ed] [their] bits and spurs with gold and silver and precious stones," insisting that ornamenting spurs so fashionably turned them into "the trinkets of a woman" that would inevitably lead the knight who wore such baubles to ruin.[27] It appears that no more than 20 percent of spurs were gilded or tinned at this time (Graph 5.2), so Bernard's targets may have been the spurs cast from copper alloy. This early use of spurs as knightly accoutrements and symbols of virile manhood carried a new sort of tension that would later recur as spurs resurged in the early modern – they were seen, and understood as displays of manly prowess, but only to a degree. Once they were gilded and pierced, spurs moved from being power objects to a contested medium for fashionable display.

In the English Later Middle Ages, the spur was still coupled to active masculinity, violence, and rank. In the thirteenth-century manual of chivalry *The Buke of the Order of Knyghthood*, spurs are described as tools to keep the knight "busy and diligent," so that "he sleep not" when faced with enemies or "wicked misdoers."[28] In this paragraph spurs and swords are directly associated, the description of spurs ending with a note that the reader has already been informed about swords. Sometimes, these pieces of armorial kit were treated as extensions of each other, as in trials for treason where the sword and spurs would both be broken away from the traitor's body as a sign of his expulsion from the ranks of the honourable.[29] The spur was directly equated to the knight's honour and valour, masculine traits integral to his social identity. Amanda McVitty writes about the "slippage between the gendered identities of knight and traitor," a homosocial negotiation where traitors to the crown were unmanned. These punishments show the clear connection between stripping the sword and spur away from the body in a public ceremony and destroying the knight's public self.[30]

By virtue of their physical nature and their use in the real world, spurs became a literary and visual device expressing control, power, active engagement, and an elite masculinity that stemmed from spurs' long European association with

---

[26] Oxford, Bodleian Library, Wing / D1154, "A Description of the Ceremonial Proceedings," 15.
[27] Bernard of Clairvaux, *In Praise of the New Knighthood*, 130–134.
[28] Llull, Hay, and Botfield, *The Buke of the Order of Knyghthood*, 40.
[29] McVitty, "False Knights and True Men," 459.
[30] McVitty, "False Knights and True Men," 459.

Spurs and Negotiations of Masculinity in Early Modern England

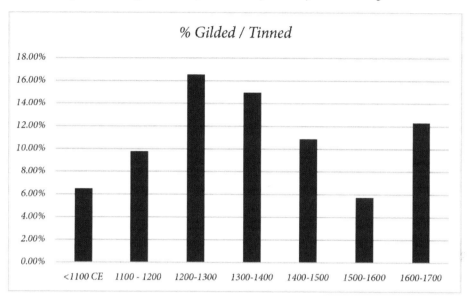

Graph 5.2. Percentage of tinned or gilded spurs, variation over time. Same data set as Graph 5.1.

knighthood and aristocracy. The separation of the spur from the body set them apart as spurs, unlike beards, could carry manhood from body to body, the symbol maintaining its meaning even in circumstances far removed from the original context. While this idea emerges in full force in later centuries, its elements exist in the medieval period as well – Chaucer described the Wife of Bath as wearing "on hir feet a paire of spores sharpe."[31] The Wife of Bath is presented as a controlling woman, especially over her husbands, and as something of a gender non-conformist, marrying multiple times and displaying tropes associated with masculinity of the time rather than those of proper medieval womanhood. Chaucer's use of spurs as a symbol for the Wife of Bath drew upon these associations.

EARLY MODERN SPURS AND THE PORTABILITY OF MANHOOD

In early modern times spur use split into two categories: the functional and the symbolic. At the start, they were a potent marker, intrinsically associated with royal vestments as well as with the trappings of chivalry. They were parts of clothing that could be treated as parts of the body, as seen in a traitor's divesture of his vestments followed by dismemberment of the corpus

---

[31] Skeat, *Pierce the Ploughmans Crede*, 424–425.

beneath.[32] During the early to mid-sixteenth century the functional spur receded in popularity as a fashion item, the forms and surface decoration becoming simpler as the spur became more ambiguous in its use. Spurs were still worn for practical purposes, but most were utilitarian in design, the percentage of gilded, tinned, and decorated spurs dropping off considerably (Graph 5.2). On the other hand, spurs remained the symbol of theoretical knighthood, referenced in the names of chivalric orders such as the papal Order of the Golden Spur (1357–841), an award given for service that was not necessarily martial in nature. As functional knighthood waned as a social and martial force, the semiotics of spurs became open for negotiation.[33] Literature acknowledged this tension, as we see in the play *The First Part of the True and Honorable Historie, of the Life of Sir Iohn Old-Castle* (1600). Murley, a brewer, finds a pair of gilt spurs and in response to his friends' exhortations for him to don them replies optimistically: "thou speakest treason to knighthood, dare any weare golden or siluer spurs til he be a knight? no, I shall be knighted to morrow, and then they shall on."[34] The gold and silver are the important aspects here, making a visual distinction between social ranks. Despite the apparent trend in artifacts toward simplicity and functionality, interestingly enough, spurs also came under regulation. Both Henry VIII and Mary I restricted damasked spurs – spurs decorated with intricate patterns of silver filigree – to use by those of the rank of knight or above, or "Captains in Her Majesties' pay."[35] This may indicate official acknowledgement of this division, formalizing the distinction between plain spurs for practical purposes, and decorative spurs for cultural ones.

The domestication of the spur into an article of fashionable dress escalated in the seventeenth century. Sumptuary legislation in England was removed in James I's repeal act of 1604, and with that retraction went any restrictions on spur-wearing.[36] Boots and spurs entered fashionable dress prior to the Civil War and their use expanded from there. We can see these changes in a few different arenas. The number of surviving spurs and fittings from this period increased. Literature made more reference to spurs and spur-wearing, both in the literal and metaphorical sense. In images, particularly in portraits of unarmoured men, spurs appeared far more frequently and artists drew much more attention to them. The prick spur, numbers dramatically reduced in artifact assemblages between the thirteenth and sixteenth centuries, also underwent a fashionable resurgence. Now known as "scotch spurs," these new

---

[32] Sponsler, "Narrating the Social Order: Medieval Clothing Laws," 266; Westerhof, "Deconstructing Identities," 103–104.
[33] Ellis, "Spurs," 1037.
[34] *The First Part of the True and Honorable Historie*, Scene viii.
[35] Elizabeth I, *Whereas the Queenes Maiestie*, 2.
[36] Jac. I, c. 25, "An Acte for continuynge and revivinge of divers Statutes, and for repealinge of some others." In *Statutes of the Realm*, 1050–1052.

Spurs and Negotiations of Masculinity in Early Modern England

versions of the medieval spur had a yoke and attachments similar to the rowel spur, but with an immovable goad rather than a turning, star-shaped rowel.[37] Many of the spurs and yokes from the seventeenth century were small, some potentially for women, some small enough that a child might wear them. Others were delicate, flimsy, or designed with goads too short to reach the horse's side; still others were lacking functional goads at all. Large, butterfly-shaped spur leathers completed the design, sitting across the top of the booted foot in place of the ribbon rosette on a shoe.

For men in the later sixteenth and early seventeenth centuries the boot became a fashionable statement, replacing the shoe. The boot represented active masculinity in stark contrast to the court masculinity of the soft shoe; it suggested a manhood engaging in outdoor life and physical pursuits. In the first half of the seventeenth century spurs worn with leather boots and streetwear were the major noisemaker of the wardrobe, the clink and jangle of metal on metal an accompaniment that announced the arrival of a well-dressed man. Or, of course, an ill-dressed and exaggerated one, as in *The Picture of an English Antik* from 1646, which mocked "The tops of his boots very large, turned down as low as his spurs," and "A great paire of spurres, gingling like a Morrice-dancer."[38]

In the early years of the seventeenth century, prior to the Civil War, the spur was still strongly associated with warfare and knighthood, as well as constancy and self-control. The frontispiece of Samuel Ward's sermon *Woe to Drunkards* of 1622 (Fig. 5.4) uses familiar rhetoric in contrasting older forms of masculinity with modern ones. The frontispiece of his sermon places the spur (sober, masculine, and respectable) in direct visual and ideological contrast with the rosetted shoe (debauched, feminized, and dissolute). By the 1630s the arrival of spurs as a fashion item for young men disconnected from horseback riding became a target for satirical commentary from writers like Thomas Nash who disdained the practice: "If thou be a Student of the Lawes, & they behold thee walking in the streets in thy boots and gingling spurres, they presently conclude, there goes *Hotspur* the Law|yer, that thinkes the time never flyes fast enough, vn|lesse he puts spurres vnto it."[39] They also signalled high status, enough so that in fiction they were often a symbol co-opted by those who wanted to appear to be of an elevated social level, spurs appearing as part of disguises along with fancy cloaks and "my good sword," in ballads through at least the 1670s.[40]

We can see a snapshot of the rapid rise of the boot and spur as fashionable accessory for fashionable men in images from dancing manuals of the

---

[37] Ellis, "Spurs and Spur Fittings," 129.
[38] Anonymous, *The Picture of an English Antick*, 23–24.
[39] Nash, *A Fourefold Vvay to a Happie Life*, 171.
[40] Crimsal, *A Pleasant New Dialogue*, 1; Harvard University Library, Wing / C6777, *The Crafty Maid of the West*, 1.

Figure 5.4. Frontispiece from Samuel Ward, *Woe to Drunkards. A Sermon by Samuel Ward preacher of Ipswich* (1622). Photograph courtesy of Sotheby's.

period. There are no English dancing manuals for the sixteenth century, but *Orchésographie*, a foundational early French dancing manual from 1588, contains images of men in military contexts, armed and in armour, with no sign of spurs on their feet.[41] The text covers various positions of the feet extensively and in detail, but no mention is given of boots, shoes, or spurs. The fashion is instead for soft shoes and long, lean legs, a manhood centred in the codpiece and the visible, turned-out calf. Contrast that with the frontispiece from *The English Dancing Master: or, Plaine and easie Rules for the Dancing of Country Dances*, with the tune to each Dance, the first English country dancing manual from 1651. The woodcut shows an elegantly dressed gentleman dancing with a be-gowned lady. While his partner's legs are hidden beneath her gown the gentleman has turned his leg out, not to display the well-shaped muscle of his calf – hidden under looser breeches that extend three-quarters of the way down the leg – but the obvious presence of the large rowel spurs buckled over his soft-topped leather boots.[42] Marie-Josèphe Bossan describes a kind of leather-wheeled spur worn with the highly fashionable short and lightweight ladrine boots from the mid-seventeenth century. According to Bossan, this spur design would have been worn to balls to avoid tearing dresses on the metal prongs of the rowel sitting at the back of a functional spur.[43] Extant examples of spurs from the period with ineffectively short necks and goads suggest similar behaviours, as does an example recorded in the Portable Antiquities Scheme database where a break in a spur arm was repaired with a wrap of gold foil, thereby rendering it visually intact but structurally useless except as jewellery.[44] In these images and artifacts the spur has moved entirely into the realm of the symbolic. The new designs had rendered its original purpose physically impossible.

Art of the period changed emphasis from short portraits to longer ones, and many more of these included the male feet. In sixteenth-century portraiture we see many images set from the waist up and, when longer, the artist does not call attention to the feet. Masculinity – when it is defined in these portraits by clothing and imagery – is focused on the codpiece, an explicitly phallic symbol for a time period that heavily prized male fertility and the ability to father sons. When we do see feet in portraits from the sixteenth century spurs are not often included in the forefront, even when other armour pieces draw visual focus. By the last decade of the century, however, interest in medieval chivalry and knightly romance had expanded in Elizabethan England and the imagery followed suit. The spurs are present in some of these new long-body images, but not as prominently displayed nor as central a focus with the pose

---

[41] Arbeau, *Orchésographie*, fol. 17r.
[42] Playford, *The English Dancing Master*, 1.
[43] Bossan, *The Art of the Shoe*, 266.
[44] See, for example, LANCUM-2CC1D7 and SUSS-0662DE in the Portable Antiquities Scheme database.

as they would later become. The lounging figure in Isaac Oliver's portrait *A Young Man Seated Under a Tree* (c. 1590–1595) wears rowel spurs on his thigh-high black boots, but the leathers are subtle straps, the metal is dulled, and the vibrant yellow of the sitter's extremely fashionable doublet draws the eye up and away from the feet. By contrast, portraits of fashionable young men of the 1630s–1640s include poses with the foot and calf turned out to put the spur into focus, butterfly spur leathers twice the width of the boot, and gleaming brass that catches both the painter's light and the viewer's attention.[45] Portraits of men in specifically military contexts, on the other hand, as with Peter Lely's portrait of Sir Edward Massey (1647), tend to de-emphasize the fashionable aspects of the spurs while maintaining the turned-out pose.

The cessation of the royal tournaments in 1622, replaced by the theatrical chivalry of the masque, marked the end of a particular form of demonstrative knighthood.[46] Chivalry taken seriously became more the domain of the puritans, while royalists mocked the old forms of knighthood with satirical orders such as the Order of the Blue, whose membership rolls boasted such names as "Giant Drunkzadoge" and "Giant Neverbegood."[47] In the first decades of the century spur-wearing gallants became targets of ridicule, both as self-imposed irony and as caricatures in dramas and satirical epigrams.[48] By the 1630s, when the old forms of chivalry were something of a political embarrassment, we see the spur appearing more and more frequently in portraiture. The further toward the eighteenth century we go, the more often they appear in images, with the paintings' composition and the turn of the leg calling attention to the presence of the accessory. This new political environment contributed to the change in perceptions. Now the dancing halls were filled with carousing men in spurs, the image associated with an evening of entertainment rather than knighthood and sobriety. Spurs and their attendant masculinity had been moved into an entirely new symbolic realm. This trend of being painted in fashionable dress, without many other military trappings or horses but *with* the spurs, continued through the seventeenth century. Only tangentially associated with the fashionable knights of the fourteenth century in their gilt rowel spurs, seventeenth-century spurs become fashion pieces once more, taking the role in portraiture that used to be filled by suits of breastplates, gorgets, and helms.

After Charles I's accession to the throne the great tournaments and fictionalized chivalry that typified the previous reigns ended, and yet spurs

---

[45] See, for example, the portraits of King Charles I by Daniel Mytens (1631); John Belasyse (Bellasis), 1st Baron Belasyse of Worlaby by Gilbert Jackson (1636); and William Style of Langley by an unknown artist (1636).

[46] Adamson, "Chivalry and Political Culture," 165, 171.

[47] Adamson, "Chivalry and Political Culture," 166.

[48] See, for example, Niccols, *The Furies· with Vertues Encomium*, Epigrams III, X, XII, and XXV.

Spurs and Negotiations of Masculinity in Early Modern England

remained. As early as the 1590s spurs were used as symbolic protectors of masculinity as embodied through this realm of violence. In a tract called *The most Horrible and Tragicall Murther of the Right Honorable, the Vertuous and Valerous Gentleman, Iohn Lord Bourgh, Baron of Castell Connell Committed by Arnold Cosby*, the murderer, Cosby, is described as using trickery and lies to win a duel – he only manages to win when he suggests that Lord Bourgh put off his spurs.[49] On the literal side, asking Bourgh to remove his spurs puts Bourgh's head low and his attention elsewhere, and gives his opponent the opportunity for a surprise strike. On the metaphorical side, this is a symbolic removal of Bourgh's protection as a knight from the wiles of the dishonourable. Another text in 1641 describes how a man is literally unmanned by the removal of his spurs, comparing them in the same breath to his head and his blood, and to the ermine robes that mark his status.[50]

The sixteenth century saw spurs disassociated from horse ownership by a rising aspirational social class. The transition period in the seventeenth century saw the decorated spur move from symbol of knighthood into civilian status symbol and mark of fashionable dress. Spurs did not discard their gendered nature, however, but stayed as a signpost for a particular kind of man and man's body.[51] What that kind of manhood was, however, changed as gender itself became a growing site for anxiety. Scholarship has come to approach men as gendered beings rather than assuming their experience as the default setting from which femininity digresses.[52] In order to do that here, we must look at how the various forms of masculinity in medieval and early modern Europe were constructed and expressed. Clare Backhouse's recent work on fashion in the popular ballads in the eighteenth century speaks to this – how a genteel notion of masculinity was on the rise, and how cutting-edge fashions emphasized this particular practice of being an adult European man.[53] The ideal was then shifting from the chivalric knight toward the elite philosopher, as would come to fullest fruition later. Alexandra Shepard has shown the ways in which the range of available types of masculinity expanded in the seventeenth century and caused rising tensions around how to express those different masculinities.[54] In this period self-control served to prove

---

[49] R., *The most Horrible and Tragicall Murther*, 7.
[50] Anonymous, *The Discontented Conference*, 1.
[51] On the symbolism of spurs, see Smith, "Saints in Shining Armor"; Nickel, "Arthurian Armings"; Hodges, "Costume Rhetoric in the Knight's Portrait"; Leonard and Nelson, *Masculinities, Childhood, Violence*. The pamphlet *Hic Mulier*, 1620, specifically calls out spurs as a sign by which men could broadcast their profession: "Are not Bishops knowne by their Myters, Princes by their Crowns, Iudges by their Robes, and Knights by their Spurres?" Anon., *Hic Mulier*, 8.
[52] Hadley, *Masculinity in Medieval Europe*, 2.
[53] Backhouse, *Fashion and Popular Print in Early Modern England*, ch. 4.
[54] Shepard, "From Anxious Patriarchs to Refined Gentlemen?," 284, 292.

manhood and the spur, used to control both horse and man, provided the visual evidence.[55]

The gendered nature of spurs made them a site for tension as anxieties around gender expression grew. A century and a half after the Wife of Bath's spurs served as a warning about women usurping the roles of men, the investiture of Mary I in 1553 saw the connection made explicit. Spurs were a part of the regalia used during the investiture of royalty, specifically for kings and – beginning with Mary I – for queens regnant. Mary I had spurs fastened on her feet by the Bishop of Winchester before he girded her with the sword that represented martial leadership, in effect taking on the king's role as military leader along with the queen's role that her sex assigned her.[56] The polemic pamphlet *Haec-Vir*, a defence of those who broke gendered roles, was illustrated by a woman wearing terrifyingly large spurs – and a man in spur leathers but not the spurs themselves.[57] By the seventeenth century a single spur was acceptable wear for women when riding side-saddle, but women wearing a pair of spurs could be seen as seizing masculine privilege.[58] Nathaniel Ward referenced Chaucer in a short poem directed at contemporary fellow poet Anne Bradstreet, suggesting that the male poets of her acquaintance had better watch out for her: "And chode by Chaucers Boots, and Homers Furrs, / Let Men look to't, least Women wear the Spurrs."[59] The masculinity inherent in the spurs and in riding astride was now something to caution others about – putting on this coded accessory could transport a woman into a man's world.

Active masculinity and the rights and privileges that were conveyed by spurs could be as transient as the spurs themselves and, more importantly, could be removed along with them. This conceit of portable gender attributes is not unique to spurs. Butler's work on gender theory and particularly on the performative nature of gender suggests that gender is a construct that places the body under tension – and that said tension can be resolved through the outward signs and signifiers of gender performance.[60] Fisher argued that beards acted as a form of prosthetic, manifesting gender identity on the face as part of that outward performance, and Simons that the types of beards in which men were depicted in early modern art conveyed vital information

---

[55] Reinke-Williams, "Manhood and Masculinity in Early Modern England," 690.

[56] Account from Simon Renard to Philip of Spain: "The Bishop of Winchester, who officiated, gave her the sceptre and the orb, fastened on the spurs, and girt her with the sword." Calendar of State Papers, Spain, Volume 11, 3 October 1553, Simon Renard to Prince Philip.

[57] Anonymous, *Haec-Vir*, frontispiece.

[58] Rivers-Cofield, *A Guide to Spurs*, 59–60.

[59] Ward, "Mercury shew'd Apollo, Bartas Book," v.

[60] Butler, Judith. "Performative Acts."

about the wearers' specific expressions of masculinity.[61] Spurs fit into that same space, a physical projection from the body that served as an indication of the kind of body beneath the clothes, and of the kind of masculinity being created. In the mid-seventeenth century boots and spurs were intertwined and inseparable in fashion and, as has been noted, footwear was one of the major ways by which gender identity was constructed in the period.[62] The symbolism in the eighteenth century conveyed an image of potent, outdoor-oriented, active masculinity, and the spur enhanced that identification.[63]

CONCLUSION

Bolting themselves into a physical reminder of the link between elite genteel masculinity and external power and control, spur-wearers in the early modern period displayed their inner selves and how their fashion defined them. While stays and skirts reshaped the female body, spurs reshaped the male one – and, in some cases, added a masculine body part to the female. Spurs represented control not only over one's own body, but over the bodies of other creatures – the physical means of directing the actions of a powerful animal, a sign of mastery important beyond its literary connections with knighthood. Spurs were practical pieces of equipment for cavalry, but as warfare changed and ideas of successful manhood changed, spurs acquired the leftover symbolism from armour and themselves shifted to represent the *idea* of a warrior rather than literal warrior-ship. They became fragile and decorative pieces worn for fashion, pieces of resurrected chivalry separated from their original purpose.

The physical nature of the spur is vital to the process. Wearing spurs requires boots, and heavy boots have been associated with active masculinity for centuries. Once the spur became a symbol, it could be removed and appropriated. The practical value of the accessory gave a legitimate excuse for the spur to be "borrowed" by women and deployed as part of their own struggles for control and autonomy. Spurs played a role in the redefinition and renegotiation of masculinities in early modern Europe, a topic that was the subject of profound anxiety. Serving as a mediator, a pair of spurs was a way to transfer aspects of genteel masculinity from the elite male to the aspirational male and to the female, a carrier of masculine traits that moved with the hard steel, leather boots, and gleaming buckles from body to body.

Returning to the Melanson site in Acadia in the first half of the eighteenth century, we can now understand the spur-owner's choices a little differently. None of the Melanson men were knights, none rode a charger into battle for

---

[61] Fisher, "The Renaissance Beard," 157; Simons, "Marked Differences," p. 89.
[62] Riello, "The Material Culture of Walking," 49, 51.
[63] Steele, *Shoes. A Lexicon of Style*, 132; McCormack, "Boots, Material Culture and Georgian Masculinities," 468.

king and country, but the likelihood is high that the wearer was trying to make an impression on a very specific audience. Living so close to Fort Anne, and himself engaged in delicate political negotiations with the British leadership in the region, the Melanson male may have used the spur to reinvent himself. Wearing his shining brass spurs and buckles, he took the transitive properties that had, by this point, become imbued in the image of the spur, and created himself as a man of quality and self-control, buckling on the physical signs and symbols of the masculinity he wanted to uphold.

Dalhousie University

CITED WORKS

Manuscript Sources

Oxford. Bodleian Library
    Wing / D1154; Reel position: Wing / 1685:15, "A Description of the Ceremonial Proceedings at the Coronation of Their Most Illustrious, Serene, and Sacred Majesties, King James II and His Royal Consort Queen Mary Who Where [Sic] Crowned at Westminster-Abby, on Thursday the 23th. of April, 1685."

Cambridge. Harvard University Library
    Wing / C6777; Reel position: Wing / 1483:04. "The Crafty Maid of the West, or, The Lusty Brave Miller of the Western Parts Finely Trapan'd a Merry New Song to Fit Young-Men and Maids. : Tune of Packingtons Pound." (1672)

Printed Sources

Adamson, John S. A. "Chivalry and Political Culture in Caroline England." In Kevin Sharpe and Peter Lake, eds, *Culture and Politics in Early Stuart England*. Stanford, CA: Stanford University Press, 1993, 161–197.

Anonymous. *A Spectacle for Vsurers and Succors of Poore Folkes Bloud Whereby they may See, Gods Iust Dislike and Reuenge, Vpon their Vncharitable and Vnciuill Oppression, with a Horrible Murther Committed by a Young Man, that Hanged His Owne Mother in August Last, 1606*. London: For Iohn Wright, 1606.

——. *Hic Mulier: Or, the Man-Woman and Haec-Vir: Or, the Womanish-Man*. Exeter, UK: The Rota at the University of Exeter, 1973.

——. *The Discontented Conference Betwixt the Two Great Associates, William Archbishop of Canterbury, and Thomas late Earle of Strafford.*: [London: s.n.], 1641.

——. *The First Part of the True and Honorable Historie, of the Life of Sir Iohn Old-Castle, the Good Lord Cobham as it Hath been Lately Acted by the Right Honorable the Earle of Notingham Lord High Admirall of England His Seruants*. London, Printed by Valentine Simmes for Thomas Pauier, 1600.

Spurs and Negotiations of Masculinity in Early Modern England

———. *The Picture of an English Antick, with a List of his Ridiculous Habits, and Apish Gestures. Maids, Where are your Hearts Become? Look you what here is!* 1646. Woodcut, Oxford Text Archive. Online at www.proquest.com/books/picture-english-antick-with-list-his-ridiculous/docview/2240953295/se-2.

Arbeau, Thoinot. *Orchésographie. Et traicte en forme de dialogve, par leqvel tovtes personnes pevvent facilement apprendre & practiquer l'honneste exercice des dances.* Par Thoinot Arbeau demeurant à Lengres. Lengres: Imprimé par Iehan des Preyz, 1589. Online at www.loc.gov/item/55003658/.

Backhouse, Clare. *Fashion and Popular Print in Early Modern England: Depicting Dress in Black-Letter Ballads.* New York: Bloomsbury Publishing, 2017.

Bernard of Clairvaux. *On Grace and Free Choice. In Praise of the New Knighthood.* Trans. Conrad Greenia. In *The Works of Bernard of Clairvaux.* Vol. 7. Cistercian Fathers Series no. 19. Kalamazoo, MI: Cistercian Publications, 1977, 127–145.

Biddle, Martin. *Artefacts from Medieval Winchester.* Pt 2, *Object and Economy in Medieval Winchester.* Oxford: Oxford University Press, 1990.

Bossan, Marie-Josèphe. *The Art of the Shoe.* New York: Parkstone International, 2004.

Butler, Judith. "Performative Acts and Gender Constitution: An Essay in Phenomenology and Feminist Theory." *Theatre Journal* 40.4 (1988): 519–531.

Calendar of State Papers, Spain. Vol. 11, 1553. Ed. Royall Tyler. London: His Majesty's Stationery Office, 1916.

Cohen, Thomas V. "Masculinity as Competence." In Konrad Eisenbichler and Jacqueline Murray, eds, *Premodern Masculinities in Transition.* Woodbridge, UK: The Boydell Press, 2024.

Crépeau, Andrée, "Lot Summaries, Melanson 17B: 17B2" (Field note summaries taken during 1985 digs. Original writers unnamed), handwritten. Parks Canada, 1985.

Crépeau, Andrée and Brenda Dunn, "The Melanson Settlement: An Acadian Farming Community (ca. 1664–1755)." Research Bulletin, 250. Ottawa: Environment Canada–Parks, 1986.

Crimsal, Richard. *A Pleasant New Dialogue: Or, the Discourse between the Serving-Man and the Husband-Man the Lofty Pride must Bated Bee, and Praise must Goe in Right Degree. to the Tune of, I have for all Good Wives a Song* London: for F. Coules, 1640.

Dean, James M., ed. *Medieval English Political Writings.* Kalamazoo, MI: Medieval Institute Publications, 1996.

Elizabeth I. *By the Queene. Whereas the Queenes Maiestie, for Auoyding of the Great Inconuenience that Hath Growen and Dayly Doeth Increase within this Her Realme, by the Inordinate Excesse in Apparel.* London: By the deputies of Christopher Barker, 1597.

Ellis, Blanche M. A. "Spurs." In Biddle, Martin. *Artefacts from Medieval Winchester,* pt 2: *Object and Economy in Medieval Winchester.* Oxford: Oxford University Press, 1990, 1037–1041.

———. "Spurs and Spur Fittings." In John Clark, ed., *The Medieval Horse and its Equipment*. Woodbridge, UK: The Boydell Press, 1995, 124–156.

Fisher, Will. "The Renaissance Beard: Masculinity in Early Modern England." *Renaissance Quarterly* 54.1 (2001): 155–187.

Goodall, I. H. "The Medieval Blacksmith and his Products." *Medieval Industry* 40 (1981): 51–63.

Great Britain et al. *The Statutes of the Realm: Volume 4, Part II, 1586 to 1625*, ed. John Raithby [s. l., 1819].

Hadley, Dawn, ed. *Masculinity in Medieval Europe*. London: Routledge, 2015.

Harvey, Karen and Alexandra Shepard. "What Have Historians Done with Masculinity? Reflections on Five Centuries of British History, circa 1500–1950." *Journal of British Studies* 44.2 (2005): 274–280.

Hay, Sir Gilbert, Beriah Botfield, and David Laing. *The Buke of the Order of Knyghthood*. Abbotsford Club, 1848.

Herrup, Cynthia. "The King's Two Genders." *Journal of British Studies* 45.3 (2006): 493–510.

Hodges, Laura F. "Costume Rhetoric in the Knight's Portrait: Chaucer's Every-Knight and his Bismotered Gypon." *The Chaucer Review* 29.3 (1995): 274–302.

Karras, Ruth Mazo. *From Boys to Men: Formations of Masculinity in Late Medieval Europe*. Philadelphia, PA: University of Pennsylvania Press, 2003.

Korvemaker, E. Frank. "Archaeological Excavations at the Roma Site, Brudenell Point, P.E.I., 1968–1970." Report #90, National Historic Sites Service. Parks Canada / Parcs Canada, 1980.

Kuchta, David. *The Three-Piece Suit and Modern Masculinity: England, 1550–1850*. Oakland, CA: University of California Press, 2002.

Lacy, Charles de Lacy. *The History of the Spur*. London: The Connoisseur, 1911.

Leonard, Amy E. and Karen L. Nelson. *Masculinities, Childhood, Violence: Attending to Early Modern Women-and Men: Proceedings of the 2006 [sixth] Symposium*. Newark, DE: University of Delaware Press, 2011.

Lukas, Benjamin. "From the Knightly Bayard to Captain Monluc: Representations of Masculinity in Sixteenth-Century French Military Literature." In Konrad Eisenbichler and Jacqueline Murray, eds, *Premodern Masculinities in Transition*. Woodbridge, UK: The Boydell Press, 2024.

Mathias, Catherine. "Boot Spurs: A Form of Accessory or a Tool?" *Global Journal of Archaeology & Anthropology* 3.3 (2018): 43–48.

———. "Bootspurs of the Early Modern Period Newfoundland." *Material Culture Review / Revue de La Culture Matérielle* 80 (2014). Online at https://journals.lib.unb.ca/index.php/MCR/article/view/25563.

McCormack, Matthew. "Boots, Material Culture and Georgian Masculinities." *Social History* 42.4 (2017): 461–479.

McNeil P. and Giorgio Riello. "The Art and Science of Walking: Gender, Space and the Fashionable Body in the Long Eighteenth Century." *Fashion Theory* 9.2 (2005): 175–204.

McVitty, E. Amanda. "False Knights and True Men: Contesting Chivalric Masculinity in English Treason Trials, 1388–1415." *Journal of Medieval History* 40.4 (2014): 458–477.

Millar-Heggie, Bonnie. "The Performance of Masculinity and Femininity." *Mirator* 1 (2004): 1–14.

Nash, Thomas. *Quaternio Or A Fourefold Vvay to a Happie Life Set Forth in a Dialogue Betweene a Countryman and a Citizen, a Divine and a Lawyer. Per Tho: Nash Philopolitem* London: Printed by Iohn Davvson, 1633.

Niccols, Richard. *The Furies· with Vertues Encomium. Or the Image of Honour. In Two Bookes of Epigrammes, Satyricall and Encomiasticke*. London: Printed by William Stansby, 1614.

Nickel, Helmut. "Arthurian Armings for War and for Love." *Arthuriana* 5.4 (1995): 3–21.

Playford, John. *The English Dancing Master: or, Plaine and easie Rules for the Dancing of Country Dances, with the tune to each Dance*. London: Printed by Thomas Harper, 1651.

R., W. *The most Horrible and Tragicall Murther of the Right Honorable, the Vertuous and Valerous Gentleman, Iohn Lord Bourgh, Baron of Castell Connell Committed by Arnold Cosby, the Fourteenth of Ianuarie. ogether with the Sorrowfull Sighes of a Sadde Soule, Vppon His Funerall: Written by W.R. a Seruaunt of the Said Lord Bourgh* [London: Printed by R. Robinson], 1591.

Reinke-Williams, Tim. "Manhood and Masculinity in Early Modern England." *History Compass* 12.9 (2014): 685–693.

Rivers-Cofield, Sara. "A Guide to Spurs of Maryland and Delaware ca. 1635–1820." *Northeast Historical Archaeology* 40.1 (2011): 43–71.

Roach-Higgins, Mary Ellen and Joanne B. Eicher. "Dress and Identity." *Clothing and Textiles Research Journal* 10.4 (1992): 1–8.

Shepard, Alexandra. "From Anxious Patriarchs to Refined Gentlemen? Manhood in Britain, circa 1500–1700." *Journal of British Studies* 44.2 (2005): 281–295.

Simons, Patricia. "Marked Difference: Beards in Renaissance Europe." In Konrad Eisenbichler and Jacqueline Murray, eds, *Premodern Masculinities in Transition*. Woodbridge, UK: The Boydell Press, 2024.

Skeat, Walter W. *Pierce the Ploughmans Crede: To Which is Appended God Spede the Plough (about 1500 AD)*. London: Paul, Trench, Trübner & Company, 1895.

Smith, Katherine Allen. "Saints in Shining Armor: Martial Asceticism and Masculine Models of Sanctity, ca. 1050–1250." *Speculum* 83.3 (2008): 572–602.

Sponsler, C. "Narrating the Social Order: Medieval Clothing Laws." *Clio* 21.3 (1992): 265–283.

Spufford, Margaret. *The Great Reclothing of Rural England: Petty Chapman and Their Wares in the Seventeenth Century*. London: Hambledon Press, 1984.

Steele, Valerie. *Shoes: A Lexicon of Style*. New York: Rizzoli International Publications, 1999.

Westerhof, Danielle. "Deconstructing Identities on the Scaffold: The Execution of Hugh Despenser the Younger, 1326." *Journal of Medieval History* 33.1 (2007): 87–106.

White, Carolyn L. "Constructing Identities: Personal Adornment from Portsmouth, New Hampshire, 1680–1820." PhD, Boston University, 2002.

———. "Knee, Garter, Girdle, Hat, Stock, and Spur Buckles from Seven Sites in Portsmouth, New Hampshire." *International Journal of Historical Archaeology* 13.2 (2009): 239–253.

Electronic Sources

"Portable Antiquities Scheme." Finds Reporting Guide: Spurs. https://finds.org.uk/counties/findsrecordingguides/spurs/.

"Portable Antiquities Scheme." Archaeological finds database. https://finds.org.uk/database.

"Renaissance Dance." Library of Congress. www.loc.gov/collections/dance-instruction-manuals-from-1490-to-1920/articles-and-essays/western-social-dance-an-overview-of-the-collection/renaissance-dance/.

6

MARS ASLEEP: DISCARDED SWORDS IN SEVENTEENTH-CENTURY DUTCH ART

Martha Hollander[1]

In seventeenth-century Europe, fighting was everywhere. The right to keep and use arms, once restricted to nobility, had become fundamental for both military and civilian men. As a result, in the seventeenth and eighteenth centuries fighting with bladed weapons became the chief form of aggressive behaviour, especially among younger men. Armed disputes between men could happen at any time, whether spontaneous or formalized in the form of duels.[2] At the same time, instruction in the art of combat, with or without weapons, was provided in the fight books that proliferated throughout the early modern period.[3] These popular books, reprinted and translated throughout Europe, were available to various social groups, from elites to middle-class fraternities and guilds. The practice of fencing was encouraged, even required, among young men of the middle and upper classes as well as the nobility. Most ritualized fighting was in defence of personal honour (including masculine identity) and intended to wound, rather than to kill.[4]

---

[1] I'm grateful to Konrad Eisenbichler and Jacqueline Murray for the opportunity to realize the longstanding ideas in this essay. Thanks also to Hilary Doda and Lisa Thoms for some exhilarating exchange of ideas, and to Elizabeth Hollander for her editorial expertise.
[2] On the culture of violence among young men, see Roberts, *Sex and Drugs*, 101–140. On duelling, see Spierenburg, "Knife Fighting."
[3] The term "fight book" is used to denote "a vast and heterogeneous collection of manuscripts and printed books, destined to transmit on paper (or parchment) in a systematised way a highly complex system of gestures or bodily actions, often, but not always, involving the use of weapons of different sorts," including "manuals in the classical sense, but also works on unarmed combat, mounted combat, combat in armour, combat against multiple opponents, and combinations of those." Jaquet, *Fight Books*, 9.
[4] On fencing and training, see Roodenburg, *Eloquence of the Body*, 92–102. On the connections between fighting and notions of honour relating to longstanding codes of chivalry, see Jones and Coss, *Chivalry*, especially the article by Peter Sposato and Samuel Claussen, "Chivalry and Violence," 100–118.

Figure 6.1. Gabriel Metsu, *Music Party*, 1659. Metropolitan Museum, New York. Marquand Collection, Gift of Henry G. Marquand, 1890.

While the art of fencing was also taught as a form of deportment and exercise, its chief goal was the most efficient way to disable one's opponent.[5]

Public life in the northern Netherlands, as elsewhere, would have an undercurrent of potential violence: men had their swords at the ready, schooled in the art of defence. In seventeenth-century Dutch depictions of daily life, where men interact with women in scenes of leisure, there can be found an intriguing detail: a discarded sword. The sword, sometimes

[5] Anglo, *Martial Arts*, 273.

Mars Asleep: Discarded Swords in Seventeenth-Century Dutch Art

accompanied by a cloak, may appear variously hanging by its baldric (sword belt), from the wall, on the back of a chair, or lying across a table or on the floor. It may appear in scenes of cardplaying, flirtation, eating and drinking, and music-making, and occasionally in portraits of men.

Gabriel Metsu's elegant genre scene known as *The Music Party* (Fig. 6.1) depicts a woman and two men playing music at a table covered with books and scores. The woman grasps the neck of a lute and, with her other hand, holds up a score for a man standing at the window, who sings and beats time. The other man sits across from them at the table, turned slightly away from as he tunes his viol. Aside from the figures, a complex little still life at the bottom of the picture is an intriguing mix of martial and amorous associations. An abandoned sword rests on an embroidered cushion, entwined with its fur-trimmed baldric. Its diagonal position mirrors that of the neck of the man's viol directly above it, which intrudes into the space where the maidservant stands in the doorway and is juxtaposed with the oval shape of the woman's lute. The handle points to the viol player's buttoned cloak, which hangs off the bench he sits on. At the left another sword stands against the wall, pointing at the open chest of songbooks. A score on the floor bears Metsu's signature.

The composition as a whole is a clever harmonizing of elements: the two seated figures facing and turning away from the viewer, the lute (pointing upward to the maidservant in the doorway, bringing in a tray), the viol (pointing downward, echoing the sword handle). Metsu has also arranged spilled, crumpled, or folded objects: the draped fabric of the woman's skirt, the man's blue cloak, and the carpet on the table; the sheets of music on the floor and table, echoed by the looseness of both men's white shirts and the viol player's white canons.

In Metsu's refined and ambitious composition, a weapon is cushioned in luxury, linked with music and flirtation, robbed of its function. It is also sexually suggestive, slicing through the baldric's fur and leather, the tip just visible. In the absence of any documentation regarding what people thought about genre scenes, we can assume that the placement of the motif was a way of heightening the appealing ambiguity of the scene rather than indicating an absolute key to its meaning.[6]

The man at the left wears a plumed beret. This type of hat was not worn in the 1660s but is an element of fantasy costume, often appearing in history scenes to denote the past.[7] Such a detail, like the sword, further indicates a level of contrivance and playfulness enhancing the essential realism of the scene. Metsu originally trained in Leiden but moved to Amsterdam in 1654

---

[6] On the limits of interpretation, see Muizelaar and Phillips, *Men and Women*, 123–125.

[7] On the sixteenth-century hat, see Hollander, "Vermeer's Robe," 189.

for a larger network of clients. Among them were distinguished collectors who were also important citizens of Amsterdam.[8] Completed in 1659, this ambitious work, with its wit, complexity, and brilliance of execution, would appeal to the tastes of these well-heeled patrons.[9]

The sword, removed from its context of violence and defence, attached to a baldric and sometimes accompanied by a cloak, often appears in scenes like Metsu's. The discarded-sword motif began to make an appearance around 1615–1620 and persisted into the early 1700s. Flemish artist David Vinckboons popularized the subject of elegant alfresco parties, based on earlier Flemish imagery, in the first decade of the century in Haarlem. A typical scene depicts a gathering of luxuriously dressed men and women in a park (Fig. 6.2). Seated around a richly set table, three couples flirt, play music, dance and sing, while more couples sit on the grass in the distance. In the centre is an empty chair with a man's hat resting on the seat; underneath it, a sword sticks through the gap below the chair back. It is not clear to whom these accessories belong. Rather, this conspicuous still life appears like a gloss on the company's activities: the removal of cloaks and swords for leisure, indicated by the playing cards scattered in the grass below them. Vinckboons painted several known variations on this scene, in which discarded swords, along with cloaks and hats, lie in the grass, next to stacks of songbooks ready for use. (Metsu's pairing of a cast-off sword and musical scores echoes this motif.)

Artists working in the second decade of the century began to develop on these scenes, often outdoors, of well-dressed men and women, often at tables. Dutch audiences called them *gezelschappen* or companies. The sumptuous details in these scenes – servants, dogs, fanciful backgrounds, food, flowers, and displays of gilt and silver plate – sometimes include one or more swords resting on the ground, sometimes with a cloak or a hat. In depictions of leisure from the turn of the century, no swords appear at all; at the very least, one or two men are shown wearing their swords. Presumably the use of the discarded-sword motif expanded as a larger market for these *gezelschappen* developed during this period and artists were coming up with elements of visual and thematic interest.

During the 1620s and 1630s, some artists began experimenting with the motifs of swords and cloaks, along with other material objects. In images of leisure by painters such as Dirck Hals, Jacob Duck, Willem Duyster, Pieter Codde and Anthonie Palamedesz., swords – with or without cloaks – appear resting on the floor or on tables, leaning against railings, hanging on walls, window shutters, or over the backs of chairs. At mid-century, Metsu's

---

[8] Waaiboer, *Life and Work*, 146–147.
[9] On the responses of artists to the tastes and demands of the market, see Franits, *Genre Painting*, 2–3.

Figure 6.2. David Vinckboons, *The Outdoor Party* (1610). Rijksmuseum, Amsterdam.

Figure 6.3. Nicolaes Maes, *The Listening Housewife (The Eavesdropper)* (1656). Wallace Collection, London, UK © Wallace Collection, London, UK / Bridgeman Images.

contemporaries Pieter de Hooch, Cornelis de Man, and Emanuel de Witte continued the use of this motif. Most of these scenes feature men and women together. (It should be noted that the combination of discarded sword and cloak could appear in images of men at their leisure, without women, as in Jost

Mars Asleep: Discarded Swords in Seventeenth-Century Dutch Art

Cornelisz. Droochsloot's *Elegant company of gentlemen playing music, eating and drinking in an interior of 1645*).

The sword and cloak also appear in scenes where the men, their presumed owners, are absent, hidden, or in the distance. In *The Eavesdropper* (1656) Nicolaes Maes depicts a woman on a staircase, listening to the activities taking place above and below her (Fig. 6.3). At her right, a sword and cloak rest on a chair; the cloak is a vibrant red and adorned with buttons. As is often the case in *gezelschappen*, it is not clear whom do these objects belong. The bright red and gold brocade trim of the jacket rhyme nicely with the red coat and cockade of the man sitting at table in the room behind the listener: do they belong to him? Or to the other man who flirts with the maid in the kitchen below? In pictures where the men are absent, or in the distance, these objects function as metonymic signs of masculine power, stand-ins for men in general rather than belonging to any one man. At the same time, they suggest the shedding of this power – or at least, the lowering of defence – in the safe environment of an interior.

Finally, the abandoned sword can appear all by itself. *The Terrace* (c. 1660, artist unknown) depicts a scene through a window (Fig. 6.4). On the sill in the foreground rests a sword and ornate baldric, overlapping a still life of musical instruments and songbooks on a chair in the near distance. Behind these elements, standing on a terrace, is a couple with a wineglass; a second couple appears in the window above them. Meanwhile, the courtyard below expands off to the left through a wall into a sunny landscape. This elaborately erotic picture uses the sword as a suggestive visual introduction for the courtship scene: the sword handle sticking out from a pile of fur-trimmed fabric threatens to slice into the picture. The sword's shape mimics the edge of the window at the right and the necks of the viols in the background. The abandoned trappings of public masculinity draw our eyes into the story beyond. This unusual composition is related to other isolated images of unworn (notably women's) clothes, such as Hendrik van der Burch's *Dutch Interior* (c. 1660) and Samuel van Hoogstraten's *Slippers* (1658). These are likewise demonstrations in erotics and perspective where cast-off garments are placed at the threshold of a tantalizing space further inside the picture.

Is the discarded sword grounded in the social realities of its use? Does the presence of a cast-off sword on a chair or on the floor reflect how men actually treated their outer garments and equipment? What did men do with these items when entering a space? The literature on behaviour appears to be silent on these small moments of everyday life. It seems unlikely that a man would let his long, sharp sword, even in its scabbard, drop on the floor or lie perilously across a table. A close look at interior scenes reveals occasional depictions of hooks and hangers on walls, sometimes empty, sometimes with swords, cloaks, hats, and gloves hanging on them. Maes and de Man, for example, both depict hooks on walls and cabinets. Also noticeable in these scenes is the absence of *women's* outer clothing: veils, hats, muffs, short cloaks. In the fictive, deeply conventional

Figure 6.4. Dutch (Delft), *The Terrace* (c. 1660). The Art Institute of Chicago®.

world of Dutch pictures, elements of outdoor public apparel strewn around the room belong to men. Women's unworn clothes, as in the examples above, are more intimate: shoes, jacket, cap.[10]

---

[10] The more general motif of discarded clothing, beyond the scope of this essay, is also typical of Dutch painting's contrived fictions. As Wayne Franits observes, "Conventionality […] refers not only to the repetition of specific styles and motifs

Mars Asleep: Discarded Swords in Seventeenth-Century Dutch Art

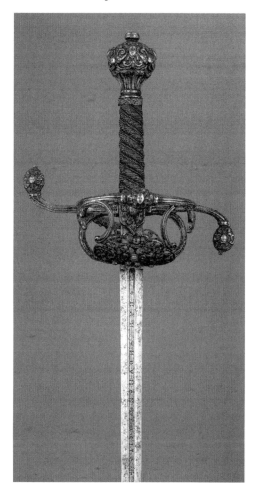

Figure 6.5. Rapier. Blade by Johannes Moum. German hilt (ca. 1630–40); blade, 17th century. Metropolitan Museum of Art, New York. Rogers Fund, 1904.

What kind of swords appear in these scenes? The type of sword in general use in the seventeenth century was the rapier, a long, narrow double blade designed for cutting and thrusting, with a guard of complex design to protect the user's hand (Fig. 6.5).[11] By the late sixteenth century this sharp and dangerous weapon was in standard use and easily available to ordinary citizens. The swords featured in these scenes vary in style. The sword lying

---

    but especially to the restricted number of themes that artists depicted, ones that were used continually, often over several generations. Artists fashioned them in response to personal aesthetic interests, to pictorial traditions, and especially to the demands of the market." Franits, *Genre Painting*, 1–2.

[11] On the rapier and its variations, and on the nomenclature of bladed weapons in general, see Anglo, *Martial Arts*, 99–102.

in the foreground in Metsu's picture has a long handle and simple crossguard, looking somewhat more old-fashioned. The same sword type appears in Barend Fabritius's image of an artist at work in his studio (Fig. 6.9). Meanwhile, Maes depicts a hilt of a different design, with a simple knuckle guard. The rapier in Rembrandt's portrait of Jan Six (Fig. 6.10) has a stylish swept hilt. These variations suggest that artists depicted different types of hilt design, depending on the need for emphasis. The swords in Metsu's and Fabritius's works would stand out more distinctly than the smaller design in Maes's picture. Presumably artists used prop swords from their collections of studio objects or copied sword designs from prints or fight books.[12]

The repetition of sword types and the arbitrary, often ostentatious placement of a sword without a clear owner further reinforce the artifice and rhetorical character of the discarded sword. (The unworn-sword motif also appears frequently in emblem books, generally representing physical courage, steadfastness, and honour.)[13] Its use in paintings is twofold. On the one hand, like other material details in pictures, it offers a display of skill, in this case, rendering folded fabric and gleaming ornamented steel. At the same time, it adds a note of social or erotic commentary: a man shedding his public accoutrements for private pleasures. Such multivalent uses of imagery like the sword clearly had great appeal for art owners and viewers. The longevity of this motif in works produced in various Dutch cities attests to its popularity.

MARS DISARMED

The discarded sword in genre scenes, evoking disarming and sometimes even disrobing for love, appears to be a modern version of the Venus disarming Mars motif. This classical trope originates with Lucretius, whose opening invocation to Venus in *De rerum natura* calls on the goddess to use her seductive power, which has overwhelmed Mars, to bring about peace. Most depictions of the adulterous lovers include the detail of his cast-off armour

---

[12] De Winkel, *Fashion and Fancy*, 343–345 offers some examples of bladed weapons in artist's inventories, ranging from sabres and old-fashioned longswords to rapiers.

[13] The solo-sword motif, like many other everyday objects in Dutch visual culture, developed and was distributed widely in early Dutch emblem books. Roemer Visscher's influential *Sinnepoppen*, for example, includes a fair number of swords. "Alter alterius poscit opem" (one asks the help of the other) depicts a sword and a spindle, metonymically, as contrasting symbols for a man and his wife in an ideal of equal marriage. Visscher, *Sinnepoppen*, II, 51 "Voor lichte eere / lamme leden" (lame limbs for the sake of soft honour) mocks those who would constantly fight for honour despite frequent wounds I, 7. Later in the century, Daniel de la Feuille's multilingual *Devises et emblemes* (1691), includes a sword pointed down on the ground, with the motto "Progite lauros" (show me but laurels), suggests that honour is the chief reason to take up a resting weapon. "Une Epée la pointe en bas." De la Feuille, *Devises et emblems*, 15, Number 4.

Mars Asleep: Discarded Swords in Seventeenth-Century Dutch Art

and weapons. They also include the figure of Cupid, or several putti, removing Mars's weapons and playing with them, rendering them useless as instruments of war. In the late fifteenth century Botticelli created an image of Mars asleep, not only stripped of his armour, but also of his clothes (1485). In the early seventeenth century, Joachim Wtewael transforms the myth into a domestic satire by depicting Mars and Venus as adulterous lovers discovered in bed by the other Olympian gods (1604–1608).

The Return from War: Mars Disarmed by Venus (1612), a collaboration by Pieter Paul Rubens and Jan Brueghel the Elder, depicts a naked Venus removing Mars's helmet as he stands rapt, posing with a baton like a parody of a military portrait, while putti relieve him of his gear (Fig. 6.6). The couple occupy only the right part of the picture; to the left is a scattered mass of elaborate state-of-the-art weaponry.[14] Along with cannons, spurs, a crossbow and a gun, there are two suits of armour in pieces. Exquisitely decorated and modern, the armour does not belong to Mars, who still wears his classical-style armour. Rather, it stands for military might in general, shed and dismantled for the sake of love and peace. This motif of unused and user-less weapons is similar to the discarded swords in *gezelschappen* with their uncertain ownership. In the early seventeenth century in Holland, this popular classical subject was associated with the Twelve Years' Truce, the period of ceasefire during the Eighty Years' War between the northern Netherlands and Spain.[15] Adriaen van de Venne's *Allegory of the Truce* (1616) depicts Cupid leading the Spanish nobleman and the Maid of Holland in a celebratory procession of love and peace. A heap of useless weapons, similar to that in Rubens's painting, sits at once side. Along with the mock-wedding of the two allegorical figures, the cast-off paraphernalia of violence signals the end of war.[16]

Yet, life after the Truce was not necessarily so peaceful. Netherlandish cities were still billeting troops. It has been observed that only after the Treaty of Münster in 1648 and the creation of the Dutch Republic did the theme of the tamed, disarmed soldier (as opposed to a civilian) become a subject of genre scenes. Soldiers, as well as civilian men, appear in genre scenes with their swords removed or unused. Aside from guardroom scenes where soldiers are shown at leisure, often unarmed and undressing and sometimes with women in taverns, they appear, especially after the Treaty of Westphalia (1648) in more elegant settings. In these later courtship scenes, particularly depicted by Gerard ter Borch, the soldier was transformed from aggressor to a romanticized, courtly figure, moving from the guardroom to beautifully appointed houses.[17]

---

[14] On this painting, see Rosen, *Soldier at Leisure*, 132–134.
[15] On discarded swords and the truce, see Chapman, *Propagandist Prints*, 60.
[16] See Woodall, "Love is in the air."
[17] Kettering, "Gerard ter Borch's Military Men," 100–119 and Kunzle, *From Criminal to Courtier*, 600–620. On the "domestication" of military men, see Rosen, *Soldiers at Leisure*, 127–149.

Figure 6.6. Pieter Paul Rubens and Jan Brueghel, *The Return from War: Mars Disarmed by Venus* (1612–16). The J. Paul Getty Museum, Los Angeles. Acquired in honor of John Walsh.

Mars Asleep: Discarded Swords in Seventeenth-Century Dutch Art

IDLE AND SLEEPING SOLDIERS

Mid-century artists used swords, worn and unworn, to expressive effect in scenes of soldiers at rest. In Caspar Netscher's comic scene *The Sleeping Soldier* (c. 1660), from an original by Gerard ter Borch, a soldier has fallen asleep before getting around to removing his sword and now it hangs uselessly at his side. The sleeping-soldier motif derived from wartime "guardroom" scenes of the 1630s and early 1640s.[18] It may have topical implications: the ravaged state of the military after 1650. Aside from this specific resonance, the ineffectual sword reveals how these men have abandoned the strict code of masculinity set forth in fight books in favour of idleness and love. Militarism was a vital component of ideal masculinity in Holland, so much so that the virtues of a soldier were recommended for ordinary men as well as for aristocrats. Their abandonment for pleasure, even temporarily, signals a threat to manliness itself.

Meanwhile, the subject of Mars disarmed by Venus persisted throughout the century. It is one of several popular historical subjects drawn from the Bible and Ovid's *Metamorphoses* involving a woman's subjugation of a warrior: Samson and Delilah, Judith and Holofernes, Hercules and Omphale.[19] In Jan Steen's 1668 version of the Samson story Delilah reaches for a pair of shears, which are placed in the composition above his discarded sword, its point hidden under a turban. Steen's scene, like other representations of this story, is marked by the transfer of an active bladed weapon from the man – whose weapons and armour are now useless – to the woman, a titillating inversion for the viewers of pictures.

Modernized and domesticated, the enduring trope of warlike men overpowered by women endured in the scenes of erotically suggestive leisure already discussed. The soldier, sometimes identifiable by military clothing or armour, becomes a fashionable man; the heap of weapons becomes the single abandoned sword. These men are not necessarily asleep, of course, just enjoying themselves. Flirtation, feasting, dancing and games are, however, surrogates for the sleep of Mars: these men have abandoned their defence and the symbol of this abandonment – the discarded sword – underscores their vulnerability.

---

[18] The "sleeping soldier" type is identified by Kunzle, *From Criminal to Courtier*, 603–604.

[19] On imagery of the disarmed Hercules, see Rosenthal, *Gender, Politics, and Allegory*, 122 ff. Also echoed in some Dutch courtship scenes is an early modern literary version of this trope: the story of Rinaldo and Armida from Tasso's *Gerusalemme Liberata* (1582). See Hollander, "Cavalier at a Dressing Table," 141–142.

Martha Hollander

SWORDS AND MASCULINE IDENTITY

By the late sixteenth century throughout Europe and England, sword-wearing, as well as fighting, were understood as essential to masculine identity.[20] When going about in public most men, civilian or military, noble or middle class, wore swords. Sword-wearing was associated not only with defence, but also with social status.[21] The contemporary discourse on sword-wearing and sword use in seventeenth-century Europe reflects the clashing cultures of civility and violence. Baldassare Castiglione, writing in 1510, is specific about the need for knowledge of arms and for having a sword at the ready: "I judge it his first duty to know how to handle every kind of weapon, both on foot and on horse, and know the advantages of each kind; and be especially acquainted with those arms that are ordinarily used among gentlemen, because […] there often arise differences between one gentleman and another, resulting in duels, And quite often those weapons are used which happen to be at hand."[22] Jacques Faret, in his influential *L'Honnete Homme ou l'art de plaire a la court* ("The Honest Man, or the Art of Pleasing at Court," 1630), writes: "in my opinion there is not any more fitting not more essential for a gentleman, than that of arms. […] Nobility is chiefly gotten by arms, and must be preserved by arms, and opens a way to great reputation, and so to great honours. It seems then, that the strongest ambition which he can have that wears a sword, is, to be esteemed a man of courage and hardy, and consequently to be held a man of government, and good."[23]

As Faret claims, arms are associated not only with honour but also with vigorous manliness. "A man is never comely, but when he believes it not […] and ye shall many times see one that seems more pleasing to the eyes of a troop of ladies, all sunburnt, and covered with sweat and dust, that is returned from the war, or from hunting, then these men of wax, which dare never show themselves in the sun, nor approach near the fire for fear they should melt."[24]

Such "men of wax" are cannily described in Roemer Visscher's *Sinnepoppen* (1614), one of the earliest emblem books to be written originally in Dutch; it went through three editions in the seventeenth century alone and was widely popular and influential. Just as the text is in the vernacular, the images are based in contemporary life. This Dutch satire complements the French, English, and Italian views of armed masculinity and its obverse, luxury and weakness. In the

---

[20] Tlusty, "Martial Identity," 554. Aside from its ubiquitous functionality, the sword had a special mystique in chivalric culture; see Ralph Moffat, "Arms and Mormour," in Jones and Coss, *Chivalry*, 160–162.

[21] For the spur, the other element of arms at once essential and appropriated as a symbol of masculine authority and social rank, see Doda, "Spurs and Negotiations of Masculinity" in this volume.

[22] Castiglione, *The Book of the Courtier*, 27.

[23] Faret, *The Honest Man*, 24–26. I have modernized the spelling.

[24] Faret, *The Honest Man*, 359–360.

Figure 6.7. Claes Jansz. Visscher, "Ad pompam tantum." Illustration for Roemer Visscher, *Sinnepoppen*. Amsterdam 1614, p. 54. Rijksmuseum, Amsterdam.

emblem *Ad pompam tantum* ("Only for show"), Visscher writes "These young men strutting with plumes on their heads, silk clothing and gold chains around their necks, gilded swords by their side, are not men who exert their bravery in war, but are fit only to strum on a lute and sing, and to stand out in a procession like a figurine on a stick."[25] The illustration by Claes Jansz. Visscher (no relation) depicts a man in an exaggerated parody of the day's fashionable look (Fig. 6.7). He strolls gracefully in huge breeches, one arm akimbo, the other hand wrapped in a cloak and carrying a pair of gloves. A wavy plume adorns his hat, his pointed beard is perfectly shaped, and his thin waxed moustache curls up to his eyes.[26] Roemer Visscher refers to the sword as gilded, that is, for decoration, not combat. The man's slender sword is almost entirely hidden behind his ballooning breeches. Only the elegant hilt and a bit of the tip are visible.

The sword in tandem with a cloak, the unworn pair so often depicted in genre scenes, completed the outfit for a well-dressed man. Carrying a sword without a cloak could be especially inappropriate. (Half a century later, Samuel Pepys, whose social self-consciousness appears frequently in his diary, recounts an embarrassing episode when he left for an official business without his cloak and had to ask his servant to bring it from home; in the meantime, he hid in a corner.)[27] To carry a sword without a cloak when traveling in official/court circles where the etiquette stakes were high suggested a threat; thus the cloak subdued the sword and completed a gentleman's kit.

SWORDS IN PORTRAITS

In formal male portraiture, the sword – with or without a cloak – suggested qualities of boldness and prestige. Portraitists offered a repertory of sword-wearing: caressing the hilt; an authoritative arm-akimbo pose on the same or opposite side of the sword; keeping the sword at one's side and holding a staff. In half-length portraits, the sitter's torso might be shortened to show the elegant workmanship of handle and hilt. In one forceful instance, the Haarlem cloth merchant Willem van Heythuysen, painted by Frans Hals in 1625, poses outdoors, hand on hip, the other grasping his large, beautifully ornamented sword point downward (Fig. 6.8). Dressed in sumptuous black brocade, he has wrapped his cloak around his sword-bearing arm, while a cloth of honour is

---

[25] "Dese Jonckerkens die haer opproncken met Pluymagien op het hooft, gouden Ketens op zyden kleederen om den hals, vergulde Swaerden op de zyde, zijn de mannen niet die in het oorloogh de vroomheydt te wercke stellen, en zijnder oock niet nut toe: maer op een Luytken te slaen, een Musijckjen te singhen, dat past haer beter, en in een Processie uyt te munten als een Beeltjen op een stockjen." Visscher, "Ad pompam tantum," *Sinnepoppen*, III.32, 154. All translations from Dutch sources are mine.

[26] For the association of facial hair with masculine virtue, as well as style consciousness, see Simons, "Marked Differences" in this volume.

[27] Pepys, *Diary*, 3:241.

Figure 6.8. Frans Hals, *Portrait of Willem van Heythuysen* (1625). Alte Pinakothek, Munich. bpk Bildagentur / Bayerische Staatsgemäldesammlungen / Art Resource, NY.

draped behind him – a typical aristocratic prop for aspirational portraits. His pose echoes that of military men and monarchs; the portrait is full-length, which in former times would have been reserved for nobility. The sword itself, seeming to pierce the ground and casting a keen shadow, evokes a readiness to defend honour, while tamed by the folded cloak, rumpled drape, and spray of roses on the ground.

The unworn sword, pointed downward, is especially pervasive in emblems as a sign of brave tenacity at the ready. An emblem from *Sinnepoppen*, "Jussa fortiter meum est" (I must carry out my orders resolutely), features a sword, standing on end, being clamped in a vise to strengthen it.[28] Further, this sword-as-fortitude motif was also often featured in images of St Paul. Rembrandt, for example, depicted the saint writing in his prison cell, an old-fashioned longsword propped against the wall behind his bed (1657). It was not only the instrument of Paul's martyrdom, but it also refers to his use of military rhetoric. In his exhortations to live a Christian life he exhorts followers to "fight the good fight" (I Tim. 6:12) and "put on the armour" (Rom. 13:12). This element of fortitude was expressed in the seventeenth-century revival of the medieval Christian Knight theme. It is likely that van Heythuysen's imposing sword, pointed downward but ready to be taken up, embodies this concept.[29]

Unused swords sometimes appear in scenes of artists in their studios. These include portraits, self-portraits, and generalized allegorical images of artists. Such images were forms of professional self-promotion, articulating the glorification of painting and its elevation to intellectual status.[30] Painters depicted themselves, or artists in general, not only with objects that refer to the study of art, such as plaster casts and sheafs of paper, but also with instruments of learning, such as globes and books. Swords often appear as exotic props, like curved sabres, or varieties of modern swords. They hang on walls, with or without cloaks and gloves. In his image of a young painter at work (1655–1660), Barend Fabritius includes a sword and baldric, together with a pair of boots, hanging on the wall, next to an unframed portrait of a man (Fig. 6.9). The juxtaposition of these objects (boots were worn at court, and as military and riding gear) suggest the gentlemanly ideal to which the artist might aspire in his search for a career. Swords also rest in piles with other weapons and armour, evoking a military metaphor for figuring the artist. Writers on art such as Philips Angel and Samuel van Hoogstraten exhort the painter to marshal his skills as if on a battlefield.[31]

---

[28] Visscher, *Sinnepoppen*, I, 43.
[29] On the Christian Knight revival, and Hals's portrait, see Nevitt, *Art and the Culture of Love*, 173–182.
[30] See Dixon, *The Dark Side of Genius*, 123–142 on how artists represented themselves; 151–171 on artists' studios.
[31] On the piles of weaponry in artists' studios, see De Boer, "Martial Arts," 127.

Figure 6.9. Barend Fabritius, *Artist in the Studio* (1655–60). Musée du Louvre, Paris. © RMN-Grand Palais / Art Resource, NY.

Martha Hollander

REJECTING THE SWORD: CONTEMPLATION AND MELANCHOLY

The unused, unworn sword also appears in images of contemplation. Distinct in tone from the useless ornamental sword worn by Roemer Visscher's dandies, these weapons are set aside for intellectual or spiritual pursuits. Rembrandt's etched portrait of the cloth merchant and playwright Jan Six (1647) shows Six's intellectual life dominating, for the moment, over his other interests (Fig. 6.10). His hunting gear hangs on the wall, and his fashionable rapier, with its elegant spun hilt, rests on a table under a baldric.[32] These attributes of prestige and physical action are held in reserve during a sedentary interlude of reading. In an extraordinary detail, Six's fur-lined cloak has just fallen from his shoulders and rests on the sill, crumpled behind him; the other end partly covers his rapier. He barely notices, as if he could not wait to finish removing his public attire before settling down to read.[33]

English and European portraitists responded to the market for male meditative images throughout the century, influenced by the sixteenth-century cult of melancholy. Reflected in behaviour and dress, this mental state involved social withdrawal, intellectual pursuits, and pining for love, the obverse of physical and martial power. Rather than wearing their swords, as in more public portraits, men were depicted with their swords at rest, nearby, or lying conspicuously on the floor or in the grass. The roots of the fashionable melancholy type extend back to a portrait imagery disseminated at the English court. In Isaac Oliver's famous depiction, a young man leans against a tree with his ankles crossed in repose (Fig. 6.11). His sword hangs from a silver belt, but he refuses to touch it. Instead, he folds his arms, abdicating from action and response. His left forearm is encased in a sumptuous black glove, while the other glove rests next to him on the grass. In a similar mode – a man alone in nature, laying aside public accoutrements – Oliver's teacher Nicholas Hilliard created two recumbent portraits of Henry Percy, Earl of Northumberland, known for his scholarly and scientific pursuits. The earl lies on the grass, head on resting on his hand, his gloves beside him.[34] Like swords, gloves evoke the trappings of class and authority. Both are well-made luxury items, functional yet

---

[32] De Winkel refers to the rapier as a sign of status, given Six's membership in the civic militia; De Winkel, *Fashion and Fancy*, 98.

[33] Rembrandt's unusual portrait shows a rare moment of privacy, a new concept in Baroque life and thought. Smith, "I Janus," 50. On the melancholy aspects of Six's image, see Dixon, *The Dark Side of Genius*, 107–108.

[34] On melancholy portraiture at the English court, see Dixon, *The Dark Side of Genius*, 55–80; on the portraits by Oliver and Hilliard, see 64–65.

Figure 6.10. Rembrandt van Rijn, *Portrait of Jan Six* (1647). Metropolitan Museum, New York. Gift of Henry Walters, 1917.

Figure 6.11. Isaac Oliver, *A Young Man Seated Under a Tree* (c.1590–1595). Royal Collection Trust, London. Bridgeman Images.

Figure 6.12. Jan De Heem, *Interior of a Room with a Young Man Seated at a Table* (1628). Ashmolean Museum, Oxford. Bequeathed by Daisy Linda Ward, 1939. Image © Ashmolean Museum, University of Oxford.

Martha Hollander

essential for self-presentation. The removal of gloves, like that of swords, signals a retreat from agency and reputation.[35]

Jan de Heem's *Interior of a Room with a Young Man Seated at a Table* (1628) offers more a detailed narrative of withdrawal (Fig. 6.12). A young man sits at a table in a typical melancholic pose of head resting on hand. Books are piled on the table in artfully arranged chaos, along with his hat and cloak. On the wall behind him is a portrait of the German Protestant military leader Christian of Brunswick, who died in battle in 1626. Next to the picture is a coat of arms, half-covered by a bag. On the other side of the picture is a map and below it a rapier and baldric rest against a chest. On the other side of the doorway is a second sword: a cavalry sabre hanging up on the wall. All these material details suggest war, honour, reputation, self-sacrifice. Is Christian's image here meant to suggest determination in the face of defeat? The young man sits framed by the two swords, one for peacetime, one for war. At the edge of the table nearest to him is an unsealed letter. Perhaps a call to action? Whatever the message, he appears to turn away, for the moment.

Discarded swords can be attributes of the melancholy look, expressing a meditative state of retreat, a lack of aggression and resolve. It was a trope in literature as well as art. In his 1665 poem "Gedachten op Mijn Kamer" (Thoughts in my room), the Dutch poet Willem van Focquenbroch expresses the withdrawal from sword-wearing as a relief from the burdensome display of status. Observing the objects on a table in front of him, he writes:

> I look at the weapons at the side
> which show me my ancient nobility.
> I find myself free from those troubles
> that dwell always around the courts,
> and mock all that slavery.
> Or, as I see a picture before me
> of Charles, the old British King,
> I think it matters little;
> life is but show, where each plays his part.[36]

His reference to a picture of Charles I recalls Jan De Heem's young man facing away from his sword and the portrait of the war hero Christian of Brunswick.

---

[35] See Stallybrass and Jones, "Fetishizing the Glove," especially 119–123 on the aristocratic portrait tradition of discarded gloves.

[36] "Zie ik de wapens aan ter zy, / Die my myn ouden adel toonen, / Ik vind my van die zorgen vry, / Die steets omtrent de Hooven woonen, / En spot met al die slavery. / Of zie ik voor my op het beeld / Van Karel, d'oude Britsche Koning, / Zo dunkt my, dat het niet veel scheelt, / Of 't leven is maar een vertooning, / Daar ieder mensch zyn rol in speelt." [First published in *Thalia, of geurige sanggoddin*. Amsterdam: Johannes van den Bergh, 1665.] Focquenbroch, *Bloemlezing*, 23.

Mars Asleep: Discarded Swords in Seventeenth-Century Dutch Art

In Focquenbroch's poem, as in De Heem's picture – and Rembrandt's portrait of Jan Six – the discarding of a sword is displayed with the same rhetorical weight as the wearing of one.

CONCLUSION: AN IDEA OF MASCULINITY

The brooding or reading man who has laid aside his sword might express a tension evoked between the active and contemplative life.[37] In reality, however, a man was not meant to choose, except in the moment; the active and intellectual life were opposed only in allegorical terms. In fact, they were complimentary aspects of cultivated masculinity, as Rembrandt's aspirational portrait of Jan Six makes clear. The discourse on maintaining the gentlemanly ideal focuses on its diversity: a great range of skills and pursuits, from fighting and riding to scholarship, poetry, and love. Echoing Castiglione, Faret points out that "A gentleman should be a good horseman [...] he should know how to handle his weapon; [...] study the politics or the morals, or the mathematics [...] he should carefully read the best authors which have written of these goodly sciences, or that he should confer with learned men." If this impressive variety seem impossible, Faret reminds the reader "This is rather an Idea of that which is possible, than an example of a thing which is commonly seen."[38]

Not just manly pursuits and skills, but manly behaviour is likewise viewed as an assemblage of opposites. While Faret writes about attractive warlike men "all sunburnt, and covered with sweat and dust," Giovanni Della Casa remarks, "A noble man must not run in the street, nor hurry too much, for this is suitable for a groom and not for a gentleman. Besides, a man will tire himself out, sweat and pant for breath, all of which are unbecoming to men of quality. Nor, on the other hand, should one proceed as slowly or demurely as a woman or a bride does."[39]

This balance between appealing vigour and raucous excess, between restraint and feminizing modesty, requires careful cultivation and watchfulness. The persistence of the discarded-sword motif in Dutch art over the course of the seventeenth century mirrors the instability of ideal masculinity. The associations of a weapon as a sign of social rank, courage, skill, and action, essential both to self-defence and to the demands of civility, is remarkably diverse. In the examples offered here, the unworn, unused sword not only suggests a withdrawal from arms, but, in the balancing act of masculinity, the potential for taking up arms again. When men are depicted in moments

---

[37] On this interpretation of De Heem's picture, see Brown, *Art in Seventeenth-Century Holland*, Cat. 53, 50.

[38] Faret, *Honest Man*, 401–403.

[39] Della Casa, *Galateo*, 91.

of pleasure or meditation, the swords are discarded, but still strategically, artfully placed. Where men are absent, the swords are conspicuous signs of vigorous action, status, and honour that defined early modern masculinity. The sleeping Mars will soon awaken.

Hofstra University

CITED WORKS

Anglo, Sydney. *The Martial Arts of Renaissance Europe*. New Haven, CT: Yale University Press, 2000.
Boer, Lisa J. De. "Martial Arts: Military Themes and Images in Dutch Art of the Golden Age." PhD thesis, University of Michigan, 1996.
Brown, Christopher. *Art in Seventeenth Century Holland*. The National Gallery, 30th September to 12th December 1976; A Loan Exhibition. London: National Gallery, 1976.
Burton, Robert. *The Anatomy of Melancholy*. Ed. Holbrook Jackson. New York: New York Review of Books, 2001.
Castiglione, Baldassare. *The Book of the Courtier*. Trans. C. S. Singleton, ed. Daniel Javitch. New York: Norton, 2002.
Chapman, H. Perry. "Propagandist Prints, Reaffirming Paintings: Art and Community During the Twelve Years' Truce." In Arthur J. Wheelock Jr and Adele Seeff, eds, *The Public and Private in Dutch Culture of the Golden Age*. Newark, DE: University of Delaware Press, 2000, 43–63.
Della Casa, Giovanni. *Galateo. A Renaissance Treatise on Manners*. Ed. and trans. Konrad Eisenbichler and Kenneth R. Bartlett, 3rd edn, rev. Renaissance and Reformation Texts in Translation, 3. Toronto: Centre for Reformation and Renaissance Studies, 2009.
Dixon, Laurinda S. *The Dark Side of Genius: The Melancholic Persona in Art, ca. 1500–1700*. University Park, PA: Pennsylvania State University Press, 2013.
Doda, Hilary. "Spurs and Negotiations of Masculinity in Early Modern England." In Konrad Eisenbichler and Jacqueline Murray, eds, *Premodern Masculinities in Transition*. Woodbridge, UK: The Boydell Press, 2024.
Du Mortier, Bianca. "Costume in Frans Hals." In Seymour Slive and P. Biesboer, eds, *Frans Hals*. London: Royal Academy of Arts, 1989, 45–60.
Faret, Nicolas. *The Honest Man: or, The art to please in court. Written in French by Sieur Faret. Translated into English by E.G.* London: Printed by Thomas Harper, for Edward Blount, 1632.
Focquenbroch, Willem Godschalk van. *Focquenbroch. Bloemlezing uit zijn lyriek*. Ed. W. F. Hermans. Amsterdam: G. A. van Oorschot, 1946.
Franits, Wayne. *Dutch Seventeenth-Century Genre Painting: Its Stylistic and Thematic Evolution*. New Haven, CT: Yale University Press, 2004.

Mars Asleep: Discarded Swords in Seventeenth-Century Dutch Art

Jaquet, Daniel, "Introduction." In Karin Verelst and Timothy Dawson, eds, *Late Medieval and Early Modern Fight Books: Transmission and Tradition of Martial Arts in Europe (14th–17th Centuries)*. Leiden: Brill, 2016, 8–10.

Jones, Robert W. and Peter Coss. *A Companion to Chivalry*. Woodbridge, UK: The Boydell Press, 2019.

Hollander, Martha. "Adriaen van de Venne's Cavalier at a Dressing Table: Masculinity and Parody in 17th-century Holland." In Arthur J. Di Furia, ed., *New Perspectives in Early Modern Northern European Genre Imagery*. London: Routledge, 2016, 131–159.

——. "Vermeer's Robe: Costume, Commerce, and Fantasy in the Early Modern Netherlands." *Dutch Crossing* 35 (2011): 177–195.

Kettering, Alison M. "Gerard ter Borch's Military Men: Masculinity Transformed." In Arthur J. Wheelock Jr and Adele Seeff, eds, *The Public and Private in Dutch Culture of the Golden Age*. Newark, DE: University of Delaware Press, 2000, 100–119.

Kunzle, David. *From Criminal to Courtier: The Soldier in Netherlandish Art 1550–1672*. Leiden: Brill, 2002.

Muizelaar, Klaske and Derek Phillips, eds. *Picturing Men and Women in the Dutch Golden Age*. New Haven, CT: Yale University Press, 2003.

Nevitt, H. Rodney. *Art and the Culture of Love in Seventeenth-Century Holland*. Cambridge, UK: Cambridge University Press, 2003.

Pepys, Samuel. *Diary of Samuel Pepys*. Ed. Robert Latham and William G. Matthews. 10 vols. Berkeley, CA: University of California Press, 1970–1983.

Roberts, Benjamin. *Sex and Drugs before Rock 'n' Roll: Youth Culture and Masculinity during Holland's Golden Age*. Amsterdam: University of Amsterdam Press, 2012.

Roodenburg, Herman. *The Eloquence of the Body. Perspectives on Gesture in the Dutch Republic*. Zwolle: Waanders, 2005.

Rosen, Jochai. *Soldiers at Leisure: The Guardroom Scene in Dutch Genre Painting of the Golden Age*. Amsterdam: University of Amsterdam Press, 2011.

Rosenthal, Lisa. *Gender, Politics, and Allegory in the Art of Rubens*. Cambridge, UK: Cambridge University Press, 2005.

Simons, Patricia. "Marked Differences: The Beard in Renaissance Europe." In Konrad Eisenbichler and Jacqueline Murray, eds, *Premodern Masculinities in Transition*. Woodbridge, UK: The Boydell Press, 2024.

Smith, David R. "I Janus: Privacy and the Gentlemanly Ideal in Rembrandt's Portraits of Jan Six." *Art History* 11 (1988): 42–63.

Spierenburg, Peter. "Knife Fighting and Popular Codes of Honor in Early Modern Amsterdam." In Pieter Spierenburg, ed., *Men and Violence: Gender, Honor and Rituals in Modern Europe and America*. Columbus, OH: Ohio State University Press, 1998, 103–127.

Stallybrass, Peter and Ann Rosalind Jones. "Fetishizing the Glove in Renaissance Europe." *Critical Inquiry* 28:1 (2001): 114–132.

Tlusty, B. Ann. "Martial Identity and the Culture of the Sword in Early Modern Germany." In Daniel Jaquet, Karin Verelst and Timothy Dawson, eds, *Late Medieval and Early Modern Fight Books: Transmission and Tradition of Martial Arts in Europe (14th–17th Centuries)*. Leiden: Brill, 2016, 547–570.

Visscher, Roemer. *Sinnepoppen*. Amsterdam: Willem Jansz., 1614.

de Winkel, Marieke. *Fashion and Fancy: Dress and Meaning in Rembrandt's Paintings*. Amsterdam: Amsterdam University Press, 2006.

Woodall, Joanna. "Love is in the Air: *Amor* as Motivation and Message in Seventeenth-century Netherlandish Painting." *Art History* 19 (1996): 208–246.

TRANSFORMING MASCULINITIES

7

MILITARY MASCULINITIES IN
LA CHANSON DE BERTRAND DU GUESCLIN

Sarah Wilk

The lengthy *chanson de geste* that mythologizes the life of the French knight Bertrand du Guesclin (c. 1320–1380) sends a strong message about military masculinities and the kind of man who is worthy of praise. It comes as no surprise, then, that du Guesclin responds quite firmly against a charge of cowardice levelled against him when he advises Henry of Trastámara against engaging in the Battle of Nájera:

> Mais pour tant que parlé en avez ensement,
> Et ainssi reprouvé m'avez villainement,
> Foy que je doy a Dieu le divin sacrament,
> Demain leur liveroy bataille et content
> Et seroy le premier a mon commencement!
> La poura on veoir de moy le bon talent,
> Ne se je suis traïtres ne coars ensement.[1]
>
> (But since you have talked about it, / and so villainously reproach me, / by the faith in the divine sacrament which I owe God, / tomorrow I will give them battle and satisfaction / and I will be the first from my command! / Then you will see my good intentions, / that I am neither a traitor nor a coward either.)

Consistently loyal to whichever cause he was fighting for, the historical Bertrand du Guesclin very much earned his reputation and the rewards that came to him. The poem that commemorated and mythologized his life has a strong message about military masculinities that shows why he was so respected. His unwavering loyalty meant that he could act as he saw fit,

---

[1] Cuvelier, *Bertrand du Guesclin*, vv. 12,357–12,376. All translations from this work are mine, though a translation exists, Nigel Bryant's *The Song of Bertrand du Guesclin*. My thanks to Thomas V. Cohen and Dorothea Kullmann for their help with the tricky bits. Further verse references to this text will be incorporated parenthetically into the text.

even when his actions were questionable. This loyalty is part of the poem's argument: those who are consistently loyal are the worthiest of praise. This article explores more of the poem's arguments about military masculinities.[2]

The historical Bertrand du Guesclin (c. 1320–1380), a minor Breton noble, was one of the most famous of the French soldiers of his generation, valuable enough to be mythologized both in his lifetime and in subsequent centuries. He proved himself so useful that he served the last ten years of his life as Constable of France, a military position hitherto reserved for someone of the higher nobility. When the Hundred Years' War between England and France escalated after 1369, he managed to retake much of the territory lost to the English after the Battle of Poitiers (1356) and the subsequent Treaty of Brétigny (1360). He was captured for ransom twice, at the Battle of Auray in 1364 and the Battle of Nájera in 1367, which will be discussed below. He also won four battles where he was in command. When he died, he was buried in the tomb next to the kings of France at Saint-Deny until it was destroyed during the French Revolution. His heart was interred at Saint-Sauveur at Dinan, in Brittany. Given his career and the respect given after his death, it is a natural consequence that his life would be used as a political argument in favour of the French crown and its interests.

The main source for du Guesclin's life, the *Chanson*, is a puzzling work in many ways. It was commissioned anonymously around 1380, when du Guesclin died. The poet is Cuvelier, about whom nothing is known besides this poetic work. The poem survives in nine manuscripts. The 1990 edition by Jean-Claude Faucon is just over 24,345 lines long;[3] for comparison, the eleventh-century *Chanson de Roland* (*Song of Roland*) is about 4,000 lines long. The comparison with Roland is significant, because there are references to Roland, among other heroes of the *chanson de geste* genre peppered throughout the work. The poem also makes an argument for making du Guesclin a Tenth Worthy, that is, another archetype of chivalry and knighthood.[4] Besides the nine poem manuscripts, two versions of a prose version of the *Chanson* have survived as well.[5]

---

[2] For more about the influence of military masculinities in a later period in France, see Lukas, "From the Knightly Bayard," in this volume.

[3] Faucon's edition includes a lengthy discussion of who Cuvelier might be.

[4] The Nine Worthies include three pagans: Hector, Alexander the Great, and Julius Caesar; three Jews: Joshua, David, Judah Maccabee; three Christians: King Arthur, Charlemagne, Godfrey of Bouillon. See Vernier, *The Flower of Chivalry*, for more about the mythologizing of Bertrand both in his lifetime and through this poem.

[5] Jones, in *An Introduction to the Chansons de Geste*, 137–141, explains that prose versions of *chansons de geste* were part of a trend that saw almost half of surviving Old French verse reworked into prose by the end of the Middle Ages. This trend was a reflection of changing tastes, as well as the perception that verse was more truthful.

Military Masculinities in La Chanson de Bertrand du Guesclin

There has been speculation as to the purpose of this poem. Some scholars hold that this is a very political work. Yvonne Vermijn, for example, argues that the poem could have been written for the French royal court, which in 1380–1385 was experiencing some turmoil after the death of King Charles V.[6] She also argues that Cuvelier manipulated du Guesclin's importance and influence because the point was not to write historical truth as we understand it, but rather to emphasize the moral truth (*la vérité morale*).[7] The "moral truth" that this poem shows, is that loyalty to a larger cause is more important than individual actions. This theory makes sense in conjunction with military masculinities; a political poem needs a steady hero who is a good example. But in this *Chanson*, the idolization of du Guesclin must refract blunders and setbacks and reflect them back to the reader as positives.

Alongside its political message, this poem has much to say about gender, particularly military masculinities. An examination of how the poem constructs the masculinities of military men, both positive and negative, reveals that the poem is showing its audience that military men can be a positive example of masculinity, provided they are motivated by loyalty. A man who is consistently loyal to a larger cause has the freedom to pursue his internal motivations for wealth or honour. This means that antagonists can be praised when they display the traits commonly associated with knighthood, such as honesty, loyalty, or generosity. However, it is also possible for protagonists to have those traits and lose, or get captured, or die, and still be seen as a positive example of military masculinity. Du Guesclin is therefore portrayed positively even when his individual actions were unsuccessful or not what we would consider moral.

The poem's account of the Nájera campaign shows the complexity of its title character. In this middle section of the poem du Guesclin's story includes failure, which makes the author's use of him as a shining example of knighthood as well as a propaganda tool for the kings of France all the more interesting. The poem does not demand perfection from its main character, possibly because it was written so soon after his death that Cuvelier could not stray too far from history.

As Judith Butler argued in *Gender Trouble*, gender is a performance, and that was the case in the Middle Ages as well.[8] For military men, this meant competence at violence.[9] Conversation with older, experienced men was a way boys learned expected behaviour, while literature, whether read or heard,

---

6   Vermijn, "«De quoy juqu'a mille ans bien parlé en sera»," 34, 36–40.
7   Vermijn, "«De quoy juqu'a mille ans bien parlé en sera»," 55.
8   Butler, *Gender Trouble: Feminism and the Subversion of Identity*.
9   See Braudy in *From Chivalry to Terrorism*, 56–62, Bourdieu, *La Domination Masculine*, or Karras, *From Boys to Men*. For more about competence as a masculine ideal, see Cohen, "Masculine Competence," this volume. For more about the inverse, where "effeminate" men are portrayed as failed military men and so

could reinforce behaviour and emotional expression.[10] Both performance and violence as tools to impress certain values are present in this *Chanson*. Violence, in this poem, can include verbal threats and shaming along with physical violence or theft. What this poem does is frame such violence as a positive trait when it is used in a way that supports Cuvelier's intentions. The main positive example is, of course, the character of du Guesclin. Du Guesclin the man and du Guesclin the character both had setbacks, such as being captured and ransomed. Neither the man, nor his poetic representative conducted himself consistently as an ideal of knighthood. The poem leans into this imperfection and does not expect either protagonists or antagonists to be the epitome of what they represent. Briefly put, the characters are human.

THE POEM

Everything about this poem serves its political purpose. The work is a mix of panegyric for du Guesclin and propaganda for both King Charles V of France and his ally Henry of Trastámara. For reasons scholars can only guess, Cuvelier chose to write his poem in the style of earlier *chansons de geste*, which had somewhat fallen out of fashion by this period.[11] In spite of this, it somewhat defies the genre. First, the title character is a Breton and, as has been noted by Robert Levine, "When they appear in *chansons de geste*, Bretons are typically gluttons, buffoons, boasters, and cowards."[12] Levine argues throughout that the marriage of a Breton protagonist in a genre of poetry that historically had favoured the French was a deliberate decision intended to stimulate cohesion in French-controlled territories in the face of continuing conflict with England. If this is so, then it was certainly fortunate that du Guesclin's life followed such a useful trajectory. Second, the great length of the poem, six times longer than the *Chanson de Roland*, suggests that it was not meant to be sung in front of an audience.

This long poem has a complex structure. It has three parts, representing different, important periods of du Guesclin's career. The first 7,000 lines are about his childhood and his military exploits in Brittany and Normandy. The second, about his involvement in the Castilian Civil War, comprises about 10,000 lines. The third, about du Guesclin's turn as Constable of France up until his death in 1380, is 6,000 lines long. The plurality of du Guesclin's character's actions and loyalties is on display in the second section. He is a knight, but also a soldier for hire. The poem depicts him as a flawed, but

---

unlike militant Roman or "chivalric" men, see Milligan, "The Effeminate Man," also in this volume.
[10] See Andrew Taylor, "Chivalric Conversation and the Denial of Male Fear" and Craig Taylor, "Military Courage and Fear."
[11] For more information, see Levine, "Myth and Antimyth," 262–266.
[12] Levine, "Myth and Antimyth," 262.

fundamentally good man. He is loyal to his king and to his men. He provides good advice when asked and is harsh against those the poet believes deserve it. He does his utmost in the pursuit of his goals, even when his actions have a negative impact on others. His character is used to show a positive portrayal of someone who made a successful living through war.

However, regarding the Castilian Civil War, Cuvelier had to work to apologise for du Guesclin's failings. Rather than gloss over blunders and questionable behaviour, he rewrote those instances to argue that they were understandable in the circumstances.

FROM THE SPANISH ADVENTURE TO THE BATTLE OF NÁJERA (1367)

The Castilian Civil War (1351–1369) that forms the background to this section was fought between two sons of King Alfonso XI of Castile, When, in 1350, the king died, his legitimate son, Pedro (the Cruel, according to his detractors; the Just to his supporters), succeeded him. His half brother, Henry of Trastámara (the Fratricidal, if one favours Pedro), wanted the throne for himself. One reason Henry's claim gained support was because of Pedro's attempts to assert Crown authority. Another was Pedro's perceived reliance upon the Jews and Muslims in his court. For these reasons, Henry was able to gather enough support to be crowned king. Pedro had an existing alliance with England, Navarre, Majorca, and Granada, while Henry found aid from France and Aragon. In 1366, Henry successfully captured Burgos, where kings of Castile were traditionally crowned, and forced Pedro to flee. Pedro travelled to English-controlled territory in France to petition Prince Edward for aid. Together, they forced Henry to retreat to France in 1367, a result of the Battle of Nájera. This victory was short-lived, however. Not long after the battle, Edward also returned to France after Pedro reneged on his promise of payment. Henry was able to secure more help from France in return for a fleet of ships, and returned to Castile in 1369. The final battle of the conflict, the Battle of Campo de Montiel, gave victory to Henry who, after killing Pedro, ruled Castile.

The corresponding section of the poem opens with du Guesclin hiring the Great Company (*Grande Compaignie*) and threatening the pope at Avignon for funding. Pedro the Cruel struck an alliance with Edward, Prince of Wales (The Black Prince). Armies starved, and levies proved they were not as trustworthy as professionals. Since the poem is propaganda, it follows that the justifications Cuvelier raises for Henry's coup are suitably dramatic. At the beginning of the Spanish Adventure portion of the poem, starting at line 7,479 in the Faucon edition, he explains that King Pedro's wickedness was threefold. The first problem was that he was seduced away from his flawless wife, Blanche, sister of the queen of France, by means of herbs and potions (*par herbe, par venin*) administered by Juana de Castro, Pedro's mistress and later wife, daughter of the Galician noble, Pedro Fernández de Castro. Potions aside, historically, Pedro lived with Juana openly, while Blanche was a virtual prisoner and died under mysterious circumstances.[13] In the poem, Blanche sent a wealthy Jew away in disgust after he paid homage to her, which led Pedro to believe that Blanche was against him and everyone he favoured. In retaliation, Pedro had a group of Jews enter Blanche's castle and smother her in her bed, but publicly denounced the murder (vv. 7,900–7,954). Historically, Blanche's death was more mysterious and contributed to the eventual diplomatic separation of France and Castile when Pedro made an alliance with England in 1362. The second problem with Pedro suggested in the poem was that he was too trusting of the Jews in Castile, to the point of loving the Jews more than the Christians:

> or avoit de Coustume Pietre qu'il se fia
> Aus Juïfs de sa terre, et trop plus les ama
> Au'il ne fist Crestiens (vv. 7,516–7,519)
>
> (it was Pedro's custom to trust / the Jews of his land, and love them too much / more than the Christians)

The third problem the poem identifies is a falsehood: that Pedro was younger than Henry and illegitimate, while Henry legitimate. Henry was, in fact, older than Pedro, but there is no doubt that he was the fourth of Alfonso XI's ten illegitimate children by his mistress, Eleanor de Guzmán.[14] The poem tells the story that another wealthy Jew, enraged at Blanche's death, asked to be converted and then told his story, saying that Henry's mother and father were married, and after his mother died, Alfonso's new wife only had daughters. The unnamed convert claimed that Alfonso threatened to love his new wife no longer if her fourth child was another daughter so, when her baby turned out to be another girl, she sent for a Jewish baby boy to replace her. That baby was Pedro (vv. 7,954–8,017).

All this shows that the poem did not shy away from invention when selling its audience on Henry of Trastámara as a legitimate alternative to the wicked Pedro. The poem also claimed that Henry was the legitimate son of Alfonso XI and Pedro was the bastard, alleging that Henry's mother had married Alfonso before Pedro's mother, which was untrue. This, in conjunction with the aforementioned changeling story, is how the poem attempts to convince its audience that there is no choice but to support Henry (vv. 7,983–8,024).

After the Treaty of Brétigny (1360), which temporarily re-established peace between England and France, another military problem faced France: a mix

---

[13] Vernier, *The Flower of Chivalry*, 84.
[14] Cuvelier, *Song of Bertrand*, 154.

of unemployed mercenaries from England, Scotland, Brittany, Normandy, and Hainault had banded together and was roaming the countryside, stealing and burning crops, and demanding payment in return for protection. There were several attempts to lead them out of France, but only du Guesclin succeeded, partly because he secured funding from both the pope and the kings of France and Aragon.[15] With funding came support and planning, and soon thereafter an army for Henry of Trastámara.

A problem with the Great Company marching off to Castile was that a significant portion of the soldiers were English, or allied with the English, and at this time, England's King Edward III was allied with Pedro. Edward III decreed that English soldiers should not join du Guesclin and Henry, but the decree came after his son, Prince Edward, who was ruling Aquitaine at the time, granted the Great Company permission to cross his territory on the way to Castile.

There are two important points to highlight in the poem's discussion of du Guesclin's hiring of the Great Company. The first is the explanation for why the unemployed mercenaries wanted to stay in France and fight for themselves:

> Par le paÿs aloyent prendre leur mencion,
> Et prenoient par tout leur gent a raançon.
> .XXX. capitaines trouver y peüst on,
> Voire touz les plus grans,
> d'autres y ot foison.
> Chevaliers, escuiers y avoit, se dit on,
> Qui de France essilier orent devocion
> [...]
> Tout pillart, traïteur, mordreour et larron. (vv. 8,109–8,116)

> (They roamed the country, plundering everywhere / and seizing people for ransom. / There were thirty captains seen leading them, / who were the mightiest, / with a host of others. / Knights and squires all bent on ruining France / [...] They were all looters, traitors, murderers, and thieves).

The poem continues, explaining why these men were roaming and behaving poorly:

> La en y ot de liez, s'en y ot de dolans,
> Car il y ot assez pilars et faulx tirans,
> Qui n'avoient pitié de fenme ne d'enfans,
> Ne des maisons ardoir nyent plus que mescreans.
> S'y avoit des bastars et d'autres mescheans,
> Qui redoubtoient moult et peines et ahans,/

---

[15] Fowler, *Medieval Mercenaries*, 143.

Sarah Wilk

> Des montaignes monter et les <u>fiers</u> desrivans,
> Car li pays de France est beaux et deduisans,
> S'y a bonnes viands et des bons vins frians. (vv. 8,329–8,340)

> (Some of them were happy, others were unhappy, / because a lot were thieves and false torturers, / who had no more pity than infidels for women nor children, / or for burning down their houses. / Some were bastards and others were wicked, / who greatly dreaded toil and suffering, / or climbing mountains and steep cliffs, / because the land of France is beautiful and pleasant,/ there is good food and good delicious wines).

Cuvelier describes the unemployed mercenaries: the destruction of France; the dread of toil and suffering. Namely, they were enriching themselves because they did not have to travel far or suffer much because France was lovely and relatively easy pickings. These men's acts of violence were not in service of their king's goals, so it was negative, and therefore they could justifiably be named looters, murderers, traitors, and thieves.

In the poem, du Guesclin rides to meet the Great Company where they are staying at a house they had captured and offers to make everyone there rich if they would join him. One of the leaders, the English Hugh Calveley (an important character in this part of the poem, also based on a real person) agrees on behalf of the Company, but with an important caveat:

> Tres bonne compaignie li miens corps vous fera
> En toutes les manieres que fere on le pourra!
> Et yray tout par tout ou aler vous plaira,
> Guerrier tout le monde et deça et dela,
> Fors le prince de Gales; mais ja ne m'avenra
> Que soye contre lui, car, si tost qu'il vorrea,
> G'iray avecques lui, juré lui ay pieça. (vv. 8,225–8,233)

> (My soldiers will be very good companions to you / as much as we are able / And will go anywhere or wherever you wish to go, / to fight anyone in the world on either side of the mountains, / except the Prince of Wales; but it will never come about / that I should be against him, because, as soon as he wished, / I would go with him, I have already sworn to him).

This point is reiterated several times while the English are fighting for du Guesclin. Because Calveley was forthright and insistent about this potential conflict of interest, the poem portrays him in a positive way. He is happy to take employment, but his clarity about where his loyalties ultimately lie shows that he is in possession of the prized traits of loyalty and honesty.

Military Masculinities in La Chanson de Bertrand du Guesclin

Not everyone in the Great Company is pleased about joining du Guesclin. Despite Calveley's enthusiasm for du Guesclin's venture, some in the company needed coaxing. Du Guesclin was able to persuade those who would have preferred to continue taking advantage of that part of France's nice weather and good wine by underscoring their crimes:

> Efforciees les dames et arses leurs maisons,
> Honmes, enfans occis et mis a raançons,
> Conment mengiet avons vaches, brebis, moutons;
> Conment avons pillet oyes, poucins, chappons,
> Et beü les bons vins, faiz les occisions,
> Eglises violees et les religions" (vv. 8,291–8,298)

> (We have violated ladies and burned their homes, / killing men, infants, and putting them to ransom, / how we have eaten cows, ewes and rams, / pillaged geese, chickens, capons, / and drank good wines, committed killings, / violating churches and monasteries.)

Du Guesclin includes himself in this list of crimes. The poem does not show him actively participating in these crimes, but his alignment with the men under his command is consistent throughout the poem and is consistent with what the historical du Guesclin wrote about those under his leadership.[16] By agreeing to use their violence in service of a larger goal, these murderers and thieves become better men. The construction of masculinities is fluid.

What persuaded the Great Company was du Guesclin's comparison to other men:

> Nous avons fait trop pis que ne font les larrons;
> Les larrons vont emblant, c'est pour leur enfançons,
> Pour vivre, car qui est de povreté semons
> A peine puet il ester en cest siècle preudons;
> Pis valons que larrons, que les gens murdrissons. (vv. 8,299–8,303)

> (We have committed crimes worse than thieves; / when thieves steal, it is for their children, / to live, because he who is living in poverty / is hardly able to be a worthy man in this day and age; / we are worth less than thieves, than murderers.)

Again, thieves might be thieves, but their need to keep their children alive makes them better than soldiers who steal and murder for no purpose other than to enrich themselves. Again, violence that is in service of one's family, in this case, is justified and positive. The portrayal of this violence depends also

---

[16] See Jones, *Letters, Orders and Musters of Bertrand du Guesclin*, for examples.

on how other men perceive it. When a larger, external goal is visible, violence is permissible.

The Great Company have a purpose, but it still needs funding. The pope at Avignon (Urban V, r. 1362–1370) had both money and absolution. This is an instance where du Guesclin does not entirely act with honour, but the poem excuses it with anticlerical sentiment. The pope, "sitting in his mighty state" (*moult ot seignorie*), worries about the large army that has shown up on his doorstep, and sends a cardinal out to see what the soldiers want. The cardinal, understandably, is nervous to talk with the soldiers, and

> s'en tost et hasteement,
> bienvoulsist qu'il eüst acompli son talant
> Et qu'il fust revenus a son conmandement;
> Mieulx amast a chanter sa messe haultement" (vv. 8,487–8,490)

> (was quick and hasty / to wish he had accomplished his task / and that he had returned to his job; / he much preferred to sing his high mass.)

The cardinal is told that the Great Company is there to receive absolution for their sins as well as the sum of 200,000 francs. The cardinal agrees to absolution but is not convinced to provide funding. Du Guesclin argues that the money is necessary, pointing out that many of the soldiers in the Great Company are not the epitome of knighthood:

> Car je vous di pour vray qu'il en y a granment
> qui d'absolucion ne parollent noyent;
> Il ameroient mieulx a avoir de l'argent;
> nous les menons tretouz en droit essilement. (vv. 8,561–8,565)

> (I tell you that there are lots of them / who say not a word of absolution; / they would much rather have the money; / we are leading the traitors into appropriate exile.)

Du Guesclin might have convinced the Great Company to follow him to Castile, but that hardly meant that the soldiers' taste for plunder and coin was transformed. The exchange shows that while du Guesclin is portrayed as gathering this army for a practical purpose, he did not expect the same of everyone else. Nor does he shy away from pointing out that fact when it could secure papal funding.

With a last parting shot from Bertrand that he could not promise to keep all the soldiers in line, the cardinal returns to the pope with the soldiers' demands. The pope is willing to grant absolution to the Great Company but is much less enthusiastic about paying the army to leave. At this point Cuvelier displays more anticlerical opinions, accusing the papacy of hoarding treasure when the pope, "in his well-paved palace" (*en son palays pavé*), exclaims that

Military Masculinities in La Chanson de Bertrand du Guesclin

"They are trying hard to go to hell" (*Pour aler en infe se sont forment pené*; vv. 8,646–8,648).

Ultimately, the pope agrees to pay the sum, but took the funds from the citizens of Avignon rather than from his own treasury (vv. 8,628–8,629). Cuvelier seizes the opportunity to show off how his du Guesclin displays the virtue of generosity by refusing to take money that was not from the pope's treasury, saying,

> Amis, ce dist Bertran, au pape me direz
> que ses grans tresors soit ouvers et deffremez.
> A ceulx qui payé l'ont, il leur soit restorez,
> Et dictes que jamais n'en soit nulz reculez
> Car se je le savoye, ja n'en soiez doubtez
> Et fuisse oultre la mer bien passez et alez
> Je m'en seroye ainçois par deça retournez
> Que li papes n'en feust corrociez et yrez. (vv. 8,695–8,702)

> ('Friends', said Bertrand, tell the pope / that his great treasury be opened and unlocked; / to those who have paid it, it should be restored; / and say that never shall anyone be refused. / For if I were to know it, have no doubt about it, / even if I had crossed the sea and were gone far away, / I would be back here from afar sooner / than the pope could be angry and cross about it.)

It is not just anyone who can threaten to turn a boat around if the pope is angry about having to return money. Though faced with a literal external motivation of an army on his doorstep, the pope is internally motivated to keep his treasury full when he chooses to tax the rich citizens people of Avignon rather than pay off the Great Company himself. This is why, though threatening a pope and a cardinal is certainly not best behaviour, the pope's greed makes du Guesclin's actions justified. Vermijn argues that Cuvelier was defending the nobility's exemption from taxes as long as they used funds they received from the Crown to defend their land. The pope was shirking his duty by taxing the rich folk of Avignon to pay off the Great Company rather than use this fund.[17] Another possibility is that, given the references to the cardinal preferring to sing his high mass, or the pope's nicely paved palace, the poem's point was that the pope had the funds to pay off the army without taking it from others.

After the shakedown, the Great Company marches to Castile and joins Henry of Trastámara. The poem relates how the Great Company learned of Pedro's wicked ways, and how Pedro, learning of this new threat to his rule, flees to Burgos. Henry, du Guesclin, and their army make their way towards

---

[17] Vermijn, "«De quoy juqu'a mille ans bien parlé en sera»," 87–88.

Burgos, stopping to lay siege to towns like Briviesca and Borja that refused to open their gates to Henry out of fear of Pedro's revenge. In the poem, Henry and du Guesclin are able to take Burgos without a fight because the leaders of the Christians, Jews, and Muslims in the city all agreed that Pedro had deserted them, and so it is fitting for them to accept Henry as their king. Henry is crowned at Burgos on 5 April 1366. At this point Pedro flees Castile to seek help. Du Guesclin is rewarded for his aid and is granted Henry's home county of Trastámara, as well as the title of King of Granada. Granada, of course, was still under Muslim rule at the time (the Nasrids) so the title was just a title, not a reality.[18]

At this point in the poem, Prince Edward (the Black Prince), becomes another main character. Both historically, and in the poem, Edward was in Aquitaine enjoying some of the benefits of having captured the French king Jean II at the Battle of Poitiers (1356). Although England and Castile were allied, Edward did not stop du Guesclin and his forces from crossing his territory. King Edward III sent word that no English should join du Guesclin, but this missive arrived after the companies had left. It was a gesture toward the treaty.[19] Pedro had to see Prince Edward himself to get his English allies to help him.

In the poem, Pedro stops to stay with the king of Portugal on his way to see Prince Edward, and the king advises him that he should promise whatever it takes to reverse the shame of having lost his kingdom in the first place. The king also says that:

> Li princes est si grans et si fiers chevalier
> Et tant a a despendre et de terre a baillier
> Qu'il ne doubt nul honme, conte, duc ne princier,
> Roy ne empereour ou c'on puist chevauchier. (vv. 10,806–10,809)

> (The prince is a great and proud knight / and has so much to spend and so much land to grant / that he fears no man, count, duke, nor prince, / king, nor emperor where one can go campaigning.)

Cuvelier is perhaps implying that there was almost no price too steep and that it would take a large payment to persuade someone who already had so much. Meanwhile, Henry is reminded again that the English soldiers in his army would leave him if Prince Edward decides to fight, though they agreed to stay with Henry until it is known what the Prince is going to do (vv. 11,241–11,259). Continuing his vilification of Pedro, Cuvelier has Pedro show Prince Edward more deference "than he would show God in heaven" ("Qu'il ne l'eüst pas fait a Dieu de paradis"; v. 11,540).

---

[18] Jones, *Letters, Orders and Musters*, 56.
[19] Sumption, *The Hundred Years War*, 2:544.

Military Masculinities in La Chanson de Bertrand du Guesclin

Since Prince Edward was alive at the time the poem was written, he would have been known to the audience. As a result, Cuvelier does not portray him as an antagonist, but rather as someone who possesses many of the qualities prized in military men, though his major flaw, pride, caused his illness and death. This is all exemplified in how Edward was served at his court:

> Dont aportent le vin li chevalier <u>loé</u>,
> Car li princes estoit de telle auttorité
> Que nulz ne le servoit de vin ne de <u>claré</u>
> Ne d'espice ensement ne d'autres biends planté,
> S'il n'estoit chevaliers a esperon doré,
> Tant estoit ourguilleux et de grand fierté,
> Ne il ne doubtoit honme tant eüst poesté;
> Tant par l'avoit orgueil esprins et alumé!
> Le plus grant se tenoit de la crestienté
> [...]
> Et par son grant orgueil qui l'avoit enchanté
> Perdi vie et honneur et sa noble duchié. (vv. 11,604–11,619)

> (The knights brought him wine / because the prince was of such authority / that nobody served him wine nor claret, / nor spicy dishes nor meat in plenty, / if he was not a knight with golden spurs. / Such was his pride and great power. / He feared no man, no matter how strong; / so much was he fired and lit with pride! / He thinks himself the greatest in Christendom / [...] and because of the great pride which had bewitched him / he lost his life and honour and his noble duchy).

Edward reaped the benefits of his competence at war and had many prized qualities, but his pride is why he suffered his disastrous victory at Nájera. Edward may have won the battle, but he contracted the illness which that would kill him on this campaign, and Pedro reneged on his promises of payment. In Cuvelier's view, Edward was someone who allowed his success to go to his head and therefore was not as good a model of military masculinities as du Guesclin.

Both in the poem and historically, Edward agreed to aid Pedro. In return, he was offered Viscaya, which would be annexed into Aquitaine, as well as reimbursement for the entire cost of the expedition. Pedro had to have been either reasonably certain of success, or desperate.[20] The English and Gascon soldiers who had been with Henry were recalled. To prevent this army from returning to Castile, Henry made a deal with Charles of Navarre, who controlled the pass through the Pyrenees. Unfortunately for him, Edward and Pedro had previously made their own deal with Charles, so their army

---

[20] Sumption, *Hundred Years War*, 2:545. See Sumption for more details.

was able to return.[21] Edward and Pedro made their way toward Burgos, but because Edward was unfamiliar with the territory his army soon ran out of provisions. On 1 April 1367, the Prince and his army camped by the town of Logroño, while Henry and his army shadowed them and camped by the town of Nájera, both near the River Najerilla. Henry's French captains suggested starving out Edward and Pedro, but Henry's hand was forced because his political position was not steady. Many towns had elected to help Edward and Pedro. Elsewhere, rebellions against Henry were rising. Henry simply lacked the time to wait for the opposing army to retreat or starve.[22]

At this point the poem once again goes into detail describing the skirmishes and jostling for position between the armies. While it makes for a good story, it is, of course, not an entirely reliable account of what happened. When it came to the question of whether to starve out the enemy or fight, Cuvelier shows that action is better than waiting, when the count of Armagnac advises Edward to push for a battle: "Let our people be fully armed tomorrow, and so we shall fight the rebels because it is better enough to die by the sword than to die of hunger like a deranged beast" ("Car il vault miex assez de mourir par espee / Au'ainsi mourir de fain conme beste dervee"; vv. 12,309–12,310). Prince Edward takes this advice and prepares his army for battle. Henry's army heard about their oppositions' dearth of supplies, and du Guesclin suggested that, since hunger would prompt action, it would be better for Henry to refuse to fight and wait for Edward and Pedro to retreat. Another advisor to Henry, the count of Denia, accuses du Guesclin of cowardice:

> "Or voy certainement
> C'on vous tient a hardi; mais c'est bien pour noient
> Car vous avez paour, je le voy clerement,
> Ou vous amés du roy bien pou l'avancement.
> Ja avons nous eü l'estreine richement
> De quoy li autre sont esbahi duramen.
> Qui croire me voura, j'en diray mon talent,
> Bataille liverons bien et hardiement."
> Dist Bertran de Glaiquin: "Par le mien seirement!
> Se demain conbatons, je vous dy vroiement,
> Nous serons desconfi trestout entirement
> Et seray mort ou prins, par le mien sairement!
> Grant mischief avenra sur le roy et sa gent.
> Mais pour tant que parlé en avez ensement,
> Et ainssi reprouvé m'avez villainement,
> Foy que je doy a Dieu le divin sacrament,

---

[21] Sumption, *Hundred Years War*, 2:548–549.
[22] Sumption, *Hundred Years War*, 2:550–554.

Military Masculinities in La Chanson de Bertrand du Guesclin

> Demain leur liveroy bataille et content
> Et seroy le premier a mon commencement!
> La poura on veoir de moy le bon talent,
> Ne se je suis traïtres ne coars ensement. (vv. 12,357–12,376)

("Now see that we certainly / believe you brave; but it really is for nothing / because you are afraid, I see that clearly, / or you have little care for the king's advancement. / Even if we have rich gifts / about which the others are dreadfully astonished, / who will believe me, I will say my desire, / let us fight well and boldly." / Bertrand du Guesclin said: "By my oath! / If we fight tomorrow, I tell you truly, / we will all be completely defeated, / and I will be dead or taken prisoner, upon my oath! / Great harm will come to the king and his people. / But since you have talked about it, / and so reproach me villainously, / by the faith in the divine sacrament which I owe to God, / tomorrow I will give them battle and satisfaction / and I will be the first from my command! / Then you will see my good intentions, / that I am neither a traitor nor a coward either.)

Not only does du Guesclin have to defend himself against cowardice, but he also must prove that he is not a traitor in advising against battle. Perhaps Cuvelier wanted to absolve du Guesclin from the defeat that followed. The spectre of shame in the eyes of other men is an instigator. It is also a consequence of the notion that dying in battle is better than waiting to starve. Once such a charge has been leveled, the only way to dispel it is action. In both history and the poem, in the aftermath of Nájera, Henry fled, du Guesclin was captured, and many of those who could not fetch a good ransom died.[23]

Cuvelier included both the realities of war and the pageantry. Pedro and Prince Edward contend with some of the realities of moving a large force through (for Edward) unknown territory, with dwindling supplies. However, that does not stop Cuvelier from indulging in describing the pageantry of an army on the march. After the troops were rallied with the encouragement that they would have to fight for their dinner, Cuvelier then offers this comparison:

> Ains ne fu si bel ost puis le temps Pharaon
> Qu'en Egite chassa l'Israel nassion.
> La peüsiez veïr moult noble establisson,
> Bennieres ventelans et maint doré pennon;
> Les lances en leur oins et au col de blazon,

---

[23] Sumption, *Hundred Years War*, 2:555. "There could hardly have been a better illustration of how developed the hunt for prisoners had become in fourteenth-century warfare than the scale of the slaughter at Nájera combined with the almost complete survival of the rich and ransomable."

> Les hïaumes ou chief plus luisans que coton,
> Et tiennent leur aroy aussi fier que lion. (vv, 12,447–12,453)

> (There had not been such a beautiful host since the time of the Pharaoh, / who had chased the Israelite nation from Egypt. / There could you see a very noble array, / fluttering banners and many a golden pennon; / lances in their hands and shields around their necks, / the helmets on heads shining brighter than cotton, / and held their formation as fierce as a lion.)

The comparison of Pedro and the Prince to the biblical Pharaoh is another sly way for Cuvelier to suggest that Henry and du Guesclin's cause was the just one. Like the Israelites, Henry has God on his side. Transparent as the comparison may be, the pageantry also shows another side to war – it sidesteps the hardship and turns instead to a collective lack of fear when a crowd of armed men come together united against their enemy.

On the other side of the battlefield, du Guesclin expresses doubt in the resolve of his own Spaniards, saying to his men that he has no more faith in them than in "flying birds" (*oysel volant*; v. 12,074). This sentiment ties into Bertrand's advice to wait for Pedro and the English to starve. It was one of the realities of war that those who were not professionals like du Guesclin and his men might not have the same resolve. In the lead-up to the battle, du Guesclin warns both Henry and his own men many times against the Spanish resolve saying that "it will be a shame to see them flee" ("Ce sera grant domnaige quant tel gent s'en furia"; v. 12,623). Later, in his pre-battle speech to the troops Henry declares that:

> Je vous dy en convent, sur Dieu le tout puissant,
> Que se vous estes prins, mate et recreant
> Touz pendre vous feroy, ja n'y aurés garant,
> Chascun sera pendu a loy de soudoiant;
> Il ne vous demoura ne fenme ne enfant. (vv. 12,624–12,628)

> (I promise you, by Almighty God, / that if you are taken prisoner, defeated and vanquished, / he [Pedro][will hang you all, you can be sure of it. / Each will be hanged according to the law of traitors; / you will retain neither women nor children.)

Following Henry's words to his troops, Bertrand tells his own men:

> Seigneurs [...] alés moy escoutant:
> Tenons nous touz ensemble et n'alons departant.
> Avec ses Espaignolz ne vous alez boutant,
> Cair ilz sont une gent ou ne me vois fiant. (vv. 12,645–12,649)

> (Sirs [...] Listen to what I say: / let us all stand together and not fall

apart. / Do not chase the Spanish, / because they are a people whom I would not trust.)

Their warnings were well founded. It does not take long, in fact, for the Spanish to turn and flee once the battle started. The poem suggests that distrust of the Spanish stemmed from their shifting allegiances. Henry's cause might be just, but it had not been long previously that those in his army were loyal to Pedro:

> Quant les Espaignolz virent leur seigneur aprochier
> Ceulz qui devant estoient lui monstrerent derier.
> A la fuite sont mis li Espaignol lanier,
> Et le prince de Gales les fist si enchausier
> A pointe de cheval, a lance convoier,
> Que jucques a la rive les menerent banier.
> La entroient dedens com poisson en vivier,
> Qui l'eaue ne peut boire, il le convint noier.
> L'eaue fist les chevaux jusqu'au fons trebuchier,
> Et tant en y noia sans venir au gravier
> Que par dessus les mors pouoit on chevauchier.
> De .X^M. qui furent a celle eaue aprochier
> A droit port de salu n'en revint un millier,
> Et les autres .X. mille qui leur devoient aidier
> S'alerent retreant tout selon le gravier
> Et vont a sauveté aucun ou bos planier;
> Ainsi se veulent les Espaignolz desfouquier. (vv. 12,855–12,871)

(When the Spanish saw their lord approach, / those who were in front showed him their behinds. / The cowardly Spanish were put to flight, / and the prince of Wales had them all driven / in front of the horses, guided by lances, / all the way to the river and led them to plunge. / They entered therein like fish in a fish-pond. / Those who could not drink the water had to drown. / The water tumbled the horses to the bottom / and so many died without coming to the shore / that one could ride across on the dead. / Of the 10,000 who went to the water, / not 1,000 returned to safety. / And the other 10,000 who should have provided aid / all retreated along the shore / and some took refuge in dense woods. / And thus the Spaniards wanted to flee.)

Cuvelier chose to describe Pedro as the Spaniards' lord (*seigneur*), suggesting that their hearts were not really in the fight for Henry and, because they were technically traitors, they deserved death rather than mercy or ransom. Since they were deserving of death, there was little reason for Cuvelier to portray their deaths in any dignified way.

The poem's story of Nájera concludes with du Guesclin's capture after improbably leading Henry to safety and returning to the fray. Pedro, furious about Henry's escape must be restrained from killing the prisoners by Prince Edward. Despite his defeat and capture, the poet does not lay blame on du Guesclin, but on the Spaniards who fled and left their allies to counter insurmountable odds.

According to historical consensus, Henry and du Guesclin had expected the Battle of Nájera to start with a frontal attack by the English and had lined up their army accordingly. Edward and Pedro, however, unexpectedly attacked Henry's left wing. Du Guesclin tried to swing the army around, but while the division under his command managed to manoeuvre smoothly, the other divisions did so more chaotically. As a result, some Castilian light horse and infantry deserted Pedro. At that point perhaps du Guesclin felt he had no choice but to charge but was not able to break through the English lines. Henry attempted to relieve the French but found himself surrounded. The English had brought their archers who, as in previous battles, wrought havoc on their enemies. The Castilians found themselves attacked on all sides and were quickly overrun. They broke and fled. The Aragonese cavalry pursued the fleeing men, trapping them on the banks of the river. About half of Henry's forces died, while Pedro and Edward suffered few casualties.[24] Henry escaped, his bid for the kingship of Castile temporarily set back. Du Guesclin was taken prisoner. Only two years later, in 1369, were Henry and du Guesclin able to go back to Castile and defeat Pedro at the Battle of Campo de Montiel, after which Henry killed Pedro, thus securing his title.

CONCLUSION

La Chanson de Bertrand du Guesclin is consistent in its construction of ideal military masculinities. It shows that a positive image of a man is not measured by his success, but rather by his character. Du Guesclin could command brigands, lose battles, fall prisoner, and yet remain an admirable military man. He embodied the ideals of military men – competence at violence, loyalty, generosity – his individual actions mattered little, because he was loyal to the larger argument made by the poet. In this case, du Guesclin is an ideal hero, because his story parallels France's story. The acceptability of du Guesclin's behaviour and setbacks meant that it was acceptable for France to face setbacks. Simply put, du Guesclin was an ideal of military masculinity.

York University

---

[24] Sumption, *Hundred Years War*, 2:553–554.

CITED WORKS

Bourdieu, Pierre. *Masculine Domination*. Stanford, CA: Stanford University Press, 2001.

Braudy, Leo. *From Chivalry to Terrorism: War and the Changing Nature of Masculinity*. New York: Alfred A. Knopf, 2003.

Butler, Judith. *Gender Trouble: Feminism and the Subversion of Identity*. New York: Routledge, 1990.

Cohen, Thomas V. "Masculine Competence." In Konrad Eisenbichler and Jacqueline Murray, eds, *Premodern Masculinities in Transition*. Woodbridge, UK: The Boydell Press, 2024.

Cuvelier. *La chanson de Bertrand Du Guesclin de Cuvelier*. Ed. Jean-Claude Faucon. Toulouse: Editions universitaires du sud, 1990.

——. *The Song of Bertrand Du Guesclin*. Trans. Nigel Bryant. Woodbridge, UK: The Boydell Press, 2019.

Fowler, Kenneth. *Medieval Mercenaries*. Oxford, UK and Malden, MA: Blackwell, 2001.

Jones, Catherine M. *An Introduction to the Chansons de Geste*. Gainesville, FL: University Press of Florida, 2014.

Jones, Michael, ed. *Letters, Orders and Musters of Bertrand du Guesclin, 1357–1380*. Woodbridge, UK: The Boydell Press, 2004.

Lassabatère, Thierry. *Du Guesclin: Vie et Fabrique d'un Héros Médiéval*. Paris: Perrin, 2015.

Levine, Robert. "Myth and Antimyth in 'La Vie Vaillante de Bertrand Du Guesclin.'" *Viator* 16 (1985): 259–275.

Lukas, Benjamin. "From the Knightly Bayard to Captain Monluc: Representations of Masculinity in Sixteenth-Century French Military Literature." In Konrad Eisenbichler and Jacqueline Murray, eds, *Premodern Masculinities in Transition*. Woodbridge, UK: The Boydell Press, 2024.

Milligan, Gerry. "The Effeminate Man and the Rhetoric of Anxious Masculinity: Anton Francesco Doni and Scipione Ammirato." In Konrad Eisenbichler and Jacqueline Murray, eds, *Premodern Masculinities in Transition*. Woodbridge, UK: The Boydell Press, 2024.

Moal, Laurence. *Du Guesclin: Images et histoire*. Rennes: Presses Universitaires de Rennes, 2015.

Paz, Carlos Andrés González. "The Role of Mercenary Troops in Spain in the Fourteenth Century: The Civil War." In *Mercenaries and Paid Men: The Mercenary Identity in the Middle Ages*. Leiden: Brill, 2008, 331–343.

Sumption, Jonathan. *The Hundred Years War*. Vol. 2, *Trial by Fire*. London: Faber and Faber, 1999.

Taylor, Andrew. "Chivalric Conversation and the Denial of Male Fear." In Jacqueline Murray, ed., *Conflicted Identities and Multiple Masculinities: Men in the Medieval West*. New York: Garland Publishing Inc., 1999, 169–188.

Taylor, Craig. "Military Courage and Fear in the Late Medieval French Chivalric Imagination." *Cahiers de Recherches Médiévales et Humanistes. Journal of Medieval and Humanistic Studies* 24 (2012): 129–147.

Vermijn, Yvonne. "«De quoy juqu'a mille ans bien parlé en sera». La réception de la Chanson de Bertrand de Guesclin entre 1380 et 1618." PhD thesis, University of Amsterdam, 2018.

Vernier, Richard. *The Flower of Chivalry: Bertrand Du Guesclin and the Hundred Years War*. Woodbridge, UK: The Boydell Press, 2003.

8

FROM THE KNIGHTLY BAYARD TO CAPTAIN MONLUC: REPRESENTATIONS OF MASCULINITY IN SIXTEENTH-CENTURY FRENCH MILITARY LITERATURE

Benjamin Lukas

For almost seventy years, early modern historians have debated the impact of the Military Revolution on warfare, politics, and state formation.[1] Often forgotten in this debate is how the emergence of early modern armies transformed masculine norms in European societies. Medieval European societies relied upon a martial code, known as chivalry, to indoctrinate noblemen into conforming to gendered behaviours. These behaviours in turn facilitated their participation in warfare. In France, the Military Revolution, along with other social changes, altered the nobility's role in combat and transformed chivalry into an obsolete masculine code. As the Military Revolution led to larger armies comprising primarily men from the Third Estate, knighthood ceased to reflect the role of noblemen in combat. The nobility soon became an officer class, and their new role required the construction of gender representations that redefined the relationships between nobility, masculinity, and martial violence.

Martial violence refers to certain forms of violence that enable warfare in a particular society. Martial violence is always culturally specific, because societies glorify only those forms of violence that they deem acceptable in warfare. In French society, the Military Revolution contributed to the emergence of the captain as the predominant depiction of noblemen in combat. Militarily active noblemen-turned-authors, who adopted the norms of the Military Revolution, transformed the representation of the nobility at war. In military memoirs, biographies, and treatises, these authors outlined the gender expectations of noblemen in combat. The tales of two of the most famous noblemen from the sixteenth century, Pierre Terrail, *chevalier de Bayard*, and Blaise de Monluc, *maréchal de France*, offer snapshots of this transition in the representation of noble masculine norms in sixteenth-century France.

Existing studies present the Military Revolution as a watershed in the history of European warfare. Coined by Michael Roberts in the 1950s, the term originally

---

[1] Roberts, *The Military Revolution*, 1–12, 21–23; Parker, *The Military Revolution*, 1–26; Black, *A Military Revolution*, 1–8, 20, 35.

referred to the increased size of armies, the development of new bureaucratic systems, and the introduction of gunpowder technologies in western European states.[2] In the 1980s, Geoffrey Parker sparked a heated debate over the nature of these changes when he proposed an earlier starting date for Roberts's Military Revolution and argued that the introduction of quadrilateral-angled bastions in European fortifications had provided its catalyst.[3] Since then, other historians have questioned the western European-centric focus of the term, emphasising that, at least until the onset of the Industrial Revolution, the economic scale, technological developments, and organisation of armies in other parts of Eurasia were equal to, and even greater than, those in the states examined by Roberts and Parker.[4] This chapter does not engage in this debate directly, but examines instead an aspect of warfare that has been overlooked by most historian: the relationship between the Military Revolution and masculine expectations. It argues that the changes associated with the Military Revolution led to alterations in the masculine norms of French noblemen who participated in the wars of the sixteenth century.

Many historians have presented Pierre Terrail, *chevalier de Bayard*, as an exemplar of the early sixteenth-century French nobility.[5] His biographer and sometime subordinate, Jacques Mailles, gave him the title of the "good knight without fear and reproach."[6] To justify this title Mailles traces the events of Bayard's life in chronological order. His text, with its emphasis on knighthood, tournaments, and courtly romance, represents the last hurrah of chivalric masculinity in French warfare. In contrast, Blaise de Monluc's memoir, titled *Commentaries* after that of Julius Caesar, is far removed from any chivalric ideals.[7] Rather than presenting himself and his peers as knights, this famed French marshal prefers to represent noblemen as captains whose role was to lead members of the Third Estate into battle. Throughout the text, Monluc stresses tactics, technology, and logistics over chivalric tropes.

UNDERSTANDING CHIVALRY

Before explaining the disappearance of chivalry in the sixteenth century it is crucial to explore the development of chivalric masculinity. The construction of chivalry was fundamentally tied to the emergence of feudalism and the nature

---

[2] Roberts, *The Military Revolution*, 5–14, 21.
[3] Parker, *The Military Revolution*, 6–12, 24–26, 39, 63, 115.
[4] Black, *A Military Revolution*, ix, 10, 17, 19, 33, 59; Eltis, *The Military Revolution*, 2–8, 10, 25; Parrott, *The Business of War*, 1–20; Sharman, "Myths of Military Revolution," 491–494.
[5] Susane, *Histoire de l'infanterie française*, 63; Schalk, "The Appearance and Reality of Nobility," 19.
[6] "le bon chevalier sans paour et sans reproche"; Anonymous, "Très-joyeuse, plaisant et récréative histoire," 489. Although it is labelled as Anonymous, antiquarians agree that Jacque Mailles was its author.
[7] Monluc, *Commentaires*, 22.

of warfare during the final wave of the barbarian invasions around the eleventh century. The political instability caused by the Viking, Muslim, and Magyar incursions, together with a lack of currency, led regional nobles and rulers in western Europe to ally with non-noble fighters for mutual protection. The various narratives of feudalism suggest that lords either parcelled out land to non-noble warriors or worked with local strongmen in exchange for military support. In both cases, these male warriors dominated the local population.[8] Their power came from their control of lances, a feudal military unit comprising a mounted heavy cavalryman (*miles*) and between one to six supporting soldiers, such as light horsemen, infantrymen, or archers. When required to defend their lands, noble magnates would call on their cavalrymen and group the supporting soldiers from each *lance* together according to their type for battle. The primary role of the *miles* in combat was to serve as elite shock troops, not necessarily to command men.[9]

There was no universal model for how these non-noble warriors came to possess political power across Europe.[10] What was common was that these men formed the core of feudal armies. Over time, these warriors were absorbed into the nobility as Carolingian noblemen came to embrace knighthood as part of the cultural identity of the Second Estate. In the process, the Latin term *miles* was later replaced by the vernacular terms of knight and the *chevalier*.[11] The right and ability of these men to use violence also came to justify their privileged position in European societies and the overwhelming wealth and social inequality of the medieval period.

As my colleagues Thomas V. Cohen and Sarah Wilk have already stressed in their earlier chapters in this volume, gender is performative, with competing acceptable variations in the performance.[12] The integration of warrior-knights into the nobility led to a series of conflicting interpretations of the relationships between nobility, masculinity, and martial violence. Chivalry evolved as a collection of competing ideals that signified these relationships, with chivalric literature acting as a database of gender performance options for noblemen. As Richard Kaeuper's work shows, authors representing the interests of the Western Christian Church called on knights to militarily support its institutions. Authors representing the interests of monarchial rulers encouraged knights to fight for their princes, while authors representing the fraternity of knights emphasised the political independence of the knightly class. All their interpretations invariably

---

[8] Painter, *French Chivalry*, 3; Bouchard, *Strong of Body*, 11, 13, 20; Bisson, "The 'Feudal Revolution,'" 6–9, 21–22, 28–33. There are also competing periodisation for when these changes started; see Charles West, *Reframing the Feudal Revolution*, 1–3; Débax, "L'Aristocratie languedoieenne," 99–100; Gerd, "Establishing Bond," 102–103.

[9] Painter, *French Chivalry*, 1–6; Redlich, *The German Military Enterpriser*, 8. Oman, *The Art of War in the Middle Ages*, 106.

[10] Bartlett, *The Making of Europe*, 27–36, 45–57, 60–69, 87–95.

[11] Kaeuper, *Chivalry and Violence in Medieval Europe*, 11, 13, 20.

[12] Cohen, "Masculinity as Competence," 32; Wilk, "Military Masculinities," 157–158.

rested on an assumption that nobility, masculinity, and martial violence were connected. Whether defending the Church, fighting for their king, or supporting the brotherhood of their fellow knights, authors defined the noble knight by his perceived superior fighting ability and right to use violence.[13]

Regardless of their authors, all chivalric representations constructed ties between nobility, masculinity, and martial violence in ways that reinforced the socioeconomic privileges of the Second Estate. For example, the image of the noble knight jousting for the favour of his lady stands as a classic chivalric trope demonstrating one version of these connections. The knight is a male member of the nobility and his participation in jousting is more than mere sport. It is practical training for his role in medieval combat as an elite shock troop that in turn justifies his socioeconomic status in medieval society.[14] Essential to chivalric representations was the way in which authors positively reinforced noblemen's participation in warfare by stressing the idea that their ability to inflict martial violence would impress potential sexual partners. In other words, chivalric authors used representations of noblemen engaging in certain forms of violence to construct gendered expectations for male members of the nobility. Their depictions of nobility presented the nobleman as an individual warrior who was skilled with certain types of weapons and whose primary role in battle was to serve as an elite warrior. In the minds of contemporaries, these facts legitimised the nobility's dominance of medieval society.

The chivalric emphasis on noblemen as individual warrior-knights did not mean that medieval noblemen were not also commanders – throughout the medieval period, it was noblemen who developed campaign strategies and led armies on the battlefield. However, the majority of noblemen served as individual warriors rather than commanders, and chivalric representations of masculine norms among the nobility reflected this reality, with the knight errant serving as the standard protagonist in most chivalric narratives.[15] The term knight banneret (*chevalier banneret*) denoted a knight who commanded a group of *lances*. However, most chivalric authors favoured the representation of the knight errant rather than the knight banneret in their texts, as the former better represented the functional role of most noblemen in combat.[16] Therefore, authors' emphasis on the characteristics of the knight errant became the foundation of masculine norms in medieval chivalric military literature.

---

[13] Kaeuper, *Chivalry and Violence*, 3–4, 39; Bouchard, *Strong of Body*, 105; Taylor, *Chivalry and the Ideals of Knighthood in France*, 6–11.

[14] Watanabe-O'Kelly, "Tournaments and their Relevance," 452; Gies, *The Knight in History*, 150, 165–66, 196; Verbruggen, *The Art of War in Western Europe*, 25.

[15] Taylor, *Chivalry and the Ideals of Knighthood*, 4; Painter, *French Chivalry*, 1–7; Bouchard, *Strong of Body*, 11–24; Keen, *Chivalry*, 1–2; Kaeuper, *Chivalry and Violence*, 189.

[16] Wagner, *Encyclopedia of the Hundred Years' War*, 22–23; Verbruggen, *The Art of War in Western Europe*, 25.

Representations of Masculinity in French Military Literature

THE DECLINING RELEVANCE OF CHIVALRY

Military literature continued to use chivalric imagery and nomenclature into the sixteenth century, but this use had probably already peaked in the twelfth and thirteenth centuries.[17] In the French context, military authors abandoned traditional representations at the end of the Hundred Years' War (1337–1453) because many knightly families whose existence had until then perpetuated chivalric values among the nobility had been annihilated. Between 20 and 50 percent of the French nobility were killed in the second half of this conflict, as French knights failed to adapt to the English use of longbowmen and dismounted men-at-arms formations.[18] These battlefield losses began a slow reform of gender performance expectations, which was accelerated by similar losses during the Italian Wars (1494–1559). In other words, the declining numbers of French warrior-knights contributed to chivalric masculinity's loss of relevance, convincing authors of sixteenth-century military literature to construct new gender norms that better suited the new role of the nobility in combat.

In addition to the loss of many knightly noble families, new economic opportunities and changes in social patterns allowed the nobility to achieve economic advancement, leading to a decline in the percentage of noblemen willing to engage in warfare.[19] In France, the gradual creation and expansion of judicial and administrative bureaucracies offered one alternative economic path, while the noble courtier provided another venue for socioeconomic advancement.[20] Other noble families possessed means to live comfortably as country gentlemen, thereby obviating the need to participate in combat.[21] At the same time, the opening of a limited number of trades to the nobility at the end of the medieval period provided additional economic opportunities for poor noblemen to benefit from their privileged positions in society without having to pursue a career as a warrior-knight.[22]

By the beginning of the sixteenth century, France's nobility was far more diverse and less defined by military service than its medieval counterpart. It was

---

[17] Painter, *French Chivalry*, 36–41. The nobility profited either from war or by exploiting members the Third Estate living on their lands their lands; Bartlett, *The Making of Europe*, 24–29, 86–87.

[18] With geographical variations accounting for the 30 percent discrepancy. Taylor, *Chivalry and the Ideals of Knighthood*, 152–158.

[19] By the French Wars of Religion (1562–1598), 70–85 percent of the nobility were abstaining from combat even as a civil war raged around them. Constant, "The Protestant Nobility in France during the Wars of Religion," 76.

[20] Kaeuper, *Chivalry and Violence*, 308–309; Wood, *The Nobility of the Election of Bayeu*), 44–58; Dewald, *The Formation of a Provincial Nobilit*), 76–78; Painter, *French Chivalry*, 13, 29.

[21] Beik, *A Social and Cultural History of Early Modern France*, 10–12, 71–72, 81–86; Taylor, *Chivalry and the Ideals of Knighthood*, 53, 152–158.

[22] Salmon, *Society in Crisis*, 95–96.

no longer a single monolithic group connected by its members' martial role in society, but rather a heterogeneous collection of nobles who pursued a variety of occupations. The diversity of male gender performances in the nobility were no longer limited to representations of martial violence. Evidence suggests that these different noble subgroups developed gender norms specific to their new functions in society.[23] Despite the decline of noble participation in warfare, French military literature maintained the term *chevalier* and its corresponding noble masculine standards into the early sixteenth century, even though these norms no longer corresponded to the nature of warfare or the behaviour of much of the nobility. Up until that point, most of the authors of military literature were not militarily active noblemen. However, once veterans began to write about their own and others' experiences in the late fifteenth century, masculine representations in these texts shifted towards the image of the captain.

The transformation of the nobleman's combat role from that of an individual warrior into that of an officer was the result of changes attributed to the Military Revolution, in particular the expansion of armies. France's experience of the Military Revolution has often not played a central role in historiography. However, the kingdom developed the first standing army in Europe since the Roman period when Charles VII created the *compagnies d'ordonnance* (gendarme companies) to drive out the English at the end of the Hundred Years' War. In 1479, Louis XI added infantry companies to his standing army. Later known as *les vieilles bandes*, these units consisted of men from the Third Estate and were led by members of the nobility. Gradually, the gendarme companies evolved into the training grounds of the French noble officer class, as the French army, like the rest of western Europe, embraced the expansion of forces through increased reliance on non-noble combatants.[24]

BAYARD AS AN EXEMPLAR OF MASCULINE NORMS

Mailles lived in a period when the masculine performance models of the knight and the captain coexisted. Following French victories in the first years of the Italian Wars, François I's court tried to relaunch chivalric pageantry. However,

---

[23] Cox's work demonstrates that the courtier was at least one other form of masculine norms among the nobility; Cox, *Aristocratic Masculinity in France*, 1–59: Wood's and Dewald's works on the *noblesse de robe* suggest that these men also had masculine norms specific to their profession; Dewald, *The Formation of a Provincial Nobility*, 17, 66–67; Wood, *The Nobility of the Election of Bayeux*, 156, 163.

[24] I disagree with Wood's assessment that France had an incomplete Military Revolution; Wood, *The King's Army*, 1–8, 134–135; The work of Susane, Oman, and Love demonstrates that France embraced the Military Revolution prior to the French Wars of Religion. The collapse of the Crown's ability to fund the war does not negate that France used the tactics, technology, unit organisations, and terminology of the Military Revolution. Oman, *A History of the Art of War in the Sixteenth Century*, 43–45, 59–62, 222; Susane, *Histoire de l'infanterie française*, 55, 69, 72–3, 77–78, 87–88, 121–122; Susane, *Histoire de la cavalerie française*, 15, 40–49; Love, "All the King's Horsemen," 513, 517, 521–522.

the widespread destruction of most of the French army's noble leadership at the Battle of Pavia in 1525 and France's desperate fight for survival in the late 1520s led to a fundamental rethinking of the thrust of French military literature. In an attempt to change France's fortunes on the battlefield, authors reimagined the representations of the nobleman at war in order to alter institutional culture and, with it, gender norms. These authors never directly attacked chivalry – they rarely mentioned or used chivalric nomenclature in their writings. Instead, their texts constructed representations of noblemen as officers who led common men into combat rather than as individual warriors.[25]

Mailles' depiction of Bayard's life demonstrates the final death thralls of medieval chivalry as a functional martial code. He begins his description of Bayard's life with a vivid tale about him wanting to "learn the skill of arms" (*apprendra le train des armes*) just like his male ancestors. His father realises that he will need to be placed in the household of a great family in order to learn the skills of war. He considers the houses of Bourbon and Valois, before ultimately deciding that the house of Savoy should have the honour of training his son.[26] Shortly thereafter, Mailles claims that, while still a teenager, Bayard possessed the horsemanship of a man of thirty. His skills were so impressive, according to Mailles, that the king of France brought him into his service after seeing him ride at a tournament.[27] The king made him an *archer* (light cavalryman) in a gendarmerie company and sent him to Picardy. One of Bayard's first acts upon his arrival at this northern frontier was to organise a tournament. Fighting hard with both lance and axe (weapons traditionally associated with chivalry), the young man overcame his opponents to win the attention of an unnamed local lady.[28]

After recounting these tales of a young nobleman beginning to pursue his career as a knight, Mailles goes on to offer a detailed account of Bayard's military accolades. Mailles writes that at the Battle of Fornovo in 1495 Bayard had two horses killed out from under him.[29] After a feverish rearguard action near Astizanne, soldiers of Ludovico Sforza captured Bayard, leading to a gracious exchange of words between him and the famed prince.[30] Eventually, Bayard received the captaincy of a gendarme company.[31] Despite this shift from warrior

---

[25] Louis XI, *Le rosier des Guerres*, fol. 2[r–v], fol. 18[r–v]; Anonymous, *Institution de la discipline militaire*, A3, A4, 49; Fourquevaux, *The Instructions sur le faict de la guerre*, 7–9, 25, 44–46, 50–51, 58.
[26] Anonymous, "Très-joyeuse," 489.
[27] Anonymous, "Très-joyeuse," 497.
[28] Anonymous, "Très-joyeuse," 498–501. Llull, a knight turned monk, was a prominent chivalric author in late thirteenth and early fourteenth centuries. He discusses the connections between these weapons and chivalry; Llull, *The Book of the Order of Chivalry*, 1–3, 66–67.
[29] Anonymous, "Très-joyeuse," 502–503.
[30] Anonymous, "Très-joyeuse," 508–509.
[31] Anonymous, "Très-joyeuse," 514.

to officer, Mailles continued to emphasise individual combat over battlefield leadership. In various instances, Mailles describes Bayard charging recklessly into the fighting with his "armet [helmet] on his head and his sword in his fist, like a lion."[32] Mailles tells tales of Bayard holding bridges singlehandedly against the enemy or turning the course of battle with his force of arms alone.[33]

The intensity of the violence in the text is revealing as it reflects the parameters established for martial violence in French society during the period. Although Mailles glorifies chivalric combat, at the same time he fails to mention any limitations on noblemen in battle. He establishes Bayard as the archetype of the honourable male nobleman through graphic narratives of him inflicting violence on others in battle. In several scenes, Mailles glorifies Bayard's willingness and desire to kill for France, providing descriptions of him charging into battle while shouting his famed battle cry: "France! To the Death! To the Death" (*France! À mort, à mort*). He emphasises Bayard's ability to overpower and defeat his enemies, whom he regularly portrays as being "all torn to pieces" (*tous mis en pieces*).[34] Descriptions of Bayard eviscerating his enemies is more than poetic licence, as Mailles places such actions in an approving light. Even if Bayard never mutilated his enemies in this way, Mailles' inclusion of this type of behaviour has the effect of glorifying extreme aggression in battle, thereby establishing noble masculine expectations for his readers. If a knight, without fear or reproach, tears his enemies to pieces, then his actions serve as an example for other noblemen to fight with the same bellicosity and brutality.

Part and parcel of Mailles' glorification of martial violence is his emphasis on the tradition of knights engaging in chivalric battles. These were small-scale skirmishes during which equal numbers of knights and squires from opposing sides would fight each other on behalf of their respective armies. The most famous of these clashes was *la bataille de trente* fought in 1351 between thirty Breton and thirty English knights and squires in Brittany during the Hundred Years' War.[35] Mailles' biography claims that Bayard took part in a similar skirmish in Italy, with thirteen Spanish and thirteen French noblemen confronted each other in a prearranged engagement. Mailles claims that Bayard and a seigneur d'Oroze held thirteen Spaniards at bay until both sides agreed to a truce and the skirmish ended in a stalemate.[36] As with his description of Bayard's participation in tournaments, Mailles stresses individual martial prowess in a traditional chivalric context: even though he is heavily outnumbered, Bayard's skill at arms is enough to even the odds.

---

[32] "l'armet en teste et espée au poing, comme un lyon"; Anonymous, "Très-joyeuse," 520.
[33] Anonymous, "Très-joyeuse," 513, 516–517, 519, 529, 541, 543, 586.
[34] Anonymous, "Très-joyeuse," 519, 529, 541, 543, 586.
[35] Muhlberger, "The Combat of the Thirty Against Thirty," 285–294; Brush, "La bataille de trente anglais et de trente bretons," 511–528.
[36] La Marck, "Histoire des choses mémorables," 517–518.

Mailles' biography details the violence that Bayard inflicted for decades on the enemies of France before finally dying in combat from a bullet wound during a minor skirmish.[37] Despite the insignificance of the engagement in which Bayard perished, Mailles presents his death in a true chivalric fashion. As the bullet struck him, Bayard is reported to have cried out: "Jesus ... Alas! My God, I am dead ... Have mercy on me, O God."[38] Through his narrative, Mailles transforms Bayard's death into an event that was guided by the divine hand. Bayard may have died by a stray shot, but he does so with his sword in hand and as he prepares to charge the enemy. He does not lament his death and beg to live, but instead accepts his fate and turns to God for His mercy. Mailles' biography ensures that Bayard's name and deeds will endure. To this day, Bayard serves as an archetype of French knighthood.

The normative gender behaviour Mailles constructs in his biography of Bayard relies on a knightly representation of the nobleman at war. The majority of these constructions are remnants of motifs found throughout chivalric literature.[39] Bayard's noble lineage predisposes him to excel in combat, especially when fighting on horseback. Mailles glorifies Bayard's skill at arms and the joy that he finds in the act of killing. In doing so, he encourages his male readers to emulate the warrior-knight's behaviour. The biography is a celebration of chivalric combat, with a tragic hero who is killed in the final scene by a gunpowder weapon. Mailles' overarching message is that male members of the nobility should go to war and fight as knights, just like their ancestors did.

Even though chivalric tropes play a prominent role in Mailles' depiction of Bayard's life, elements of the shift from the heroic knights to the skilled captains are present in the narrative. Mailles stresses Bayard's captaincy of a gendarme company and writes that Bayard planned various skirmishes during his career, even though the climax of each of these anecdotes is Bayard proving himself in battle and not his ability to lead other men in combat.[40] Mailles does provide the names of several noble captains whom his contemporaries respected for their leadership abilities, such as seigneur de Ligny, capitaine d'Ars, seigneur d'Aubigny, Jehan Bernardin Cazache, and Jehan-Jacques de Trevolz.[41] It is difficult to trace the military careers of most of these men, though enough of the Aubigny's and Ligny's lives is known to be able to establish that both men were experienced commanders who were respected for their leadership abilities.[42] Men like these were at the vanguard of the shift

---

[37] Anonymous, "Très-joyeuse," 602–603.

[38] "Jésus! ... Hélas! Mon Dieu, je suis mort! ... Miserere mei, Deus." Anonymous, "Très-joyeuse," 603.

[39] Keen, *Chivalry*, 1–2; Taylor, *Chivalry and the Ideals of Knighthood*, 4; North, "The Ideal Knight," 111–119, 125–128.

[40] Anonymous, "Très-joyeuse," 533–535.

[41] Anonymous, "Très-joyeuse," 492, 504, 508, 510, 511.

[42] Bonner, "Stewart, Robert," 378.

in masculine norms during the sixteenth century. Despite mentioning these men and including a few fleeting examples of Bayard's leadership abilities, Mailles nevertheless chose to present Bayard as the perfect knight rather than as the model captain.

MONLUC'S INTERPRETATION OF MASCULINE NORMS

Representations of nobility, masculinity, and martial violence in Monluc's memoir are very different from those found in Mailles' biography of Bayard. Monluc's text is part memoir and part military treatise in which he regularly offers military advice to his readers. With the exception of his account of Henri II's death in a jousting accident, Monluc does not mention tournaments, chivalric battles, or his upbringing as a page, nor does he use the term knight to describe himself or any of his peers.[43] Instead, he charts his rise from a gentleman volunteer to his last battle at the age of seventy during which a gruesome facial wound forced him into retirement. Early in his memoir, he writes: "this is not a book for learned men [...] but a soldier, a captain, and maybe a royal lieutenant will be able to find something there to learn [...] it is to you, captains, my companions, that I principally address."[44] This is a sentiment that he routinely reaffirms to the reader.[45] For him, the perfect nobleman is a warrior, but his primary role is leading men to victory, not chasing individual acts of glory. He does not talk of the joy of battle like Mailles, but instead calmly affirms the reality of war: "captains, and you, lords, who led men to death, because war is nothing else."[46] The lack of romantic elements common in chivalric texts is one of the main differences between Mailles' and Monluc's writings. Monluc also has disturbing views on the place of women in warfare, though, he does not continue the medieval tradition of presenting gendered representations of men winning women through combat. In his opinion, women are a vice that distracts captains from performing their martial duties and pursuing victory, as a result, he only mentions women at a few points in his text.[47]

The contrast between Monluc's discussion of death and Mailles' celebration of it highlights the shift in representation of noble masculinity in military writing. Monluc's admission that warfare and death were inescapably connected

---

[43] Monluc, *The commentaries*, 215–216.
[44] "Ce n'est pas un livre pour les gens de sçavoir [...] mais bien pour un soldat, capitaine, et peut estre qu'un lieutenant de roy y pourra trouver de quoy apprandre [...] C'est à vous, capitaines mes compaignons, à qui principalement il s'adresse." Monluc, *Commentaires*, 22.
[45] Monluc, *Commentaires*, 22, 25, 40, 118, 158, 187, 190, 207, 217, 242, 409, 411, 423, 446, 459, 507, 571, 608, 684, 707, 742, 778, 785, 821, 829, 832.
[46] "Capitaines et vous, seigneurs, qui menez les hommes à la mort, car la guerre n'est autre chose." Monluc, *Commentaires*, 59.
[47] Monluc, *The Commentaries of Messire Blaize de Montluc*, 4–5.

reflected the dangers that noblemen faced in combat during the sixteenth century. From the beginning of the Italian Wars in 1494 until the end of the French Wars of Religion in 1598, France was at war for sixty-two years. Each generation of French nobility experienced a major battle in which significant numbers of its members were killed in combat.[48] Despite the dramatic decline in the number of noblemen willing or able to participate in combat during this period, authors maintained that engaging in combat was the duty of the nobility. Monluc believed that noblemen must accept the dangers and embrace the inevitability of death in combat in order to maintain their honour, which, for him, was indistinguishable from their masculinity.[49] His belief in these ideals explains why, at the age of seventy and despite the pain that his past wounds continued to give him, Monluc chose to lead an assault against a breach: one of the most dangerous activities in early modern warfare.[50]

The circumstances of a nobleman's death in battle were crucially important to Monluc's conceptualisation of male honour and martial violence among the nobility. Unlike Mailles' celebration of Bayard's demise in a nameless skirmish, Monluc emphasise that a nobleman must ensure that he dies only in certain types of engagements and preferably one in which his death might have an impact on the course of a campaign. These views are showcased when he discusses the Habsburg invasion of Provence in 1536. To counter the Habsburg's efforts, Monluc and Gaspard de Saulx-Tavannes led a raid behind enemy lines in order to destroy the mill at Auriol that was suppling the bulk of the imperial army's grain. During the attack, Monluc stopped Saulx-Tavannes before he could enter the mill, wishing to see the latter's soldiers lead the way. Monluc claims that Saulx-Tavannes later asked him why he denied him the honour of being the first to enter the mill. Monluc justifies himself by writing: "I knew well that he was not yet wise, and that this was not the place that a man of worth should be killed, and he should keep himself for a good death in a breach, and not for a meagre mill."[51] It is little wonder that Monluc, sensing that the end of his own life was drawing near, would embrace the opportunity to storm a breach at the age of seventy.

Although Monluc stresses the honour that certain types of death can bestow on members of the nobility, his attitude towards death in battle is very different from Mailles' glamorisation of Bayard's demise. One of the earliest anecdotes

---

[48] The battles of Fornovo (1495), Pavia (1525) and Saint Quentin (1557) are some examples. Even victories like Ravenna (1512) led to loses among the French nobility. Mallett and Shaw, *The Italian Wars, 1494–1559*, 28–31, 106–108, 150–152, 278. There was a general fear of the loss of the military power of the nobility throughout the French Wars of Religion; Wood, *The King's Army*, 125.

[49] Monluc, *Commentaires*, 447.

[50] Monluc, *Commentaires*, 21, 59–61, 776–782.

[51] "je cognoissois bien qu'il n'estoit pas encores ruzé, et que ce n'estoit lieu qui meritast qu'un si homme de bien que luy mourust, et se falloit garder pour une bonne bresche, et non pour un chetif moulin." Monluc, *Commentaires*, 63–69.

in Monluc's memoir is about the death of a close companion during the failed invasion of Naples in 1528. Monsieur Candalle was a member of the house of Foix, a family with an illustrious military reputation. During the retreat from Naples, Candalle was wounded and captured by the Spanish. The wound festered to the point that the Spanish returned him to the French so that the young man could die with his kin. Monluc describes Candalle's death as follows: "He was a brave and decent lord, as ever came from the House of Foix […] I never knew a man so meticulous and eager to learn the ways of war from old captains as him."[52] Writing his memoirs decades after these events and having witnessed countless other deaths in battle, Monluc's description of Candalle's death lacks the bellicosity of Mailles' narrative while still venerating male participation in warfare. There is no mention of the joy of killing or the hero's final words, only respect for Candalle having shown a desire to learn the art of war. Monluc uses a similar tone in the brief passages about his sons: "I was very content and happy, because, in the loss of my children, I consoled myself that they all died men of worth, sword in hand while in the service of my king."[53] For Monluc, a notable death in the service of the king was a worthy way to die.

Like Mailles, Monluc believed that the nobility should actively participate in combat. However, in his memoir, he stresses that noblemen should be both good leaders and heroic fighters. His description of the actions of his protégé, Jacques Prévot, sieur de Charry, while recapturing the fort of Camollia at Siena in 1554 offers an excellent example of Monluc's conceptualization of the nobility's role in combat. As Monluc prepared to order an escalade to overrun Camollia's defences, he claims that he turned to Charry to see if he was prepared for the assault. With a bandage still wrapped around his head from a wound that he had received only eight days earlier, Charry stood ready with "sword and rondelle [shield] in hand, a moron [style helmet] over his skullcap that covered his wounds." Monluc then said to him: "Captain Charry, I have raised you to die in the service of the king. You must be the first to mount the ladder."[54] According to Monluc, Charry, covered by arquebusier fire, led his men up the ladders and onto the battlements, and, under his command, his soldiers proceeded to overrun one of the wall's towers, leading to the recapture of the fort.

---

[52] "C'estoit un brave et honneste seigneur, s'il en sortit jamais de la maison de Foix […] Je ne cogneuz jamais homme si soigneux et desireux d' appprendre le faict de la guerre des vieux capitaines que celuy-là." Monluc, *Commentaires*, 55–56. Odet de Foix, seigneur de Lautrec was his cousin and commanded French forces in Naples at the time.

[53] "je serois tres content et heureux; car en la perte de mes enfans je me console qu'ils sont tous morts en gens de bien, l'espée en la main pour le service de mon Roy." Monluc, *Commentaires*, 622.

[54] "l'espée et la rondelle en la main, un morion sur son couvre-chef qui luy couvroit sa playe. […] Capitaine Charry, je vous ay norry pour mourir faisant grand service au Roy. Il faut que vous montiez le premier." Monluc, *Commentaires*, 287–288.

Representations of Masculinity in French Military Literature

Monluc's conceptualisation of the noble commander emphasises the ability of captains to achieve victory. His obsession with victory is so great that he claims that he "would call on all the spirits of hell to break the head of his enemy" and later hope that God will forgive him.[55] That being said, Monluc's ideal French nobleman was a skilled tactician who planned before battles and did not always rush into the fight. For example, at one point in his memoir, he recounts a discussion he had in 1544 with King Francis I. The king asked him if he believed that French forces in Piedmont could defeat their Habsburg counterparts. Monluc claims that he responded by openly challenging the competency of his fellow French captains. He believed that many commanders had demonstrated dangerous overconfidence and had even convinced the king that the French could beat their imperial opponents despite being outnumbered. Monluc defends his position by informing the king that the imperial forces consisted of seasoned veterans who knew their trade. He argues that to blindly push for battle when outnumbered by such an enemy would be militarily disastrous and advises the king that French forces required more men and supplies to achieve victory.[56] In making these claims, Monluc predicted the events of the following September, when both Charles V and Francis I sought peace due to inadequacy of resources.[57]

Throughout his memoir, Monluc offers guidance on how to become a wise captain who makes the right choices when leading men into combat. Some of his advice focuses on the importance of adopting the new military technology of the gunpowder age. Some historians have suggested that Monluc was a fierce opponent of firearms. This is incorrect. He regretted that they had been invented but nevertheless accepted their existence. He understood that gunpowder weapons were needed to achieve victory and, as a result, provides his readers with advice on how best to use them in a variety of battlefield situations.[58] In other sections of his memoir, he encourages captains to think like their enemy when devising their strategies. He wanted French captains to carefully plan as well as act, a combination that had not traditionally been associated with chivalric masculinity.[59]

Monluc also advises his readers on the social aspects of military leadership, providing guidance on how commanders can win support from both noblemen and ordinary soldiers. In his view, each group has its distinct needs. He believes that captains should listen to the opinions of their noble officers so that they feel valued and to ensure that commanders have all the information necessary to achieve victory.[60] Monluc also advises commanders to spend

---

[55] "je pouvois appeller tous les esprits des enfers pour romper la teste à mon enemy"; Monluc, *Commentaires*, 81–82.
[56] Monluc, *Commentaires*, 67–69, 142–145.
[57] Mallett and Shaw, *The Italian Wars*, 242–243.
[58] Monluc, *Commentaires*, 35.
[59] Monluc, *Commentaires*, 394.
[60] Monluc, *Commentaires*, 394.

time with their common soldiers so as to build relationships that will ensure that the latter are willing to fight and die for their captain. This advice does not mean that he was against the use of corporal or capital punishment to preserve discipline; Monluc in fact considered discipline to be critical. However, he also advises that violent disciplinary tactics are not what will cultivate the loyalty needed to motivate the common solder to fight. He instead believes that the rank-and-file must feel a personal connection to their commanders, especially the captains of their companies.[61] Monluc's focus on how to manage common soldiers reflects the shifting role of the nobility in warfare. As part of an officer class, noblemen now needed to understand how to motivate and control their men so that they, like all military resources, did not go to waste.

Monluc was not impressed by officers who did not understand the value of good soldiers. For example, during the siege of Siena (1554–1555), he despised a captain named Saint-Auban serving under his command because "he loved a teston [silver coin] more than a good man."[62] Monluc does not elaborate on this point, but Saint-Auban was probably reporting his company at full strength when it was not, then pocketing the difference between the pay allotted for its paper strength and that for its actual strength. This type of fraud was a common practice during the period.[63] Monluc's anger toward Saint-Auban reflects his determination to ensure French victories on the battlefield and an acknowledgement that the value of money lay in the quality of the men that it could provide. In his opinion, a good commander should always care more about ensuring that he had good soldiers than padding his own fortune by embezzling funds.

CONCLUSION

The contrast between these two representations of the nobility is important. Monluc inherited command of Bayard's men, so the two were near contemporaries.[64] The fact that, within a short period of time, the masculine standard shifted from men like Bayard to those like Monluc demonstrates how quickly masculine norms can adapt to fit changing circumstances. Chivalry, with its emphasis on the nobleman as an individual knight errant charging into battle, no longer matched the realities of warfare in the sixteenth century. France required noblemen to act as captains, not as knights, and ready to learn how to raise, organise, supply, and lead men from the Third Estate into battle. Authors like Monluc helped to align literary representations of masculine norms in combat to dramatically changed circumstances.

---

[61] For example, he hanged two Catholic soldiers in 1563 because they had broken the King's edict to end the first religious war. Monluc, *Commentaires*, 181–182, 581.

[62] "il aimoit mieux un teston qu'un homme de bien." Monluc, *Commentaires*, 283.

[63] Parrott, *The Business of War*, 206–211.

[64] Bayard's company was divided two new companies, one of which the king gave to Monluc. Susane, *Histoire de la cavalerie française*, 41.

Representations of Masculinity in French Military Literature

The historiographical debate over the Military Revolution has expanded scholars' understanding of the changing nature of warfare and the ways in which military conflict shaped the development of state institutions in the early modern period. However, historians have not fully explored the impact that the Military Revolution had on European societies. This chapter demonstrates that the developments highlighted by Parker, Roberts, and others also contributed to alterations in gender norms among noble male combatants. Chivalric literature constructed a collection of masculine norms that encouraged male members of the nobility to eagerly engage in warfare. It celebrated the knight as an individual male combatant and established proficiency with arms as a noble masculine ideal. As long as the primary role of the nobleman in warfare was to serve as elite warrior, chivalric representations remained a stable element in French military literature. The expansion of the scale of conflict that was brought about by the Military Revolution destabilised these chivalric masculine norms and led to the emergence of new representations in military literature. These new gender expectations preserved the requirement that noblemen participate in martial violence, but they added new elements that matched their newfound leadership roles in combat. The shift in representations of French noblemen from knights like Bayard to captains like Monluc offers a glimpse into this transition between medieval and early modern gender norms. The differences between the two versions of masculinity may at times be subtle, but they nevertheless reflect the fundamental shift in the understanding of the nobility's role in combat that took place in the sixteenth century.

Centre for Reformation and Renaissance Studies
Victoria University in the University of Toronto

CITED WORKS

Anonymous. *Institution de la discipline militaire au royaume de France. À treshault & trespuissant Prince Antoine Roy de Navarre.* Lyon: Mace Bonhome, 1559.

———. "Trés-joyeuse, plaisant et récréative histoire composée par le loyal serviteur, des faicts, gestes, triomphes et prouesses du bon Chevalier sans paour et sans reproche, gentil seigneur de Bayart." In Jean François Michaud and Jean Joseph François Poujoulat, eds, *Nouvelle collection des mémoires pour servir à l'histoire de France depuis le XIIIe siècle jusquà la fin du XVIIIe.* Vol. 4. Lyon: Guyot Frères Imprimeurs-Libraires, 1851, 479–607.

Bartlett, Robert. *The Making of Europe: Conquest, Colonization, and Cultural Change, 950–1350.* Princeton, NJ: Princeton University Press, 1993.

Beik, William. *A Social and Cultural History of Early Modern France.* Cambridge, UK: Cambridge University Press, 2009.

Bisson, T. N. "The 'Feudal Revolution.'" *Past & Present* 142 (1994): 196–223.

Black, Jeremy. *A Military Revolution? Military Change and European Society, 1550–1800*. London: Macmillan Press, 1991.

Bonner, Elizabeth. "Stewart, Robert." In H. C. G. Mathew and Brian Harrison, eds, *Oxford Dictionary of National Biography*. Vol. 52. Oxford: Oxford University Press, 2004, 743.

Bouchard, Constance Brittain. *Strong of Body, Brave and Noble: Chivalry and Society in Medieval France*. Ithaca, NY: Cornell University Press, 1998.

Brush, Henry Raymond. "La bataille de trente anglais et de trente bretons." *Modern Philology* 9.4 (1912): 511–544.

Castelnau, Michel de. "Mémoires de messire Michel de Castelnau, seigneur de Mauvissiere et de Concressaut, baron d Jonville, comte de Beaumont le roger, chevalier de l'ordre du roy, conseiller en ses conseils, capitaine de cinquante hommes d'armes de ses ordonnances, gouverneur de la ville et casteau de Sainct Dizier, et ambassadeur pour sa majesté en Angeleterre." In Claude Bernard Petitot, ed., *Collection complète des mémoires relatifs à l'histoire de France*. Vol. 33. Paris: Foucault Libraire, 1823, 1–504.

Carloix, Vincent. "Mémoires de la vie du Maréchal de Vieilleville." In Claude Bernard Petitot, ed., *Collection complète des mémoirs relatifs à l'histoire de France*. Vol. 28. Paris: Foucault Libraire, 1822, 1–361.

Cohen, Thomas V. "Masculinity as Competence." In Konrad Eisenbichler and Jacqueline Murray, eds, *Premodern Masculinities in Transition*. Woodbridge, UK: The Boydell Press, 2024.

Coligny, Gaspard de. "Discours de Gaspar de Coligny, Seigneur de Chastillon, Amiral de France, ou sont sommairement contenues les choses qui se sont passées durant le siégé de Sainct-Quentin." In M. M. Michaud and Poujoulat, eds, *Nouvelle collection des mémoires pour servir à l'histoire de France depuis le XIIIe siècle jusqu'à la fin du XVIIIe*. Vol. 8. Lyon: Imprimeurs-Libraires, 1851, 563–583.

Constant, Jean-Marie. "The Protestant Nobility in France during the Wars of Religion: A Leaven of Innovation in a Traditional World." In Philip Benedict, Guido Marnef, Henk van Nierop and Marc Venard, eds, *Reformation, Revolt and Civil War in France and the Netherlands 1555–1585: Proceedings of the Colloquium, Amsterdam, 29–31 October 1997*. Amsterdam: Royal Netherlands Academy of Arts and Sciences, 1999, 69–82.

Cox, Darrin. *Aristocratic Masculinity in France (1450–1550): From Knight to Courtier*. Lewiston, NY: The Edwin Mellen Press, 2012.

Débax, Hélène. "L'Aristocratie languedocienne et les société féodale: Le témoignage des sources (midi de la France: XI et XII siècles)." In Sverre Bagge, Michael H. Gelting, and Thomas Lindkvist, eds, *Feudalism: New Landscapes of Debate*. Turnhout, Belgium: Brepols, 2011, 77–100.

Dewald, Jonathan. *The Formation of a Provincial Nobility: The Magistrates of the Parlement of Rouen, 1499–1610*. Princeton, NJ: Princeton University Press, 1980.

Du Bellay, Martin and Guillaume. "Les Mémoires de Messire Martin du Bellay, contenant le discours de plusieurs bhoses advenues au royaume de France, depuis l'an 1513, jusques au trepas du roy François 1er; Auquel l'hauteur a inséré trois livres, et quelques fragments des ogdades de Messire Guillaume du Bellay, seigneur de Langey, son frère." In Joseph François Michaud and Jean Joseph François Poujoulat, eds, *Nouvelle collection des mémoires pour servir a l'histoire de France depuis le XIIIe Siècle jusqu'à la fin du XVIIIe.* Vol. 5. Lyon: Guyot Frères Imprimeurs-Libraires, 1851, 95–568.

Eltis, David. *The Military Revolution in Sixteenth Century Europe.* London: I. B. Tauris, 1995.

Fourquevaux, Raymond de Beccarie de Pavie, sieur de. *The Instructions sur le faict de la guerre.* Ed. G. Dickinson. London: The Athlone Press, 1954.

Gerd, Althoff. "Establishing Bond: Fiefs, Homage, and Other Means of Create Trust." In Sverre Bagge, Michael H. Gelting, and Thomas Lindkvist, eds, *Feudalism: New Landscapes of Debate.* Turnhout, Belgium: Brepols, 2011, 101–115.

Gies, Frances. *The Knight in History.* New York: Harper & Row, 1984.

Kaeuper, Richard. *Chivalry and Violence in Medieval Europe.* Oxford, UK: Oxford University Press, 1999.

Keen, Maurice. *Chivalry.* New Haven, CT: Yale University Press, 1987.

La Marck, Robert de. "Histoire des choses mémorables advenues du reigne de Louis XII et François Ier, en France, Italie, Allemagne et es Pays-Bas, depuis l'an 1499 jusques en l'an 1521." In Jean François Michaud and Jean Joseph François Poujoulat, eds, *Nouvelle collection des mémoires pour servir a l'histoire de France depuis le XIIIe Siècle jusqu'à la fin du XVIIIe.* Vol. 5. Lyon: Guyot Frères Imprimeurs-Libraires, 1851, 1–81.

Love, Ronald. "'All the King's Horsemen:' The Equestrian Army of Henri IV, 1585–1598." *The Sixteenth Century Journal* 22.3 (1991): 510–533.

Llull, Ramon. *The Book of the Order of Chivalry.* Trans. Noel Fallows. Woodbridge, UK: The Boydell Press, 2013.

Louis XI. *Le Rosier des guerres: enseignement de Louis XI Roy de France pour le Dauphin son fils.* Paris: François Bernouard, 1979.

Mallett, Michael and Christine Shaw. *The Italian Wars, 1494–1559: War, State and Society in Early Modern Europe.* London: Pearson Education, 2012.

Monluc, Blaise de. *Commentaires, 1521–1576.* Ed. Paul Courteault. Paris: Gallimard, 1964.

——. *The Commentaries of Messire Blaize de Montluc, mareschal of France.* Trans. Charles Cotton. London: Andrew Clark, 1674.

Muhlberger, Steven. "The Combat of the Thirty Against Thirty: An Example of Medieval Chivalry?" In *The Hundred Years War.* Vol 2. Ed. L. J. Andrew Villalon and Donald J. Kagay. Leiden: Brill, 2008, 285–294.

North, Sally. "The Ideal Knight as Presented in Some French Narrative Poems, c. 1090–c. 1240: An Outline Sketch." In Christopher Harper-Bill and Ruth Harvey, eds, *The Ideals and Practice of Medieval Knighthood: Papers from the First and Second Strawberry Hill Conferences.* Woodbridge, UK: The Boydell Press, 1986, 111–132.

Oman, C. W. C. *The Art of War in the Middle Ages.* Ed. John H. Beller. Ithaca, NY: Great Seal Books, 1960.

Parker, Geoffrey. *The Military Revolution: Military Innovation and the Rise of the West, 1500–1800.* Cambridge, UK: Cambridge University Press, 1988.

Parrott, David. *The Business of War: Military Enterprise and Military Revolution in Early Modern Europe.* Cambridge, UK: Cambridge University Press, 2012.

Redlich, Fritz. *The German Military Enterpriser and His Workforce: A Study in European and Social History.* Vol 1. Wiesbaden: Franz Steiner Verlag GMBH, 1964.

Roberts, Michael. *The Military Revolution.* Belfast: M. Boyd, 1956.

Sainte Marie, Anselme de. *Histoire généalogique et chronologique de la maison royale de France.* Vol. 1. Paris: Cavalier, 1725.

Salmon, J. H. M. *Society in Crisis: France in the Sixteenth Century.* London: Ernest Benn, 1980.

Schalk, Ellery. "The Appearance and Reality of Nobility in France during the Wars of Religion: An Example of How Collective Attitudes Can Change." *Journal of Modern History* 48.1 (1976): 19–31.

Susane, Louis. *Histoire de la cavalerie française.* Vol. 1. Paris: C. Terana, 1984.

———. *Histoire de l'infanterie française.* Vol. 1. Paris: C. Terana, 1985.

Sharman, J. C. "Myths of Military Revolution: European Expansion and Eurocentrism." *European Journal of International Relations* 24.3 (2018): 491–513.

Taylor, Craig. *Chivalry and the Ideals of Knighthood in France.* Cambridge, UK: Cambridge University Press, 2013.

Verbruggen, J. F. *The Art of War in Western Europe during the Middle Ages, From the Eighth Century to 1340*, Trans. Sumner Willard and R. W. Southern. Woodbridge: The Boydell Press, 1997.

Wagner, John. *Encyclopedia of the Hundred Years' War.* Westport, CT: Greenwood Press, 2006.

Watanabe-O'Kelly, Helen. "Tournaments and their Relevance for Warfare in the Early Modern Period." *European History Quarterly* 20 (1990): 451–463.

Wilk, Sarah. "Military Masculinities in *La Chanson de Bertrand du Guesclin.*" In Konrad Eisenbichler and Jacqueline Murray, eds, *Premodern Masculinities in Transition.* Woodbridge: The Boydell Press, 2024.

West, Charles. *Reframing the Feudal Revolution: Political and Social Transformation Between Marne and Moselle, 800*–1000. Cambridge, UK: Cambridge University Press, 2013.

Wood, James. *The King's Army: Warfare, Soldiers, and Society during the Wars of Religion in France, 1562–1576.* Cambridge, UK: Cambridge University Press, 1996.

———. *The Nobility of the Election of Bayeux, 1463–1666: Continuity Through Change.* Princeton, NJ: Princeton University Press, 1980.

9

THE EFFEMINATE MAN AND THE RHETORIC OF ANXIOUS MASCULINITY: ANTON FRANCESCO DONI AND SCIPIONE AMMIRATO

Gerry Milligan

In his 1512 reflections on why Florence was bound to "lose both her liberty and her state,"[1] Francesco Guicciardini bemoaned the infighting among Italians, the might of foreign princes, and the fact that civic life was out of order. This last point was evidenced by several factors, among them "the spirits of effeminate and indolent men, turned to a dainty and – relative to our means – extravagant life."[2] Guicciardini thus laid the blame for the imminent dissolution of the Florentine republic, at least in part, on "effeminate" men. It was a condemnation of effeminacy that would be echoed by writers throughout the sixteenth century.[3] Like Guicciardini, these writers argued that men had abandoned an ideal past model of masculinity (e.g. Roman or chivalric) for a lesser and "effeminate" modern substitute and that military and political ruination were the result.

My chapter will focus on two texts that constructed the spectre of the modern effeminate man in contrast to the militant man of the past.[4] These texts enact what Peter Hennen has described as the historical function of a discourse of effeminacy, where it is "deployed as a means of stabilizing a given society's

---

[1] "perdere la libertá e stato suo"; Guicciardini, "Del modo di ordinare il governo popolare" also known as the "Discorso di Logrogno." Translation by Moulakis in *Republican Realism*, 117–118.

[2] "gli animi degli uomini effeminati ed enervati e vòlti a uno vivere delicato e, rispetto alle facultá nostre, suntuoso"; Guicciardini, "Del modo." Translation in Moulakis, *Republican Realism*, 117–118 (translation altered to reflect original).

[3] See, for example, Giovio's *Notable Men and Women*, which Kenneth Gouwens states, "eloquently details the crucial failings of manhood that Giovio portrays as underlying the many defeats that Italian soldiers had suffered over the past thirty-three years." Gouwens, "Meanings," 83. On the association of effeminacy and failed militancy in the English seventeenth and eighteenth centuries, see Neocleous, "Oh Effeminacy!"

[4] On the masculinization of militarism, see Higate and Hopton, "War," 432–447.

concept of masculinity and controlling the conduct of its men based upon the repudiation of the feminine."[5] I will consider how Anton Francesco Doni and Scipione Ammirato used differing techniques to create unease about masculine gender performance by linking so-called "effeminate" dress and appearance to failed militancy. I consciously identify and name this unease as *anxiety*. The effeminophobic anxiety that I discuss herein does not describe a psychological experience of readers of texts but, rather, the discursive tool employed by authors in the social control of men.[6] My argument about the function of effeminophobic anxiety is invested in the literary, where the strategies of literature – as Jane Tylus and I wrote over a decade ago – not only represent masculinity, they *produce* it.[7]

EFFEMINATE, EFFEMINACY, AND NORMATIVE GENDER PROJECTS

The term *effeminato* circulated with sufficient frequency to appear in the 1612 *Vocabolario* of the Accademia della Crusca: "Effeminate: of feminine manners, gestures, and spirit, delicate, soft. Latin effoeminatus, muliebris, delicatus, mollis."[8] This string of adjectives might lead one to believe that there is something or someone that can objectively be defined as "effeminate." Yet, "effeminacy," as Todd W. Reeser reminds us, is culturally variable, not the opposite of masculinity, and not bound to a determined set of traits, behaviour, or appearance.[9] It is, however, a consistent mode of ridicule in Italian Renaissance literature.[10] Men were accused of being "effeminate" in contrast to hegemonic masculinity, and thus effeminacy was (and is) employed for the distribution of power, both among men and among genders.[11]

The *Oxford English Dictionary* repeats much of the four-hundred-year-old definition of the *Crusca* (e.g. womanly, delicate) and adds other ambivalent terms such as "feeble" and "voluptuous."[12] As Hennen has noted, these definitions are not only inherently misogynist, but they are also inadequate. They fail, he

---

[5] Hennen, *Faeries*, 48.
[6] The coining of "effeminophobia" is often credited to Sedgwick, "How to Bring," 20.
[7] Milligan and Tylus, *Poetics of Masculinity*, 13.
[8] "Effeminato: di costumi, modi, e animo femminile, dilicato, morbido. Lat. effoeminatus, muliebris, delicatus, mollis"; Accademia della Crusca, *Vocabolario*, 312.
[9] Reeser, *Masculinities in Theory*, chap. 5.
[10] The use of the word "effeminate" here is used in a negative connotation and is contrasted with the words that many societies gave to a privileged group of people who are often referred to as "third gender." For an alternate reading that states that "effeminacy" was also a positive trait in Machiavelli, see Becker, "Rethinking," 69.
[11] Hennen, *Faeries*, 33.
[12] *Oxford English Dictionary*: "Womanish, unmanly, enervated, feeble; self-indulgent, voluptuous; unbecomingly delicate or over-refined." Online edition accessed 2021.

The Effeminate Man and the Rhetoric of Anxious Masculinity

explains, to capture the negative connotation and operational function of the word as separate from the inherent meaning of the word.[13] A clear example of the ambivalence of such dictionary definitions is that the associated terms "delicacy" and "softness" can also be recast in their positive connotations of "refinement" and "sensitive." I have written elsewhere how these same slippages occur in Castiglione's *Book of the Courtier*, where the ideal courtier is given the unhelpful advice to dress in a "clean and dainty" ("pulito e delicato") manner but avoid a "feminine or vain fashion."[14] These terms are further destabilized once taken out of their highly specific context (e.g. the Urbino court of 1507). In order to avoid the retro-application of modern notions of masculinity to early modern men, I have employed the safeguard to only use the term "effeminate" when the lexeme *effeminato* is found in the original. As a term and a concept, it stands apart from associated words such as "delicate" or "soft," for it marks "the only gendered behavior available exclusively to men" since women "cannot be effeminate."[15]

This chapter focuses on texts that associate the "effeminacy" of aesthetics with failed militancy because this discourse takes on an outsized role in the Cinquecento. I use the term "aesthetics" loosely here to refer to the dress, hairstyle, voice pitch, bodily poses, perfume, and other aspects that are part of the way a man was experienced in the world through the senses. The sight, smell, and sound of men were fodder for some of the most vehement criticisms of masculine gender performance. Condemnations of "effeminate" aesthetics certainly did not originate in the Renaissance. Classical texts featured critiques of effeminacy associated with men's aesthetics, and this discourse often pointed to military or political success and failure.[16] Renaissance vernacular writers continued to link "effeminate" aesthetics to political and military weakness, but they also associated them with men's peril in terms of Christian morality. Clothing, for example, could be the sign of corruption or the corrupting force itself. Francesco Pontano, in his *Dello integro e perfetto stato delle donzelle* (*On the intact and perfect state of maidens*), suggested that "effeminate" dress was a sign of Christian deviance, while Silvio Antoniano's treatise, *Tre libri dell'educazione cristiana de' figliuoli* (*Three books on the Christian education of sons*), on the other hand, suggested that dress itself was what engendered moral corruption.[17] Governments presumably also believed that clothing was a corrupting force. Legislation against male dress often specified the goal of

---

[13] Hennen, *Faeries*, 34.
[14] "manera feminile o vana"; Castiglione, *Il libro del cortegiano*, II.27, p. 160.
[15] Rogoff and van Leer, "Afterthoughts," 744.
[16] Olson, *Masculinity*, passim; Phang, *Roman Military Service*, 95–101; Williams, *Roman Homosexuality*, 142–159. See also Gleason, *Making Men*.
[17] Pontano, *Dello integro*, 22. On Pontano see Marletta, "L'umanista Francesco Pontano." Silvio Antoniano (1540–1603) explains that one of the best ways to control boys' sexual behaviour was to regulate their hairstyles and wardrobes,

curbing same-sex intimacy, such as in the Florentine laws directed at gold, silk, and embroidery.[18]

While fears of Christian and moral peril remained a concern, Cinquecento vituperations of effeminacy showed a striking emphasis on the condemnation of male aesthetics as leading to political and military failure. Much like Cicero's invectives, which associated so-called effeminate clothing with military incompetence, there was a trend in sixteenth-century political writings that labelled the aesthetics of dress, hairstyles, facial hair, skin care, voice pitch, and comportment as the cause of wartime failures.[19]

The most famous Renaissance treatise about war, Niccolò Machiavelli's *Art of War* (published 1521), condemns aesthetics as corrupting masculinity. From the ornate shade trees of the garden setting to the gold and gems of the Italian princes, aesthetics, for Machiavelli, are perilous to masculinity and to military success.[20] According to Fabrizio Colonna, the *condottiere* interlocutor in the treatise, decadence, luxury, and splendour caused the occupied state of the Italians. The fault of Italy's condition, Colonna states, lies with Italian rulers. Colonna explains that before the invasion of King Charles VIII in 1494, the Italian princes were busying themselves in unwarlike activities: "how to spin a fraud, to be adorned with gems and with gold, to sleep and eat with greater splendor than others […] to decay in laziness…"[21] For Machiavelli, the adornment of jewels was both sign of corruption and a corrupting force that had contributed to the condition of Italy's rulers being vulnerable to foreign enemies. The text concludes with Colonna stating that the princes of Italy must read about and imitate ancient and masculine men. In short, the solution to Italy's woes could be resolved by reading and internalizing Machiavelli's treatise about ancient manliness:

> E se in loro, o in parte di loro, si poteva dannare troppa ambizione di regnare, mai non si troverrà che in loro si danni alcuna mollizie o alcuna cosa che faccia gli uomini delicati e imbelli. Le quali cose, se da questi principi fussero lette e credute, sarebbe impossibile che loro non mutassero forma di vivere e le provincie loro non mutassero forma.

---

    eliminating anything that might have them appear in public as "una vezzosa feminetta," *Tre libri*, Book II.93, fol. 89ᵛ.

[18] Taddei, *Fanciulli*, 58 and 60–63.

[19] Williams, *Roman*, 150. Effeminophobia is reflected in Renaissance epic as well; both Ludovico Ariosto (*Orlando furioso*, Canto VII) and Torquato Tasso (*Jerusalem Delivered*, Canto XVI) feature male warriors who are shamed for their "effeminate" dress and actions and who are incited out of feeling shame to return to militant masculinity.

[20] On the *Orti oricellari* as creating "delicate" men, see Machiavelli, *Art of War*, Book 1, 572.

[21] Machiavelli, *Art of War*, Book 7, 724. Machiavelli's source for this passage is Xenophon's *Cyropaedia*, which he changes in significant ways to reflect his position as frustrated counselor; Masi, "*Arte della guerra*," 119.

The Effeminate Man and the Rhetoric of Anxious Masculinity

(And if in them [ancient men] or in some of them we can condemn too much ambition for rule, we shall never find any softness to condemn, or anything that makes men delicate and unwarlike. These things, if Italian princes read and believed them, are such that those princes could not do other than change their form of living. Their provinces would then change their fortunes.)[22]

The author closes his book by suggesting that if rulers would only disabuse themselves of "delicate" ways, the political state of affairs would change.

This passage underscores Machiavelli's dissatisfaction with contemporary "delicate" and "soft" men as compared to ancient warlike men. Passages like this one compel Hannah Pitkin to claim that the central ambivalence in Machiavelli is "manhood: anxiety about being sufficiently masculine and concern over what it means to be a man."[23] Pitkin's language is unclear about who is experiencing this anxiety – the men described in the text or Machiavelli himself. Pitkin is right to identify anxiety in Machiavelli's works, but in my view, textual evidence suggests that this sentiment is not necessarily experienced by the men in question but is rather projected by the author onto men when they do not satisfy his normativizing masculine ideal.

After Machiavelli's *Art of War*, we find much more vehement condemnations of "effeminate" aesthetics as well as an increasing link between aesthetics and military ruin. Castiglione's *Book of the Courtier* provides some of the earliest examples of the vitriol that will typify sixteenth-century texts.[24] As I have argued elsewhere,[25] Castiglione's repeated attacks on the so-called "effeminacy" of men's dress and aesthetics were likely not meant to change men's dressing habits but rather to investigate how language about dress might motivate social groups. In my analysis, Castiglione's dialogue acts as a scripted demonstration of how finely dressed courtiers could reclaim masculinity through their damnations of the very aesthetics and comportment that they employed. They effectively denounced refined dress while being finely dressed.

Despite the centrality of masculinity to Italian sixteenth-century texts, there has been scant attention paid to the discourse of effeminacy in the works of authors beyond Machiavelli and Castiglione.[26] This chapter will discuss two lesser studied authors who upbraid men for so-called "effeminacy" and who attempt to instil an anxiety in their readers through a linkage of military failure with men's aesthetics.

---

[22] Machiavelli, *Dell'arte della guerra*, Book 7, 689; *Art of War*, Book 7, 725.
[23] Pitkin, *Fortune*, 5.
[24] On Castiglione, see Richards, "A Wanton." See also Milligan, "The Politics."
[25] Milligan, "Aesthetics," 154.
[26] Two works that discuss effeminacy in Torquato Tasso and Lorenzo de' Medici, respectively, include Schachter, "Quanto Concede" and Tylus, "Epic's Endless Deferral." On effeminacy in seventeenth-century libretti, see Melis, "'Sei troppo effeminato.'"

Gerry Milligan

ANTON FRANCESCO DONI

Anton Francesco Doni's (1513–1574) best-known work is the miscellaneous collection of dialogues, images, novellas, and epigrams named *I marmi* (1552). In this innovative book, Doni imagines a narrator who dreams he is a bird perched in a niche of the cathedral of Florence and who can hear the conversations of those below on the church's marble steps.[27] The book, penned by a Florentine author born into the working class, thus features a polyphony of (mostly) men from various walks of life, e.g. a cloth painter, a farrier, a scholar, a nobleman.[28] A substantial percentage of the book is lifted directly from three source texts, but the texts are reworked in often telling ways.[29] Lynn Westwater has aptly demonstrated that Doni rewrites his primary source-text, the *Relox de Príncipes* of Antonio de Guevara, in ways that reveal his attitudes toward gender.[30] She argues that these rewritings reframe a strongly anti-woman source-text to become philogynist and, moreover, to produce "an anxiety about masculinity and anything that threatens it."[31] Westwater speculates that these episodes about gender relations do not so much tell us about women as about power relations between men, where men were anxious about their subordinate positions to princes.[32]

Let's discuss an episode that is not part of Westwater's study because it is not a rewrite of Guevara's *Relox*. The dialogue in question is between Fiorentino, a member of the Accademia Fiorentina. and Peregrino, a member of the (fictious) Accademia Peregrina of Venice.[33] The episode is introduced by an epigram and by a woodcut image of a knight on a horseback surrounded by what appear to be sleeping soldiers in the woods.[34] Peregrino opens the dialogue with an encomiastic story of a deceased nobleman, Massimo, who, like the man depicted in the illustration, rode horses. Peregrino compares contemporary men to Massimo and then to

---

[27] On Doni and *I marmi* see Rizzarelli, *I "Marmi"* and Masi, "Quelle discordanze sì perfette."

[28] See Urbaniak on how the structure of *I marmi* allows for a pluralism of voices not found in works that are restricted to people of the same social status (i.e. *The Decameron*), 296–301. On the biography of Doni, the son of a scissors-maker, see Rizzarelli, "Introduzione," xi and n.12 and Grendler, *Critics*, 49–65.

[29] Westwater estimates that one-eighth of *I marmi* is copied from Guevara's *Relox*, "Transposing," 169.

[30] Westwater, "Transposing."

[31] Westwater, "Transposing," 180.

[32] Westwater, "Transposing," 181.

[33] Doni, *I marmi*, 412–418. On the invented academy, see Masi, "Coreografie."

[34] On the image as well as the bibliography about the woodcut itself, see Doni, *I marmi*, 412–413, n. 113. The epigram "Essendo l'uomo debitore a i sapienti e a gli ignoranti, è dovere che egli operi con quello che egli sa: a i dotti dia diletto, a gli indotti utile e all'uno e l'altro facci piacere." Doni, *I marmi*, 412.

The Effeminate Man and the Rhetoric of Anxious Masculinity

the ancients. He then quickly drops the story of Massimo in order to level a biting indictment of "modern living" (*viver moderno*) where men allow themselves to be ruled by women. The tenor of the speech increases in its rancour as Peregrino shifts from simply providing observations about men to addressing an imagined male audience by employing the second person as an orator might do. His complaint that men are subservient to women leads him to an invective against how men have become like prostitutes (describing men's bodies as soft, perfumed, and bejewelled), and further, how men have become like women because they wish to stay idle and not endure hard work (including combat).[35] For Peregrino, labour is how the sexes are most clearly divided. War is for men, textiles for women: "Arms are men's business, not weaving garments."[36] And militancy is constitutive of masculinity because men have a moral duty to provide for and defend women: "Defend her, I say, because she is of your bones, from those parts closest to your heart."[37]

Peregrino's initial complaints about men's subservience to women build to a dizzying speech of anger, negative epithets, and scolding of men's dress and behaviour. His interlocutor, the Florentine academician, calls him a "preacher" of a new kind,[38] and indeed, Peregrino's speech assumes the tone of a firebrand sermon. If effeminacy is the sin, then dress and perfumes are the signs of this sin, and militancy and governing republics are the hoped-for virtues of salvation:

> lasciami sfogare la collora che io ho con gli uomini femine diventati. O uomo, fuori di te medesimo, che t'adormenti in braccio a Dalida, in seno a Diana e in grembo alla sensualità, svegliati [...] lascia poi fare il pane a lei, fa' che ella cucia, che ella apparecchi la tavola, che lei faccia i bucati e che porti l'acqua alla cucina, non ti aviluppare in questi vili esercitii. Ah vile uomo [...] chi t'ha insegnato lasciare da parte di maneggiar l'arme e girar in quello scambio il rocchetto? [...] Reggi le republiche nel nome di Dio; ordina le milizie, solca i mari e acquistati de gli uomini, delle città popolate e non de gli ornamenti feminili. Oh che bel perdere il tempo dell'uomo dietro a un ricamo! [...] Babbioni! insensati! Vili! Di grazia, andatemi attorno con puntaluzzi, medaglini, pennacchi, cappelletti, spadini, guanti profumati, e bottoni travisati, collanini e fori e strafori: o voi parete le belle

---

[35] "[ciascuno] vorrebbe non durar fatica, ma esser femina, starsi in agi e delicatezze e aver de' danari assai per trattenersi senza un esercizio al mondo con le femine." Doni, *I marmi*, 417.

[36] "l'arme sono esercizio da uomini e non li tessere panieri"; Doni, *I marmi*, 414. All translations from Doni are my own.

[37] "difenderla, dico, perché l'è delle vostre ossa, di quelle piú prossime al cuore"; Doni, *I marmi*, 414.

[38] "Voi mi parete un predicatore in nuova maniera di predicare entrato." Doni, *I marmi*, 415.

donne novelle! L'abito dell'uomo è la celata e la toga, il reggere, il governare, l'acquistare e il difender la republica. (Doni, *I marmi*, 415–416)

(let me vent my anger about those men who have become women. Hey you, man, out of your mind, sound asleep in Dalida's arms, against Diana's breast and in the lap of sensuality. Wake up!! […] leave the making of the bread to her, make her do the sewing, set the table, do the laundry, and bring the water to the kitchen. Don't get caught up in these matters. Ah, cowardly man […] who taught you to put aside the bearing of arms and to exchange them for a spool? […] Govern republics in the name of God, command militias, sail the seas, and acquire men and thriving cities, not feminine ornaments. Oh. what a great waste of time for a man to be doing embroidery! […] Ninnies! Fools! Cowards! For heaven's sake, you circle about me with brooches, little medallions, plumes, little hats, small dress swords, perfumed gloves, and distorted buttons, tiny necklaces, and slashes and supersized slashes. Oh you look like beautiful young women! The clothes of a man are the helmet and the toga, as well as the leading, the governing, the acquiring, and the defending of the republic.)

For angry Peregrino, men have become women. This gender transition is identifiable by noting men's labour (doing work typically held by women and neglecting the labour of arms) and through men's aesthetics (jewels and dress rather than a helmet and toga). The labour of textile making and men's dress are in opposition to militancy and governing.

Peregrino will go on to compare these modern men, as had Machiavelli, to an ideal masculinity of the ancients. He will as well return to the figure of Massimo to draw a contrast with modern men. Unlike these men in brooches, plumes, and slashed sleeves, Massimo, he tells us, "had the status of man, not a woman," and he knew of armies, cavalries, captains, and the "governing of great republics."[39] This description of Massimo is accompanied by a second woodcut, where the horseman is now defeating men in battle.[40] The image and text collaborate to remind the reader that Massimo – a man rarely mentioned in the dialogue – is in fact the protagonist of this story. He is a mythical ideal of manhood who, in the pictorial program of the text, is a chivalric knight taken from a woodcut previously used in illustrations of Ariosto's *Orlando furioso*.[41]

In his last few paragraphs of the dialogue, Peregrino addresses an audience of fathers, specifically rich fathers, who have the chance to change the world for the better through their sons. He complains that fathers "instead of militancy have killed themselves to satiate their libido" and instead of raising

---

[39] "teneva lo stato da uomo non da femina"; "reggimenti di gran republiche"; Doni, *I marmi*, 416–417.
[40] The woodcut appears in Doni, *I marmi*, 416.
[41] On the woodcut of the knight in battle, see Doni, *I marmi*, 417, n. 126.

The Effeminate Man and the Rhetoric of Anxious Masculinity

their sons, send them in the care of "effeminate pedants."[42] The solution to this masculine wasteland, at least for the wealthy, is that "rich fathers" give their sons "life experience" and send them away without money to fend for themselves.[43] If not, he warns, "new people" will come and their sons will be able to defend themselves only with the "flesh of prostitutes, the knowledge of eating well, and of being heavily perfumed."[44]

The potential economic ruin that could result from effeminacy is mitigated by Peregrino's proposal for *signori* to protect their wealth from "new people."[45] Moreover, the political implications of effeminacy are underscored by the fact that three times in this dialogue Peregrino, a Venetian visiting the Duchy of Florence, refers to men's duty to defend and govern *republics*.[46] His critique of masculine failings could thus also be masking a warning to Venetians that what has happened to Florence's once proud republic could happen to the *Serenissima* as well. A return to the masculinity of, if not the ancients, at least that of the nobleman Massimo, is needed to protect both the financial and political status quo.

In 1609, when Giovan Battista Bertoni republished Doni's book in Venice, by over fifty years after its first printing of 1552, this central theme of the ideal chivalric knight Massimo versus the failed contemporary man was undermined.[47] This time, the dialogue is introduced with a new image (no longer a man on a horse) and a new descriptive subtitle that reshapes the story to possibly fit new reader expectations. The new subtitle reads "The discussion is directed against effeminate men, and against those husbands who give overwhelming license to their wives," and the new woodcut features

---

[42] "in cambio della milizia si sono straziati in saziare la libidine della meritrice e la loro stessa ancora" and "i loro fanciulli vanno sotto la disciplina d'un pedantaccio effeminato." Doni, *I marmi*, 417.

[43] "Fate voi, padri ricchi, e che alleviate i figliuoli nella bambagia, nelle mollizie, e ne' profumi, fate, di grazia, un'esperienza in vita: mandategli, senza una sostanza al mondo, lontani due miglia [...] e vedrete come vi torneranno a casa." Doni, *I marmi*, 418.

[44] "Oh, se venisse nuova gente a occupare quello che voi lasciate loro, con che lo difenderanno? O con qual via e modo n'acquisteranno eglino per i lor bisogni? Con la dolcezza della carne delle meretrice forse? O con il saper ben mangiare? O veramente con il profumarsi assai?"; Doni, *I marmi*, 418.

[45] For an alternate reading of the economic aspect of this dialogue, see Grendler, *Critics*, 88.

[46] Machiavelli also aligned masculinity with republics rather than principalities by claiming that men of greater virtue came from republics; Masi, "*Arte della guerra*," 119.

[47] On the Bertoni edition of *I marmi*, see Rizzarelli, "Introduzione"; on the new subtitle and woodcut from the Bertoni edition, see Doni, *I marmi*, 756–757.

a man with his foot on top of a distressed woman on the ground.[48] While the subtitle emphasizes that this episode is about "effeminate men," it and the woodcut together limit the parameters of effeminacy to a battle between the sexes rather than also including the contrast between men of yore and modern men. The potential political reading of the dialogue is lost. We are instead left with a familiar warning that wives who seek to lord it over their husbands will be crushed under the foot of patriarchy.

RAISING THE STAKES, SCIPIONE AMMIRATO AND THE NEAPOLITAN NOBILITY

The second text I will discuss is an oration of Scipione Ammirato. Here, I contend that there is a dormant authentic noble masculine identity beneath a weak, delicate, and ornate one. In a subtler tone than Doni, Ammirato, a courtier in the Medici Grand Duchy of Florence, admonishes Neapolitan noblemen by appealing to a masculine chivalric identity that he sees buried beneath their modern lives. He claims that while their bodies have "masculine effects," they live in sumptuous softness.[49] Unlike the authors considered above, Ammirato writes his *Orazione* (1594) with a specific purpose in mind: convincing the noblemen of Naples to leave their lives of comfort and fight in the Long War (1593–1606) between the Holy Roman Empire and the Ottoman Empire.[50] His oration exemplifies how the literary construct of the effeminate man was used to mobilize men into real-world action.

The text calls on Neapolitans to assist Tuscany and other allies who had already offered aid to Emperor Rudolph II during the Hapsburg–Ottoman war in Hungary (The Long Turkish War, also known as the Thirteen Years' War).[51] Ammirato makes it clear that the Neapolitans, as the wealthiest nobility of Italy, have a responsibility to engage in combat.[52] He claims that contemporary practices, however, associate nobility with chivalry in form but not substance. The Neapolitans believe their sons to be warriors but they do not have them fight. It has become a linguistic equivocation, he argues, that Neapolitan men are called "knights" (*cavalieri*) even though they have no order of knighthood: "not having any order of knighthood for

---

[48] "Il ragionamento è volto contro gli huomini effeminati; e contro quei mariti, che danno soverchia licenza alle moglieri." Doni, *La terza parte*, fol. 10ʳ.
[49] "fattezze maschili"; Ammirato, *Orazione*, fol. 4ʳ. Here and elsewhere all translations of Ammirato's *Orazione* are mine.
[50] On Ammirato, see De Mattei, *Il pensiero politico* and "Scipione Ammirato."
[51] Marri, "La partecipazione," 50–59.
[52] On Ammirato's and other Italians' impressions of the Neapolitan nobility, see Nuovo, *Otium e Negotium*, 361–387, particularly 372–382.

The Effeminate Man and the Rhetoric of Anxious Masculinity

your nobility and greatness, you are all indistinctly called knights."[53] The origin of knighthood, he reminds them, is the accomplishments of "military operations" (3ᵛ). Following such traditions, these men are educated from birth in the military arts:

> non cosi tosto il bambino esser uscito dalle fasce, e poter co teneri piedi toccar la terra, che per ordine de padre, e delle madri gli si cinge la spade, ne cosi tosto è da bambino e da fanciulletto uscito, che di cavalcar gli si insegna, e appena hà pur alquanto assodato e indurito l'ossa, che a barriare, e a corer lancie, e a far altri cavallereschi esercizi è ammaestrato.[54]

(not long after the baby boy has left his swaddling clothes and is able to touch the ground with his tender feet, by order of his father and mother a sword is strapped to him. And not long after he is no longer an infant or toddler he is taught to ride horses. Just as soon as his bones have adequately solidified and hardened, he is trained to fight at barriers and run with lances and to do other chivalric practices.)

Ammirato lays out an exemplary male trajectory, where a baby boy develops into an armed todler, horse-riding teenager, and ultimately a warrior, a process that includes fathers *and* mothers.[55] The author describes an ideal if impossible educational process of the Neapolitan male and implicitly alludes to the military role for which these men have been groomed, but then points out that the ultimate purpose is quite different. Once they are adults, these could-be warriors do not engage in warfare and combat, but use their military skills, instead, for festive entertainments and focus on such things as love and luxury. Ammirato characterizes the situation as something akin to a masculinity crisis in Naples, where the above-mentioned military training is perverted into displays of frivolity:

> Tutte queste operazioni benche da per se stesse nobili, e a maraviglia belle e leggiadre, niuno per cio mi dirà non ad altro fine esser indirizzate, che à quel che elle comunemente si fanno in feste, in nozze, & in mascherate, come se i fiori d'aranci, del cui soavissimo odore si sente olir tutta cotesta

---

[53] "senza haver ordine alcuno di cavalleria per la vostra nobiltà e grandezza sete tutti indistintamente chiamati cavalieri"; Ammirato, *Orazione*, fol. 3ᵛ.
[54] Ammirato, *Orazione*, fol. 3ᵛ.
[55] The importance of women in the development of men into warriors is clearly stated by Ammirato. Elshtain, *Women and War* thoughtfully discusses the (false) paradigm of women as completely uninvolved with the military, or as she calls them, "blissful souls." On women's complex relationship with militancy and pacifism, see Milligan, *Moral Combat*; Macdonald, Holden, and Ardener, *Images of Women*.

belissima città la primavera, non havendo o mai a render frutto, solo a questo fossero dalla natura stati prodotti.[56]

(All of these activities – though in and of themselves noble, marvellous, lovely, and graceful – are not for any other purpose than for what one commonly performs in feasts, weddings, and in masquerades. Just as orange flowers, whose sweet perfume pervades this entire city in the springtime, were created by nature only for this and not for ever bearing fruit.)

Just as an orange flower that never bears fruit, these men were sterile, not realizing their social purpose.[57] They must now seek the "fruit of glory," which is war against the Turks and not, he notes, against the French and Germans.[58]

Men, Ammirato states, are living among "perfume and softness," and contrasts this soft space (the "shaded," "cool," and "beautiful *piazze* of Naples") with bloody battlefields "on the plains of Hungary under the lashing sun, the dusty haze billowed by the trodden earth of so many horses, between blood and the howl of the winds, of the conquered and of conquerors."[59] Unlike Doni, he comments on the men's "masculine features" so that he might argue that they are "knights" who have neglected their "nature" (4ʳ). Their nature is bound up with their class. Nobility, he states, is not "silk and gold and pearls and amber" but "sweat, toil, vigils, hunger, love of true glory" (5ᵛ). Ammirato repeatedly remarks on the nobility's superiority at war, but he reminds them that war is also a social mobilizer. If these *cavalieri* do not fight, other men will. He adds that past upstarts are now as rich as the nobility; these *nouveau riche* infiltrate the noble class, buy their houses and marry into their families (4ᵛ–5ʳ). It is a warning that can only remind us of the "new people" who could come to take the wealth of the rich "perfumed" sons in Doni's text.

Ammirato's oration is not atypical in its cajoling of men to fight the Turks, but we should reflect on how such typical rhetoric is in fact quite extraordinary.[60] Indeed, how does one persuade men (not women) to leave their lives of urban

[56] Ammirato, *Orazione*, fol. 3ᵛ.
[57] On sterility and masculinity, see Schachter, "'Quanto concede,'" as well as Finucci, *Manly Masquerade*, 225–280. See also Ricasoli's oration that praises virginity in a warrior, stating that it makes a man's body strong, "O Dio Eterno; come la Castità non somministrerà forze corporali, tanto necessarie nella guerra?" *Orazione*, 15–16.
[58] "Ma da voi dalla state e dall'autunno sopraggiunti non piu fiori, non più ombre, e immagini, e simolacri di battaglie, ma frutti di gloria, urti fieri di cavalli, veri scontri a' ferri politi di robuste lancie non col Franzese o col Tedesco, ma co Turchi nemici della nostra religione s'attendono"; Ammirato, *Orazione*, fol. 4ʳ.
[59] "ne piani dell'Ungheria alla sferza del sole, alla polverosa caligine mossa dalla calpestata terra di tanti cavalli, tra il sangue, e le grida de vinti, e de vincitori"; Ammirato, *Orazione*, fol. 4ʳ.
[60] See Hale, *Renaissance War*, 335–358; 359–387 for a broad summary of religious and secular justifications and exhortations of war.

comfort for the brutal fields of distant lands where they will risk being maimed or killed? Ammirato himself pauses to reflect on what inspires men to fight in wars. He states that statues of great heroes are effective inspirations to their onlookers, but he emphasizes that the most effective way to send young men off to war is by mobilizing the competitive spirit of a male community: "There is nothing that stimulates men more to glorious works than to see in the same city inferiors or equals or superiors heading to glory."[61]

Ammirato compels his readers to compare themselves to recent rather than ancient examples of exemplary fighting men, among them Charles V, Ferrante Carracciolo, and Don Giovanni de' Medici (the commander of the Medici troops in the Long War). He states "and if you have read the histories of our time, they are however not dreams or fables from romances."[62] He thus seeks to bring the ideal masculinity of the ancients or chivalric past out of literary texts and into a reality of flesh and blood. Furthermore, Ammirato appeals to the complex role that capital played in aristocratic identity formation. He does not promise that war will make these moneyed men richer (a typical promise made to recruit men of the lower classes), but rather that war will allow nobles to retain their wealth because it will give them an "occupation" and turn them into better men, removing vanities from their head like "sumptuous clothing" (11^v).[63] Gold is not dismissed entirely. It can be a motivating impulse for virtue, but too much gold, he explains in a complex metaphor, is like women's cosmetics, it damages man's God-given nature.[64]

Ammirato's masculinity crisis in Naples could be resolved only if these men would leave for war. Once the Neapolitans returned from battle, fathers would bathe their cheeks in tears, young boys would be inspired, the peasants would applaud, a sweet smell would fill the streets, and women would cover the men with flowers (13^v), and most importantly, these returning soldiers, Ammirato assures them, will finally be "knights, most Illustrious and most Excellent

---

[61] "Non è cosa, che più stimoli gli huomini all opere gloriose, che veder in una medesima città l'inferiore, o il pari, o il maggiore camminare alla gloria"; Ammirato, *Orazione*, fol. 4^v. We have some proof that the *Orazione* was at least nominally effective. The Prince of Conca, of a family from Capua, writes "aver letta con molto suo gusto l'Orazione; e di aver voglia di supplicare S.M. per ottenere il permesso di passare in Ungheria"; quoted in Del Soldato, "Vita di Scipione Ammirato," xlii.

[62] "e se voi havete lette l'istorie de nostri tempi, non sono pero sogni, e favole de romanzi"; Ammirato, *Orazione*, fol. 11^r.

[63] Ammirato tells a story of the Portuguese, who, instead of sharpening arms, embroidered their clothing, and in place of cuirasses made silk jackets; *Orazione*, 12^r. On money, class, and war, see the Castiglione's *Courtier*: a man who goes to war for profit is "no more than a base merchant," (1.43) and Karras, *Boys*, 58.

[64] In an extended metaphor, Ammirato first compares gold coverings of weapons to women's makeup, and then states that to have gold and grand material goods (*pompe*) overflowing is like makeup that ruins women's nature. Ammirato, *Orazione*, 12^r.

Lords, true offspring, legitimate descendants, candid and sincere progeny of the greatest nobility that exists in the world."[65]

This procession rewards militancy with paternal and filial approval as well as erotic reward from women. Yet, if we take Ammirato at his word, one wonders how this has resolved the gender crisis that he perceived as plaguing Naples. Do not the sweet smell of flower-strewn streets and adoring family and women resemble the beautiful squares ("belle piazze") of Naples that Ammirato had so criticized before? In fact, the crisis in Naples seems to be not a failure of manhood at all, but a situation where men are not doing as Ammirato (a proxy for the Grand Duke) and the emperor would wish. Yet, like Machiavelli, Castiglione, Doni, and so many others, the way to convince men to face the bloody, dusty plains of war was to convince them that these masculine identities (signified linguistically as "knight" and "most Illustrious and most Excellent lords") could be attained only through the trials of war. This persuasion is necessitated, of course, by the fact that these lords of Naples did not agree. The only masculinity crisis that truly existed in this scenario was the fantastic one that Ammirato created on the page through his invention of the contemporary Neapolitan man who risked languishing in perfumes and pearls and not realizing his masculine potential.

THE MASCULINITY CRISIS

Scipione Ammirato, like Machiavelli, Castiglione, Doni, and many others not mentioned here, focused on the images of a crisis – not a crisis of blood, violence, and dust in the battlefields but one of coiffures, ornament, gold, and opulence in the piazzas. For some time now, such castigations of "effeminacy" have drawn critical attention from modern scholars and these early modern voices of contempt have often been framed within an *anxiety* or *crisis* model of masculinity.[66] For example, it is common to locate masculine anxiety or crisis in certain cultural or historical moments of the early modern period, including the labour shift of elite males who transitioned from medieval knights to urban court bureaucrats, the ascension of female rulers, the presence of women in court, and the loss of political sovereignty.[67]

---

[65] "cavalieri, Illustriss. & Eccellentiss. Signori vere propaggini, leggittimi rampolli, schietta, & sincera progenie, della maggior nobiltà che sia nel mondo"; Ammirato, *Orazione*, 13ᵛ.

[66] Two excellent books that rely on the anxiety model and bear titles that reflect this framework are Breitenberg, *Anxious Masculinity*, and Long, *High Anxiety*. See Allen, "Men" for an extensive bibliography of nearly twenty-five academic books that focus on masculine anxiety and crisis.

[67] Karras glibly states that a "crisis of masculinity may be like the rise of the middle class, something that seems to happen in all historical periods"; *Boys*, 8. These

The Effeminate Man and the Rhetoric of Anxious Masculinity

It also merits mention that these crises and anxiety models have become the object of much derision, particularly in modern cultural criticism, spawning glib article titles such as "Men Interminably in Crisis?" or "Crisis what Crisis?"[68] In my view, the most convincing complaint about these models of masculinity is the critique of the frequent location of the "crisis" *within* the psyche of the so-called un-masculine man. As medieval historian Frank Klaassen points out, these models "assume a dialogue between an interior state (usually a perceived deficiency) and external self-presentation (usually a compensation for that perceived deficiency), a dialogue for which there is frequently very little evidence."[69] Klaassen directs his criticism at those historians who have no evidence that men behave due to an anxiety over not feeling adequately masculine.[70] I sympathize with Klaassen's methodological concern and note that such a shift in approach would serve to nuance our discussion of elite males who, under attack for being effeminate, were not necessarily experiencing a personal sense of masculine inadequacy. Men, even non-militant ones, could identify as appropriately masculine though they might not be perceived as such by other social groups. As Ruth Karras points out, masculinity was established within discrete peer groups, so that what was considered masculine among groups as diverse as peasants, elites, courtiers, soldiers, famers and intellectuals differed widely.[71]

---

complaints are directed at works such as Biow's thesis that the beard "masks" anxieties of masculinity that were set in motion by the urbanization and courtly culture of the period as well as the invasion and occupation by the French and Spanish: "Needless to say, at a time when Italians suffered from feelings of inferiority in military prowess, wearing a beard hides a weakness inherent in the culture: these men cannot for the life of them defend themselves against the dominant powers of Europe"; Biow, "The Beard," 181.

[68] See Allen, "Men," and Edwards, *Cultures*, 6–21. Edwards informs our understanding of how we might use the word crisis by taking on the landmark study by R. W. Connell, *Masculinities*. Edwards finds fault with Connell, who claimed that although one cannot speak of a crisis of the configuration of masculinity since it is not a coherent system, there is a crisis in the gender order as a whole with the emancipation of women. On the anxiety and crisis models in early modern scholarship, see Shepard, *Meanings of Manhood*, 77–95. She states "To dub any fault line in the edifice of patriarchy a 'crisis' betrays an underlying expectation that it should be insurmountable, and belies the persistent privileging of the majority of men above the majority of women," 87.

[69] Klaassen, "Learning and Masculinity," 51.

[70] Klaassen states that in an anxiety model of criticism we might believe that a priest who wears a weapon would be characterized as compensating for a sense of feeling inadequately masculine when it could be for a myriad of other reasons, "Learning," 51.

[71] Karras argues that pre-modern social divisions make obsolete our notion that "power" is an absolute determinant of masculinity, and these social groups had discrete notions of masculinity; *Boys*, 10–11.

Renaissance scholars unaware of this debate within masculinity studies will nonetheless recognize the much older discussion around the use of the word "crisis." Following Piero Pieri's *Il Rinascimento e la crisi militare italiana* (1934) and works such as Hans Baron's landmark study on the *Crisis of the Early Italian Renaissance* (1955) a lively discussion around the preponderant use of the word "crisis" ensued in historiography.[72] An exasperated Randolph Starn reacted to this in his 1971 article "Historians and 'Crisis.'" While not dismissing the use of a crisis model entirely, Starn cautions that the model risks "persuad[ing] the observer to consider the stresses and strains of human interaction as only abnormal and 'unhealthy,'" and consequently, "academics fashion themselves as the good 'doctor' trying to find the cures to history's ills."[73]

Similarly, we can apply this sort of caution to the crisis model in masculinity studies. The figuration of masculinity "in crisis" implies a momentous deficiency in a previous and preferred condition. If applied as a description of the period, scholarship may unknowingly share an affinity with those famous sixteenth-century voices that tried to prop up a patriarchal order that was clinging to a coherence that never existed in the first place. Caution in the use of terminology, however, does not mean excising the terms *anxiety* and *crisis* from our studies of early modern masculinity. On the contrary, there were crises and anxieties within the discursive landscape. It is quite clear that the rhetoric used by authors such as Machiavelli, Castiglione, Doni, and Ammirato was meant to create anxiety, to highlight the "abrasion" that might occur between men's lived realities and more formalized ideals of manhood.[74] These authors were invested in the social control of men; their method was to invoke effeminophobia and to persuade men to follow a prescribed conduct that had the potential, according to the author, of redeeming a normative masculinity. In the cases I discuss, the desired effect was, at least on the surface, militancy. To disallow the use of words that scholars might access to describe the complex forces of social control is to silence the gender violence that was mobilized against men and

---

[72] Pieri argued that the military defeats of the Italians in the early sixteenth century were the result of inadequate infantry. This was caused, in his assessment, from the distrust that had developed between the nobility and the common people; *Il Rinascimento*, 599–607. Baron instead located a crisis among Florentine thinkers who, according to him, believed that good prevailed until this political philosophy was altered during the threatened invasion by Giangaleazzo Visconti of Milan.

[73] Starn's article points to the medical and biological origins of the word crisis, and thus he adopts this medical metaphor of the critic playing the "doctor"; Starn, "Historians," 21.

[74] On "abrasion," see Rosen: "men experience abrasion between the masculine ideal and the surrounding world, between a shifting sense of self and world and a restrictive or dysfunctional sense of role, they often try to create a new definition of masculinity"; *Changing Fictions*, xiii.

women in order to maintain a normative masculinity and patriarchy. This suppression returns us to a moment – not so long ago – when masculinity was not scrutinized, when the relations between men were not to be discussed.[75] The new direction of masculinity studies must instead take a bold and different approach, one where scholars and readers address textual evidence fearlessly in all its multivalent and controversial possibilities.

College of Staten Island – CUNY

CITED WORKS

Printed Sources

Accademia della Crusca. *Vocabolario degli accademici della Crusca.* Venice: Giovanni Alberti, 1612.
Allen, Judith A. "Men Interminably in Crisis? Historians on Masculinity, Sexual Boundaries, and Manhood." *Radical History Review* 82 (2002): 191–207.
Ammirato, Scipione. *Orazione di Scipione Ammirato scritta alla nobiltà napoletana confortandola ad andar alla guerra d'Ungheria contra i Turchi.* Florence: Gli Heredi di Iacopo Giunti, 1594.
Antoniano, Silvio. *Dell'educazione cristiana e politica de' figlioli. Libri tre.* Milan: Pogliani, 1821.
Baron, Hans. *The Crisis of the Early Italian Renaissance: Civic Humanism and Republican Liberty in an Age of Classicism and Tyranny.* Princeton, NJ: Princeton University Press, 1955.
Bayley, Charles Calvert. *War and Society in Renaissance Florence.* Toronto: University of Toronto Press, 1961.
Beauvoir, Simone de. *The Second Sex.* Ed. and trans. H. M. Parshley. New York: Vintage, 1989.
Becker, Anna. "Rethinking Masculinity and Femininity in Niccolò Machiavelli's Political Thought." *L'Homme* 23.2 (2012): 65–78.
Biow, Douglas. "The Beard in Sixteenth-Century Italy." In Julia L. Hairston and Walter Stephens, eds, *The Body in Early Modern Italy.* Baltimore, MD: Johns Hopkins University Press, 2010, 176–194.
Breitenberg, Mark. *Anxious Masculinity in Early Modern England.* Cambridge, UK: Cambridge University Press, 1996.
Bruscagli, Riccardo. *Niccolò Machiavelli.* Florence: La Nuova Italia, 1975.
Castiglione, Baldassarre. *Il libro del cortegiano.* Ed. Amedeo Quondam. Milan: Garzanti, 1981.

---

[75] On the tradition of masculinity as existing outside scrutiny, see Simone de Beauvoir's famous assertion that a man would never write a book about the human male, *The Second Sex*, xxi and Grosz, *Jacques Lacan*, 173.

Connell, Raewyn W. *Masculinities*. Berkeley, CA: University of California Press, 2005.
Del Soldato, Francesco. "Vita di Scipione Ammirato." In *Istorie Fiorentine di Scipione Ammirato con l'aggiunte di Scipione Ammirato il giovane*. Vol. 11. Florence: L. Marchini and G. Becherini, 1827, i–xlii.
De Mattei, Rodolfo. *Il pensiero politico di Scipione Ammirato*. Lecce: Centro di Studi Salentini, 1959.
——. "Scipione Ammirato." *Dizionario Biografico degli Italiani*. Vol. 3. Rome: Istituto dell'Enciclopedia Italiana, 1961, 1–4.
Doni, Anton Francesco. *I marmi*, ed. Carlo Alberto Girotto and Giovanna Rizzarelli. Florence: Leo S. Olschki, 2017.
——. *La terza parte de I Marmi del Doni fiorentino*. Venice: Gio. Battista Bertoni, 1609.
Edwards, Tim. *Cultures of Masculinity*. New York: Routledge, 2006.
Elshtain, Jean Bethke. *Women and War*. Chicago, IL: The University of Chicago Press, 1987.
Finucci, Valeria. *The Manly Masquerade: Masculinity, Paternity, and Castration in the Italian Renaissance*. Durham, NC: Duke University Press, 2003.
Gilbert, Felix. "Machiavelli: The Renaissance of the Art of War." In Peter Paret, Gordon A. Craig, and Felix Gilbert, eds, *Makers of Modern Strategy from Machiavelli to the Nuclear Age*. Princeton, NJ: Princeton University Press, 1986, 11–31.
Gleason, Maud W. *Making Men: Sophists and Self-Presentation in Ancient Rome*. Princeton, NJ: Princeton University Press, 2008.
Grendler, Paul. *Critics of the Italian World*. Madison, WI: University of Wisconsin Press, 1969.
Gouwens, Kenneth. "Meanings of Masculinity in Paola Giovio's 'Ischian Dialogues.'" *I Tatti Studies in the Italian Renaissance* 17.1 (2014): 79–101.
Grosz, Elizabeth. *Jacques Lacan: A Feminist Introduction*. London: Routledge, 1990.
Guicciardini, Francesco. "Discorso di Logrogno." In Athanasios Moulakis, ed. and trans., *Republican Realism in Renaissance Florence, Francesco Guicciardini's "Discorso di Logrogno."* Lanham, MD: Rowman & Littlefield, 1998.
Hale, John Rigby. *Renaissance War Studies*. London: Hambledon Press, 1983.
Hennen, Peter. *Faeries, Bears, and Leathermen: Men in Community Queering the Masculine*. Chicago, IL: The University of Chicago Press, 2008.
Higate, Paul and John Hopton. "War, Militarism and Masculinities." In Michael S. Kimmel, Jeff Hearn, and Robert W. Connell, eds, *Handbook of Studies on Men and Masculinities*. Thousand Oaks, CA: SAGE, 2005, 432–447.
Karras, Ruth Mazo. *From Boys to Men: Formations of Masculinity in Late Medieval Europe*. Philadelphia, PA: University of Pennsylvania Press, 2003.
Kettering, Alison McNeil. "Gentlemen in Satin: Masculine Ideals in Later Seventeenth-Century Dutch Portraiture." *Art Journal* 56 (1997): 41–47.

King, Thomas E. *The Gendering of Men, 1600-1750*. Vol. 1. Madison, WI: University of Wisconsin Press, 2004.
Klaassen, Frank. "Learning and Masculinity in Manuscripts of Ritual Magic of the Later Middle Ages and Renaissance." *Sixteenth Century Journal* 38.1 (2007): 49-76.
Long, Kathleen P. *High Anxiety: Masculinity in Crisis in Early Modern France*. Kirksville, MO: Truman State University Press, 2002.
Machiavelli, Niccolò. *Art of War*. In Allen Gilbert, ed. and trans., *Machiavelli: The Chief Works and Others*. Durham, NC: Duke University Press, 1989.
——. *Discourses*. In *Machiavelli: The Chief Works and Others*, ed. and trans. Allen Gilbert. Durham, NC: Duke University Press, 1989.
——. *Opere*. Ed. Corrado Vivanti. Turin: Einaudi-Gallimard, 1997.
Macdonald, Sharon, Pat Holden and Shirley Ardener, eds *Images of Women in Peace and War*. Madison, WI: University of Wisconsin Press, 1988.
Marletta, Fedele. "L'umanista Francesco Pontano." *Nuova Rivista Storica* 26 (1942): 32-41.
Marri, Giulia, "La partecipazione di don Giovanni de' Medici alla guerra d'Ungheria (1594-95 e 1601). *Archivio storico italiano* 99.1 (1941): 50-59.
Masi, Giorgio. "*Arte della guerra*." *Enciclopedia Machiavelliana*. Vol. 1. Rome: Istituto della enciclopedia italiana, 2014, 108-122.
——. "Coreografie doniane: L'Accademia Pellegrina." In P. Procaccioli and A. Romani, eds, *Cinquecento capriccioso e irregolare: Eresie letterarie nell'Italia del Classicismo*. Manziana: Vecchiarelli, 1999, 45-86.
——. "'Quelle discordanze sì perfette': Anton Francesco Doni 1551-1553." *Atti e Memorie dell'Accademia di Scienze e Lettere La Colombaria* 53 (1988): 9-112.
Melis, Alessandro. "'Sei troppo effeminato./ Di femmina sono nato': Infrazione di codice e fluidità di genere in alcuni libretti d'opera del Seicento veneziano." *Storia delle donne* 16 (2020): 101-124.
Milligan, Gerry. "Aesthetics, Dress, and Militant Masculinity in *The Courtier*." In Jacqueline Murray and Nicholas Terpstra, eds, *Sex, Gender, and Sexuality in Renaissance Italy*. New York: Routledge, 2019, 141-159.
——. "Masculinity and Machiavelli: How to Avoid Effeminacy, Perform Manliness and be Wary of the Author." In Patricia Vilches and Gerald Seaman, eds, *Seeking Real Truths: Multidisciplinary Perspectives on Machiavelli*. Leiden: Brill, 2007, 149-172.
——. *Moral Combat: Women, Gender, and War in Italian Renaissance Literature*. Toronto: University of Toronto Press, 2018.
——. "The Politics of Effeminacy in *Il cortegiano*." *Italica* 83.3-4 (2006): 345-366.
—— and Jane Tylus, eds *The Poetics of Masculinity in Early Modern Italy and Spain*. Essays and Studies, 22. Toronto: Centre for Reformation and Renaissance Studies, 2010.
Neocleous, Mark. "'O Effeminacy! Effeminacy!': War, Masculinity, and the Myth of Liberal Peace." *European Journal of International Relations* 19.1 (2011): 93-113.

Nuovo, Isabella. *Otium e Negotium: da Petrarca a Scipione Ammirato*. Bari: Palomar, 2007.

Olson, Kelly. *Masculinity and Dress in Roman Antiquity*. New York: Routledge, 2017.

Phang, Sara Elise. *Roman Military Service: Ideologies of Discipline in the Late Republic and Early Principate*. New York: Cambridge University Press, 2008.

Pieri, Piero. *Il Rinascimento e la crisi militare*. Turin: Einaudi, 1952.

Pitkin, Hanah Fenichel. *Fortune is a Woman: Gender and Politics in the thought of Niccolò Machiavelli*. Chicago, IL: The University of Chicago Press, 1984.

Pontano, Francesco. "*Dello integro e perfetto stato delle donzelle*." In Cesare Riccomanni, ed., *Raccolta di scritture varie pubblicata nell'occasione delle nozze Riccomanni-Fineschi*. Turin: Vercellino, 1863, 13–30.

Reeser, Todd. *Masculinities in Theory: An Introduction*. Malden, MA: Wiley-Blackwell, 2010.

Ricasoli, Pandolfo. *Orazione in lode della verginità e della fortezza militare fatta nell'occasione della morte del Principe D. Francesco Medici*. Florence: Sermartelli, 1615.

Richards, Jennifer. "'A Wanton Trade of Living?': Rhetoric, Effeminacy, and the Early Modern Courtier." *Criticism: A Quarterly for Literature and the Arts* 42.2 (2000): 185–206.

Rizzarelli, Giovanna, ed. *I "Marmi" di Anton Francesco Doni: La storia, i generi, e le arti*. Florence: Leo S. Olschki, 2012.

Rogoff, Irit and David van Leer. "Afterthoughts ... A Dossier on Masculinities." *Theory and Society* 22.5 (1993): 739–762.

Rosen, David. *The Changing Fictions of Masculinity*. Urbana, IL: University of Illinois Press, 1993.

Schachter, Marc. "'Quanto Concede la Guerra': Epic Masculinity and the Education of Desire in Tasso's *Gerusalemme Liberata*." In Gerry Milligan and Jane Tylus, eds, *The Poetics of Masculinity in Early Modern Italy and Spain*. Essays and Studies, 22. Toronto: Centre for Reformation and Renaissance Studies, 2010, 213–240.

Sedgwick, Eve Kosofsky. "How to Bring Your Kids Up Gay." *Social Text* 29 (1991): 18–27.

Shepard, Alexandra. *Meanings of Manhood in Early Modern England*. Oxford, UK: Oxford University Press, 2003.

Starn, Randolph. "Historians and 'Crisis.'" *Past & Present* 52 (1971): 3–22.

Taddei, Ilaria. *Fanciulli e giovani: crescere a Firenze nel Rinascimento*. Florence: Leo S. Olschki, 2001.

Tylus, Jane. "Epic's Endless Deferral: Vernacular Masculinities in the Florence of Lorenzo de' Medici." In Gerry Milligan and Jane Tylus, eds, *The Poetics of Masculinity in Early Modern Italy and Spain*. Essays and Studies, 22. Toronto: Centre for Reformation and Renaissance Studies, 2010, 75–100.

Westwater, Lynn Lara. "Doni's Reuse in *I Marmi* of Gendered Elements from Guevara's *Relox de Príncep*s." In Giovanna Rizzarelli, ed., *I "Marmi" di Anton*

Francesco Doni: La storia, i generi, e le arti. Florence: Leo S. Olschki, 2012, 169–181.

Williams, Craig A. *Roman Homosexuality: Ideologies of Masculinity in Classical Antiquity.* New York: Oxford University Press, 1999.

Electronic Sources

Guicciardini, Francesco. "Del modo di ordinare il governo popolare." Online at www.Bibliotecaitaliana.it/scheda/bibit001107.

Urbaniak, Martyna. "'I pronostici et le novelle, i trovati, le lettere, de' paesi strani': *I Marmi* of Anton Francesco Doni between novella and dialogue." In Alain Létourneau, François Cooren and Nicolaas Bencherki, eds, *Representations in Dialogue: Dialogue in Representations.* Proceedings of the 13th conference of the International Association for Dialogue Analysis, 2012: 293–310. Online at www.iada-web.org/download.representationsindialogue.pdf.

INDEX

Acadians 5, 101
Accademia della Crusca 194
Accademia Fiorentina 198
Accademia Peregrina 198
aesthetic sensibilities 15, 25, 27, 133n10
aesthetics and dress 195–200, 204–6
affection 24, 49. *See also* love
African attendant 79
Alexander VI, pope 91–2
Alexandrianism 25, 27
Alfonso XI, king of Castile 159
al-Gafūrī, ʿAbd al-Majīd 68
Ammirato, Scipione 10, 194, 202–6, 208
Amsterdam 76, 127–8
Angel, Philips 142
angels 79, 85
Angers, cathedral school 16
Antonello da Messina, *Portrait of a Man* 89
Antoniano, Silvio 195
anxiety 9–10, 94, 104, 117, 119, 194–8, 206–8
 effeminophobic 194–8, 208
 and gender presentation 104, 117, 119, 197–8
appraiser (*stimatore*) 39–40
Ariosto, Ludovico. *Orlando furioso* 196n19, 200
Aristotle 80, 95
armour 8, 27, 91, 94–5, 103, 107, 109, 112, 115, 119, 125n3, 134–5, 137, 142. *See also* baldric, helmet, sword
ars dictaminis 17
arte 46
ascetic, asceticism 17, 19, 86
asexual, asexuality 79, 85, 88

Astrakhan khanate 65–6
Augustine, St 82
authority 15–21, 24, 28

Baglioni, Giovanni 46
baldric (sword belt) 127–8 131, 142, 144, 148
Baron, Hans 208
Baṭṭalnāma 66–7
Baudri of Bourgueil 15–28
Bayard, Pierre Terrial, chevalier de 175–6, 180–4, 188–9
beards 7–8, 11, 43, 75–99, 103–4, 111, 118, 140, 207n67
behaviour, improper 8, 36, 60, 104, 125, 159
 proper 56, 104, 157, 182–3
Bellini, Gentile 79–80
Benedetti, Alessandro 90–1
beret, plumed 127
Bernard of Clairvaux 19, 110
Bertoni, Giovan Battista 201
Bessarion, cardinal 7, 80, 82
bin Muslīm, ʿAbd al-Mannān 67
biography 9, 58, 182–4
Black prince. *See* Edward, prince of Wales
body, the 21, 24, 75, 79, 86, 90–1, 96, 101, 103–4, 109–11, 115, 117–19, 202–4
boots 103, 105, 107, 109, 112–13, 115–16, 118–19, 142
Borch, Gerard ter 135, 137
Borgia, Lucrezia 91–2
Botticelli, Sandro 135
boy 8, 41–4, 109, 157, 160, 195n17, 203, 205
Brétigny, Treaty of 157, 161
Bronzino, Agnolo 95–7, fig. 4.10

215

Index

brotherhood 63, 178
   milk–brotherhood 47
Brueghel, Jan (the Elder) 135–6
Buonarroti, Michelangelo 97
Burch, Hendrik van der 131
Burckhardt, Jacob 3, 15
Byzantine Church 80. *See also* Greek Orthodox Church

Campo de Montiel, battle of 159
Carafa, Carlo, cardinal 39
Caravaggio, Michelangelo 46
cards, playing 127–8
Castiglione, Baldassare 138, 149, 195, 197, 205n63, 206, 208
Castilian Civil War 159–71
cathedral schools 16–17, 19
Cellini, Benvenuto 47, 89
Certeau, Michel de 20
Chanson (La) de Bertrand du Guesclin 155, 157–9, 178
charivari 37
Charles I, king of England 116, 148
Charles II, king of Navarre 167
Charles V, Holy Roman Emperor 7, 92, 94–6, 187, 205, fig. 4.9
Charles V, king of France 157–8
Charles VII, king of France 180
Charles VIII, king of France 196
Charry, Jacques Prevot, sieur de 186
Chaucer, Geoffrey 22, 103, 111, 118
Chinggis culture and society 53, 55, 58–60, 63, 65–8
Chinggis Khan 58–9, 66
chivalric knighthood 9–11, 109, 112, 117, 182–3, 200–1
   literature 103, 138n20, 176–9, 181, 183–4, 189
chivalry 2, 8–9, 11, 115–17, 175–89, 200–6. *See also* Masculinity, warrior
Chrétien de Troyes 19
Christian Knight, theme of 142
Cicero 15, 28, 196
Civil War, Castilian 158–9
   English 112–3
civility 138, 149
classicism 5, 15, 19–20, 95, 97, 134–5, 195

Clement of Alexandria 82
Clement VII, pope 83
cloak 8, 43, 113, 127–8, 130–1, 140, 142, 144, 148
cloth of honour. *See* Honour
clothes, men's 10, 15, 46–7, 49, 65, 79–80, 101, 103–4, 107, 109, 111–13, 115–17, 119, 127–8, 135, 137, 140, 144, 194–7, 199–200, 205. *See also* armour, beret, cloak, codpiece, glove, hat
   women's 131–2
clothing, male, effeminate 194–7, 205
Codde, Pieter 128
codpiece 8, 87, 115
Coëtivy, Alain de (cardinal of Avignon) 80, 82
community of practice 18, 21–2
Compendium of Qādr-ʿAlī Bek 66
competence 5, 16, 22, 31–49, 157, 167, 172
continuity and change, historical 2–4, 11
corruption, moral 19, 68, 95–6, 196
cosmetics 205
court records 5, 31–5
courts of law 31, 34–6, 40, 42–5, 49
cowardice 9, 32, 34, 155, 158, 168–9, 171, 173, 200
Cranach, Lucas 83
crime 163
Crimean khanate 57, 65
Cuvelier, poet 156–72

Daftar-e Chinggis-nāma 59–60, 66
Damian, Peter 19
Danckertsz. the Younger, Cornelis 84, fig. 4.4
Delilah. *See* Samson
Della Casa, Giovanni 149
Della Valle, Filippo 47–8
dishonour 117. *See also* honour
dissimulation 39
distrust, mistrust 39, 171, 208n72
dominance, male 4, 23n31, 104
Doni, Anton Francesco 10, 194, 198–202
Doria, Andrea 96–7, fig. 4.10
dress *see* clothing. *See also* aesthetics

216

Index

Droochsloot, Joost Cornelisz.   131
Duck, Jacob   128
Duels, Duelling   125, 138
Dürer, Albrecht   79, 89, 92, figs. 4.2, 4.7
Duyster, Willem   128

Edward III, king of England   161–2, 161, 166
Edward, prince of Wales (the Black Prince)   159, 161, 166–9, 170–3, 175, 178
effeminacy   10, 19, 80, 82, 157n9, 193–209
effeminophobia   194–8, 208
Eighty Years' War   135
emblems / emblem books   134, 138, 140, 142
England   7, 33n5, 38n15, 101–20, 138, 144
epistolography   18
eroticism   8, 16, 18, 20–1, 91, 95, 131, 134, 137, 206
eunuchs   79, 95
excess, as legal concept   36–7, 49

Fabritius, Barend   134, 142, 143, fig. 6.9
faith (*fede*), as social quality   38–40, 43, 49
fama (as reputation)   38
Faret, Jacques   138, 149
fashion   75, 82, 87, 89, 92, 94, 101, 103–4, 107, 110, 112–13, 115–17, 119, 137, 140, 142, 144
fear   48, 60, 65, 138, 166–7, 170, 176, 182, 185n48, 196
fede   5. *See also* faith; trust
femininity, femineity   1, 5, 18, 33, 110, 117
fencing   125–6
Ferdowsi, Abul-Qasem   56
Ferrand, Jacques   95
feudalism   176–77
feuds / feuding   40, 48–9
fiction   20–1, 113, 116, 132n10
fight / fighting   36, 39, 48–9, 61, 64, 68, 125, 134n13, 138, 142, 149, 161–2, 166, 168–9, 171, 177–8, 181–3, 187–8, 193, 203–5

fight books   125n3, 134, 137
fighters   60–1, 177, 186
Flemish artists   128
Florence   46, 87, 193, 198, 201–2
Focquenbroch, Willem van   148–9
Fornovo, battle of   181
Francis I, king of France   7, 92, 94, 187
Francis, Saint   86–7

gallants   116
gender binaries   3, 5, 10
   expectations   3, 10, 34, 76, 91, 175–6, 178–80, 189. *See also* masculinity, expectations
   flexibility of   104, 118–19
   norms   6, 17–18, 179–81, 189. *See also* masculinity, norms
   performance *see* masculinity, performance
genre scene   127, 134–5, 140
Geoffrey of Monmouth   19
Gezelschappen   128, 131, 135
Ghaznavid dynasty   56, 58
Giovio, Paolo   97, 193n3
gloves   131, 140, 142, 144, 148, 200
Golden Horde   6, 53, 55, 57–9, 65–6, 68
Gonzaga, Federico   95
Grande Compaignie. *See* Great Company
Grassi, Paolo di   36
Great Company   159, 161–6, 168
Greek Orthodox Church   80, 82
Grien, Hans Baldung   85, fig. 4.5
Guesclin, Bertrand du   9, 41n22, 155–7, 164, 170, 178
Guevara, Antonio de   198
Guicciardini, Francesco   193

Haarlem   128, 140
hair, facial. *See* beards
Hals, Dirck   128
Hals, Frans   140–1, fig. 6.8
Hapsburg (family)   95, 185, 187. *See also* Charles V, Holy Roman Emperor
hat   43, 127–8, 140, 148
Heem, Jan Davidsz. de   147–9, fig. 6.12
helmet   135, 170, 182, 186
Hennen, Peter   193–5

217

Index

Henry of Trastámara 155, 158–61, 165–73
Henry VIII, king of England 7, 94, 112
Hercules 137
Heythuysen, Willem van 140–2
hierarchy, as social condition 23, 40–1, 47
Hildebert of Lavardin 19, 22
Hildegard of Bingen 19
Hilliard, Nicholas 144
Hippocrates 80
historical periodization. *See* periodization
Hollar, Wenceslaus 76–7, fig. 4.1
Holofernes. *See* Judith
homoerotic poetry 91
honour, men's 4–5, 9, 37–40, 44, 47, 49, 58, 63–5, 80, 88, 92, 110, 125, 134, 138, 142, 148, 150, 157, 164, 167, 181–2, 185. *See also* dishonour
　women's 39
Hooch, Pieter de 130
Hoogstraten, Samuel van 131, 142
Horace 15–16, 18–20, 25
household / householder 5, 8, 15, 20, 36n11, 181
humanism 2, 15, 17, 19, 24
Hundred Years War 9, 156, 179–80, 182

icon, Bulgarian 79, fig. 4.3
identity 1, 16–18, 20–1, 75, 104, 110, 118, 177, 202, 205. *See also* masculine identity
immorality 68
information, scarcity of 37–9
ingenium 24–7
Islam 54–6, 58–9, 64–8. *See also* Muslim
Italian Wars 179–80, 185
Italy 4, 7, 10, 32n3, 33, 37, 38n15, 39–40, 46, 94, 196, 202
Jaeger, C. Stephen 17–18

Jāmiʿ al-Tawārīkh 58, 66
Jewel (The) Translucent Sūtra 59
jihad 67

Judith (biblical) 137
Justus van Ghent 80

Karkadann 60, 60n32
Kazan khanate 55, 57, 65–7
Khanaqah 66
Klaassen, Frank 207
knife fighting 125n2
knight 2, 9–10, 16, 101–20, 155, 158, 161, 166–7, 175–84, 188–9, 198, 200–6. *See also* masculinity, warrior
　Christian 142
knighthood 8, 113, 115–16, 155–8, 164, 171, 175–84, 201–3, 205–6

Leoni, Leone 95
Lepanto, Battle of 79
limited good 37
Loire Valley poets 15, 17, 19
Long War (1593–1606) 202, 205
Louis XI, king of France 180
love scenes 8, 125–50
love 40, 134–5, 137, 144, 149, 160, 188, 203–4
lovers 8, 32, 134–5
loyalty 5, 9, 33, 38–9, 41, 47, 49, 58, 63, 65, 155–9, 162, 171–2, 188. *See also fede*; trust
Lucretius 134
Luther, Martin 83–6, figs. 4.4, 4.5
lyric poetry 15–28

Machiavelli, Niccolò 10, 38–9, 196–7, 200, 201n46, 206, 208
Madrasa 66, 68
Maes, Nicolaes 130–1, 134, fig. 6.3
Mahmūd of Ghaznī 56
Mailles, Jacques 9, 176, 180–6
Man, Cornelis de 130
manly, manliness 18, 32n4, 36, 38, 40–1, 45, 49, 82, 96, 104, 110, 137–8, 149, 196
Marbode of Rennes 19, 22
Mars 33, 134–7, fig. 6.6
martial code 16, 28, 32n2, 55, 60, 112, 118, 127, 144, 175, 177–8
　violence 175–7, 180, 182, 184–5, 189

218

Index

Mary Tudor, queen of England 112, 118
masculine ideal 36n11, 54, 101, 117, 137, 142, 149, 157n9, 158, 172, 181, 187, 189, 193, 195, 197, 200–1, 203, 205, 208n74
   identity 1, 5, 8–9, 11, 20, 75, 118–19, 125, 138. *See also* identity
masculinity, ancient 96, 196–7, 200–1, 205
   chivalric 16, 101, 104, 158n9, 176–9, 178, 180, 187, 189, 193, 202
   clerical 16, 19
   crisis of 1, 94–5, 205–8
   elite 4, 9–11, 15–28, 49, 54, 94, 109–10, 117, 119, 206–7
   expectations 3, 10, 34, 175–6, 178–80, 182, 189. *See also* gender, expectations
   hegemonic 4–6, 10, 16, 18–19, 28, 54, 194
   hierarchical 4–6, 8, 54
   medieval 18–20, 36n11, 104, 110–11, 117, 175, 178, 184, 189
   monastic 4–5, 20, 17, 87
   norms 6, 8, 175–6, 178, 180–1, 184, 188–9
   performance of 1–2, 10, 20, 32–3, 103–4, 117–18, 157, 177, 179–80, 194–5
   practice of 19, 32–3, 36, 49
   warrior 2, 6, 8–10, 11, 18–19, 21, 53, 59, 63–5, 68, 149, 197, 199, 203
material culture 103
materiality 16, 21–2, 24–7
Medici, Cosimo I de', grand-duke of Tuscany 92, 95
Medici, Giovanni de' 205
Medici, Lorenzo de' 197n26
medicine 89–91
melancholy 144, 148
Melanson 101–2, 119–20
Metsu, Gabriel 126–8, 134, fig. 6.1
Michelangelo *see* Buonarroti, Michelangelo
militarism and dress 200, 203–4. *See also* Armour
   and literature 205
   and propaganda 204–5
   and weakness 193, 195, 197

military / militarism 155–72, 137, 148
   evolution 2, 9, 175–6, 180, 189
   iconography in pictures 135, 142
Modern period 2
monastic circles, ideas, life 4, 17, 19–21, 26, 87
Mongol empire 4, 6, 58, 64
Mongols 6, 53–5, 58–9, 63–5
Monluc, Blaise de 9, 175–6, 184–9
moral capital 35, 37–8
   compass 6, 9, 64
morality 6, 9, 17, 35, 38, 56, 59, 64, 67–8, 149, 157, 195, 199
   Christian 10, 195
Moscow 66
Moses 80, 97
Münster, Treaty of 135
murder 48–9, 117, 160, 163
music 126–8, 131, fig. 6.1
Muslim 4, 6, 53–6, 59, 64–8, 82, 159, 166, 177. *See also* Islam

Nájera, battle of 155–78
Naples 94, 186, 202–6
Native Americans 76
Neptune 79, 96–7
Netherlands 126, 135
Netscher, Caspar 137
Nine Worthies 156n4
nobility 8, 19, 55, 104, 125, 138, 142, 148, 156, 165, 175–80, 183–6, 188–9, 202–4, 206, 208n72. *See also* Second Estate
Noghay horde 65

old men / old age 5, 33, 45, 49, 88, 148, 186
Oliver, Isaac 116, 144, 146, fig. 6.11
Omphale. *See* Hercules
orality 35, 39, 45, 54, 56–8
Otto of Friesing 19
Ottoman empire 2, 7, 57, 202
   literature 57
Ottomans 40, 76, 79, figs. 4.1, 4.2
Ovid 15, 18–21, 25, 137

Palamedesz., Anthonie 128
Pallantieri, Alessandro 41–3
paterfamilias 5, 16, 20

Index

patriarchy, patriarchal   4, 11, 97, 202, 207n68, 208–9
patronage   24
Paul, St   25, 82, 142
Pavia, Battle of   181
peace-making   36, 48–9
Pedro I, king of Castile   159–61, 165–72
penitents   85
Percy, Henry, earl of Northumberland   144
performance   21, 32–5, 38n15, 45, 49
  court testimony as   32, 34–5
  masculinity as   1–2, 4, 7–10, 19–20, 32, 54, 101, 103–4, 118, 157–8, 177, 179–80, 194–5
  social   15, 17, 32–3, 103
perfume   195, 199, 200–1, 204, 206
periodization   2–3, 5, 11
Persia   6
Persian romances   56
Petrarch   15
Petrus Christus   87, fig. 4.6
phallic replacement   103–4
  symbols   8, 115
Piccolomini, Aeneas Silvius   80
Pieri, Piero   208
Piero di Cosimo   89
pilgrims   85–6
Pitkin, Hannah   197
pity   162
Plato   80
play, playing   20–1, 28, 49, 128
Pontano, Francesco   195
portraits   8, 34, 75–6, 80, 86–9, 92–3, 96–7, 103, 112, 115–17, 127, 134–5, 140–2, 144–5, 148–9
Premodern period   1, 3–5
prison   40–5, 49, 65, 85, 142
prisoners   65, 85–6, 160, 169–70, 172
prostitutes (sex workers)   34, 201
  men as   199
prostitution / sex work   31–2, 36, 39, 47
Protestants. *See* Reformation

Qahramān-i Qātil   6
Qiṣṣa-i Sayf al-Mulūk   66–7
Qiṣṣa-i Yūsuf   67

Raḥīmqūl Abubakr-ulı̈   67
Rammāl Khwaja   67
rape, sexual violation   37, 41, 163
Rasūliyya Madrasa   68
Reeser, Todd W.   194
Reformation, Protestant   7, 83, 148, fig. 4.4
Rembrandt   89, 134, 142, 144–5, 149, fig. 6.10
Robert de Molesme, St   17
Romano, Giulio   95
Rome   5, 31–48
  violence of   36
Rubens, Pieter Paul   135–6, fig. 6.6

Sahīb Girāy Khan   57
Samson (biblical)   137
Sangallo, Francesco Giamberti da   89
satire   135, 138
Savelli, Onorio   37
Savonarola, Girolamo   87
scarcity, as condition of life   37–8
Second Estate   177–8. *See also* Nobility
secrecy   18, 39
Secret (The) History of the Mongols   58–9
self, sense of   6–11, 17–18, 41, 46, 120, 140, 167
self–control, self-discipline   6–8, 19, 33n4, 54, 68, 85–6, 104, 113, 117, 120
self-defence   46, 149
self–help, as social regulation   36
self-portrait   88–9, 142, fig. 4.7
self-presentation   6–7, 9–11, 15–16, 22, 34, 63, 75, 89, 110, 120, 142, 148, 158, 176, 183–4, 207, 208n74
self-sacrifice   148
servants   21, 23, 38–9, 41, 47–9, 127–8, 140
sex (activity)   19–20, 31–2, 36–7, 41–3, 49, 89, 91–2, 95, 104, 178, 195n17, 196
  and violence   36, 49, 104
  worker *see* prostitute
sexual code   37
  exploitation   41, 43
  immorality   68
  values   20, 41

220

Index

sexuality 7–8, 19–20, 75
Sforza, Giovanni 90–2, fig. 4.8
Sforza, Ludovico 181
Shāhnāma 56, 67
shame 82, 86, 166, 169–70, 175–6, 196n19
shaving 7, 75–91, 94
shield 170, 186
 rondelle 186
Siberian khanate 65–6
Siena, Siege of 188
Simurgh 62
Sinnepoppen 134n13, 138–9, 142, fig. 6.7
Six, Jan 134, 144–5, 149, fig. 6.10
social capital 35, 37, 205
soldiers 135, 137
spurs 7, 11, 101–20, figs. 5.1, 5.2, 5.3
 symbolism of 109–10, 113, 116, 119
 worn by women 113
Starn, Randolph 208
status, marriageable 91
 military 95, 101, 109
 physiological 92
 social 4–8, 15–16, 19–21, 23n31, 62, 64, 66, 75, 79, 104, 109, 113, 117, 138, 144n32, 148, 150, 178, 198, 200
Steen, Jan 137
Suleiman the Magnificent, sultan of the Ottoman Empire 7, 76, 79, 94
sumptuary law 112
sword 7–8, 11, 48, 64, 110, 113, 118, 125–50, 182–3, 186, 200, 203
 dress 200
 dying by 168
 longsword 134n12, 142
 rapier 133–4, 144, 148, fig. 6.5
 sabre 134n12, 142, 148
Symeon, archbishop of Thessalonica 80
syphilis 95

Tarīkh-i Jahān-gushā 58
Ṭārsūsī, Abū Ṭāhir Muḥammad b. Ḥasan b. ʿAlī b. Mūsā 56
Tasso, Torquato 137n19, 196n19, 197n26
Thirteen Years War *see* Long War

threats, threatening 36, 38, 47, 140, 158, 160, 165
Titian 79
toga 200
tonsure 85–7
torture 35, 44, 49
Trente, La battaille de 182
trust, trustworthiness 5, 9, 37–9, 65, 159–60. *See also* distrust
Turks. *See* Ottomans
Twelve Years' Truce 135
Tylus, Jane 194

uncertainty, as a condition 10, 37, 40, 60
Urbino, court 195
 studiolo 80

Vacant See (papal interregnum) 36
Venus 33, 134–7, fig. 6.6
Vermeyen, Jan Cornelisz. 93, fig. 4.9
Vinckboons, David 128–9, fig. 6.2
violence 5, 19–21, 27, 31–2, 34, 36, 40, 48–9, 60–1, 104, 110, 117, 125n2, 126, 128, 135, 138, 157–8, 162–4, 172, 178, 175, 177–8, 180, 182–5, 189, 206, 208. *See also* Martial violence, Sex and violence
 and chivalry 125n4
 culture of 125–6, 128, 138
 in pictures 128, 135
Visscher, Claes Jansz. 139, fig. 6.7
Visscher, Roemer 134n13, 138–40, 144, fig. 6.7
Vitalis, Orderic 85
Volga-Ural Muslim literature 54–5, 66–8
Volga-Ural region 6, 53–68

war 2, 9–10, 25, 36, 40–1, 56, 60–1, 112, 119, 135, 138, 140, 148, 158–9, 170, 176, 181, 183–6, 196, 199, 204–6
Ward, Samuel 114, fig. 5.4
warfare 113, 119, 169n23, 175–80, 184–6, 188–9, 203
warrantor (*garante*) 38
warrior 2, 6, 9–11, 18–19, 21, 53–4, 56–60, 63–4, 66, 79, 119, 137, 177–9, 181, 184, 189, 196n19, 203
 princess 58, 61

Index

Wars of Religion, French   179n19, 180n24, 185
weapons   27, 125, 127, 134, 137–8, 148–9, 142, 183, 207n70. *See also* shields; swords

Weiditz, Christoph   96–7
Westphalia, Treaty of   135
Westwater, Lynn   198
Witte, Emanuel de   130
Wtewael, Joachim   134

GENDER IN THE MIDDLE AGES

I *Gender and Medieval Drama,* Katie Normington, 2006
II *Gender and Petty Crime in Late Medieval England: The Local Courts in Kent, 1460–1560,* Karen Jones, 2006
III *The Pastoral Care of Women in Late Medieval England,* Beth Allison Barr, 2008
IV *Gender, Nation and Conquest in the Works of William of Malmesbury,* Kirsten A. Fenton, 2008
V *Monsters, Gender and Sexuality in Medieval English Literature,* Dana M. Oswald, 2010
VI *Medieval Anchoritisms: Gender, Space and the Solitary Life,* Liz Herbert McAvoy, 2011
VII *Middle-Aged Women in the Middle Ages,* edited by Sue Niebrzydowski, 2011
VIII *Married Women and the Law in Premodern Northwest Europe,* edited by Cordelia Beattie and Matthew Frank Stevens, 2013
IX *Religious Men and Masculine Identity in the Middle Ages,* edited by P. H. Cullum and Katherine J. Lewis, 2013
X *Reconsidering Gender, Time and Memory in Medieval Culture,* edited by Elizabeth Cox, Liz Herbert McAvoy and Roberta Magnani, 2015
XI *Medicine, Religion and Gender in Medieval Culture,* edited by Naoë Kukita Yoshikawa, 2015
XII *The Unspeakable, Gender and Sexuality in Medieval Literature, 1000–1400,* Victoria Blud, 2017
XIII *Popular Memory and Gender in Medieval England: Men, Women, and Testimony in the Church Courts, c.1200–1500,* Bronach C. Kane, 2019
XIV *Authority, Gender and Space in the Anglo-Norman World, 900–1200,* Katherine Weikert, 2020
XV *Female Desire in Chaucer's* Legend of Good Women *and Middle English Romance,* Lucy M. Allen-Goss, 2020
XVI *Treason and Masculinity in Medieval England: Gender, Law and Political Culture,* E. Amanda McVitty, 2020
XVII *Holy Harlots in Medieval English Religious Literature: Authority, Exemplarity and Femininity,* Juliette Vuille, 2021
XVIII *Addressing Women in Early Medieval Religious Texts,* Kathryn Maude, 2021

XIX *Women, Dance and Parish Religion in England, 1300–1640: Negotiating the Steps of Faith*, Lynneth Miller Renberg, 2022

XX *Women's Literary Cultures in the Global Middle Ages: Speaking Internationally*, edited by Kathryn Loveridge, Liz Herbert McAvoy, Sue Niebrzydowski and Vicki Kay Price, 2023

XXI *Women and Devotional Literature in the Middle Ages: Giving Voice to Silence. Essays in Honour of Catherine Innes-Parker*, edited by Cate Gunn, Liz Herbert McAvoy and Naoë Kukita Yoshikawa, 2023

XXII *Female Devotion and Textile Imagery in Medieval English Literature*, Anna McKay, 2024

Printed in the United States
by Baker & Taylor Publisher Services